T0368972

About This Book

Why is this topic important?

Continuing education and development lie at the very heart of any successful organization. Time and time again, studies show that the best organizations, those that deliver better-than-average return on investment, also happen to be the ones with the highest commitment to training and development. Moreover, training has become a powerful ally in the war for talent. Job seekers frequently cite a strong commitment to development as one of the principal reasons for joining or remaining with an organization.

What can you achieve with this book?

In your hands is a working toolkit, a valuable source of knowledge for the training professional. Offering entirely new content each year, the Pfeiffer Training *Annual* showcases the latest thinking and cutting-edge approaches to training and development, contributed by practicing training professionals, consultants, academics, and subject-matter experts. Turn to the *Annual* for a rich source of ideas and to try out new methods and approaches that others in your profession have found successful.

How is this book organized?

The book is divided into four sections: Experiential Learning Activities (ELAs); Editor's Choice; Inventories, Questionnaires, and Surveys; and Articles and Discussion Resources. All the material can be freely reproduced for training purposes. The ELAs are the mainstay of the *Annual* and cover a broad range of training topics. The activities are presented as complete and ready-to-use training designs; facilitator instructions and all necessary handouts and participant materials are included. Editor's Choice pieces allow us to select material that doesn't fit the other categories and take advantage of "hot topics." The instrument section introduces reliable survey and assessment tools for gathering and sharing data on aspects of personal or team development. The articles section presents the best current thinking about training and organization development. Use these for your own professional development or as lecture resources.

About Pfeiffer

Pfeiffer serves the professional development and hands-on resource needs of training and human resource practitioners and gives them products to do their jobs better. We deliver proven ideas and solutions from experts in HR development and HR management, and we offer effective and customizable tools to improve workplace performance. From novice to seasoned professional, Pfeiffer is the source you can trust to make yourself and your organization more successful.

Essential Knowledge Pfeiffer produces insightful, practical, and comprehensive materials on topics that matter the most to training and HR professionals. Our Essential Knowledge resources translate the expertise of seasoned professionals into practical, how-to guidance on critical workplace issues and problems. These resources are supported by case studies, worksheets, and job aids and are frequently supplemented with CD-ROMs, websites, and other means of making the content easier to read, understand, and use.

Essential Tools Pfeiffer's Essential Tools resources save time and expense by offering proven, ready-to-use materials—including exercises, activities, games, instruments, and assessments—for use during a training or team-learning event. These resources are frequently offered in looseleaf or CD-ROM format to facilitate copying and customization of the material.

Pfeiffer also recognizes the remarkable power of new technologies in expanding the reach and effectiveness of training. While e-hype has often created whizbang solutions in search of a problem, we are dedicated to bringing convenience and enhancements to proven training solutions. All our e-tools comply with rigorous functionality standards. The most appropriate technology wrapped around essential content yields the perfect solution for today's on-the-go trainers and human resource professionals.

Pfeiffer
www.pfeiffer.com

Essential resources for training and HR professionals

The Pfeiffer Annual Series

The Pfeiffer Annuals present each year never-before-published materials contributed by learning professionals and academics and written for trainers, consultants, and human resource and performance-improvement practitioners. As a forum for the sharing of ideas, theories, models, instruments, experiential learning activities, and best and innovative practices, the *Annuals* are unique. Not least because only in the *Pfeiffer Annuals* will you find solutions from professionals like you who work in the field as trainers, consultants, facilitators, educators, and human resource and performance-improvement practitioners and whose contributions have been tried and perfected in real-life settings with actual participants and clients to meet real-world needs.

The Pfeiffer Annual: Consulting
Edited by Elaine Biech

The Pfeiffer Annual: Training
Edited by Elaine Biech

Call for Papers

How would you like to be published in the *Pfeiffer Training* or *Consulting Annual*? Possible topics for submissions include group and team building, organization development, leadership, problem solving, presentation and communication skills, consulting and facilitation, and training-the-trainer. Contributions may be in one of the following three formats:

- Experiential Learning Activities

- Inventories, Questionnaires, and Surveys

- Articles and Discussion Resources

To receive a copy of the submission packet, which explains the requirements and will help you determine format, language, and style to use, contact editor Elaine Biech at Pfeifferannual@aol.com or by calling 757-588-3939.

If your piece is published, you will receive a complimentary set of the *Pfeiffer Training* and *Consulting Annuals*.

Elaine Biech, EDITOR

The *2013*
Pfeiffer
ANNUAL

TRAINING

Pfeiffer
A Wiley Imprint
www.pfeiffer.com

Published by Pfeiffer
An Imprint of Wiley
One Montgomery Street, Suite 1200, San Francisco, CA 94104-4594
www.pfeiffer.com

ISBN: 978-1-118-30177-7; 9781118440469 (ebook); 9781118440476 (ebook); 9781118440490 (ebook)
ISSN: 1046-333-X

Acquiring Editor: Marisa Kelley
Director of Development: Kathleen Dolan Davies
Development Editor: Susan Rachmeler
Production Editor: Dawn Kilgore
Editor: Rebecca Taff
Manufacturing Supervisor: Becky Morgan

Printed in the United States of America

Printing   10 9 8 7 6 5 4 3 2 1

Contents

**Preparing Leaders for the Future Topics

Editor's Choice

---

†*Cutting Edge Topics*

Inventories, Questionnaires, and Surveys

Articles and Discussion Resources

Website Contents

Our readers are invited to download customizable materials from this book, as well as a PDF of the book text. The following materials are available FREE with the purchase of this book at: www.pfeiffer.com/go/training2013.

The following password is required for accessing these materials:

Password: 2013

Experiential Learning Activities

Are You Ready? Assessing Change Readiness
Teri-E Belf

> Are You Ready? Components for Assessing Readiness
> Contradictory Preferences: Role Playing
> *Lauri Luoto*

> Contradictory Preferences: Role Descriptions (six sheets)

The ADAPT Problem-Solving Model: Using Interviewing
Jennifer Straub, Nicole Russo, Sarah Eckstein, and Daniel Eckstein

> ADAPT: **Analyze the Gap**

> ADAPT: **Develop Resources**

> ADAPT: **Align Goals**

> ADAPT: **Plan Interventions**

> ADAPT: **Track Implementation**

> ADAPT: **Interviewing Tips**

> ADAPT Problem-Solving Model

> ADAPT Problem-Solving Model Visual

Editor's Choice

Inventories, Questionnaires, and Surveys

Articles and Discussion Resources

Preface

"Preparing Leaders for the Future" is the theme for the 2013 Pfeiffer Training and Consulting *Annuals*. Both *Annuals* offer more theme-related experiential learning activities (ELAs), articles, and even a questionnaire, than any previous *Annual*. In addition, the high quality and creativity of the submissions made it difficult to select given the limited space. You, our readers, profit the most, by reaping the benefits of some of the best contributions we've had the opportunity to publish.

Both *Annuals*, of course, continue to present a broad array of other topics as well, such as communication, problem solving, teamwork, individual development, and the other topics that have made the *Annuals* successful over the years. The vast interest in this year's theme is a healthy indication that "Preparing Leaders for the Future" struck a chord with our contributors. The Training *Annual* and the Consulting *Annual* each present you with eleven "Preparing Leaders for the Future" submissions—practical ideas and interesting approaches to help you do your job better.

Preparing leaders for the future is a concern for almost every organization. You read about it in the newspaper, business magazines, and journals, in addition to many of the recently published business books. Organizations are apprehensive about whether they have enough leaders in the pipeline, whether those future leaders have the right skills to ensure the organization's continued success, whether the current leaders are doing what's necessary to shape the organization's future, and a host of other concerns.

Organizations that are serious about preparing their leaders for the future must ask themselves several questions:

- What are the critical challenges our organization will face in the future?

- What do our leaders need to know, do, and believe differently to succeed in our industry in the future?

- How do we better prepare our leaders for success?

Many trainers and consultants are working with their organizations to help them address these questions and prepare for the future. For example, we already know that the challenges organizations will face include increased globalization shifts; rapidly escalating complexity; financial disruption; interconnected economies, societies, and governments; an even higher reliance on technology; and rethinking long-held assumptions of how they do business. We also know that leaders will need to be more creative to respond to these challenges; more adept at identifying new markets; able to reinvent their organizations; and comfortable with ambiguity, risk, and uncertainty.

Developing leaders for the future is no longer simply a matter of cultivating a pre-defined set of skills. Like organizations themselves, leadership skills have become more complex, less defined, and certainly not as orderly as they once were. How do organizations prepare their leaders for the uncertain future? This is where those of you who are in the workplace learning and performance (WLP) profession come in! And this is where the contributions in both the Training and the Consulting *Annuals* can help.

Our authors lived up to the challenge of addressing "Preparing Leaders for the Future" with a variety of ELAs, articles, and a survey. Here are several examples.

- Catherine Rezak addresses how to develop leaders who can see the big picture to ensure that they are prepared for their organizations' uncertainty, complexity, and ambiguity in the future. Her article is located in the Training *Annual*.

- Values-based leadership can lead to organizational success. In the Training *Annual*, Homer Johnson provides insight into this increasingly popular approach to leadership by explaining major approaches to this form of leadership and by clarifying the process of developing values-based leaders.

- Shirley Copeland uses an ELA to help leaders discover practical opportunities to explore and model creative leadership. You won't want to miss this one in the Training *Annual*.

- In response to a growing global economy, Patricia Cassidy and Donna Stringer offer advice in the Consulting *Annual* on how to select, support, and retain high performers for international assignments.

- Mentoring is key to having a robust pipeline of leaders. The Consulting *Annual* offers two submissions you will want to check out. Halelly Azulay has created two self-assessments that help potential candidates prepare for a mentoring partnership. Both measure the individuals' readiness for a potential relationship. In an article, Mohandas Nair delivers ideas to ensure that both the mentor and the protégé gain the most from a mentoring experience.

I mention only six of the "Preparing Leaders for the Future" submissions. That leaves sixteen more for you to discover on your own. I am sure you won't want to miss any of them, since I am certain that leadership development is important in your organization, just as it is in all organizations. You will find all of the "Preparing Leaders for the Future" contributions called out with asterisks in the Contents.

In addition to our themed contributions, I also want to highlight the Editor's Choice Section. I am grateful to the wonderful people at Pfeiffer for allowing me to create this section to publish contributions that do not easily fit into one of the other sections or that present a topic or idea that may be helpful to those of us in the WLP profession, but can't be classified as communication or leadership or one of our other standard categories. The 2013 *Annuals* have several outstanding and creative contributions in this section.

The Pfeiffer Training Annual presents Karl Albrecht's "Thinker's Test," which can be implemented in an infinite number of ways. Lily and Peter Cheng offer a lively activity that demonstrates that all employees add value to an organization in "The Cents of It All." And Lou Russell ensures that you can reduce stress and frustration from your day if you "Build a Better 'To-Do' List."

The Pfeiffer Consulting Annual includes only one submission in the Editor's Choice Section—but what a submission it is! In her distinctively, lively approach, Beverly Kaye, leader in the career development field, discusses the importance of knowing and being able to articulate one's values. She relates it to something few of us consider: finding fulfillment in your career. Bev's article talks about why it is important, and offers a way for you to assess your own values.

As you may be able to surmise, I am excited about *The 2013 Pfeiffer Training and Consulting Annuals*. Both are jam-packed with practical as well as new activities and articles you will find both fun as well as rewarding to use.

What Are the *Annuals*?

The *Annual* series had its debut in 1972. From its inception the goal was to deliver excellent as well as original content. The activities, articles, and instruments are written and designed for trainers, consultants, facilitators, and performance-improvement technologists. We know the materials are also practical, because they are written by the same practitioners who use the materials.

The series consists of two annuals. The first, The *Pfeiffer Annual: Training*, focuses on skill building and knowledge enhancement that would be used in a training setting. It also includes articles that enhance the skills and professional development of trainers and facilitators. The second annual, The *Pfeiffer Annual: Consulting*, focuses on intervention techniques, such as building teams, and organizational systems, such as implementing change or strategic planning. It also includes skill building for the professional consultant. You can read more about the differences between the two volumes in the section that follows this preface, "The Difference Between Training and Consulting: Which *Annual* to Use."

The *Annuals* have been an inspirational source for experiential learning activities, resource for instruments, and reference for cutting-edge thinking for forty-one years. Whether you are a trainer, a consultant, a facilitator, or a bit of each, you will find tools and resources that provide you with the basics and challenge (and we hope inspire) you to use new techniques and models.

Annual Loyalty

The *Annual* series has many loyal subscribers. There are several reasons for this loyalty. In addition to the wide variety of topics and implementation levels, the *Annuals* provide materials that are applicable in varying circumstances. You will find instruments for individuals, teams, and organizations; experiential learning activities to round out workshops, team building, or consulting assignments; ideas and contemporary solutions for talent management; and articles that increase your own knowledge base, to use as reference materials in your writing, or as a source of ideas for your training or consulting assignments.

Many of our readers have been loyal customers for decades. If you are one of them, we thank you. And we encourage each of you to give back to the profession by submitting a sample of your work to share with your colleagues.

For me, the most exciting element of the *Annuals* has always been that I can use all the materials without going through the arduous process of obtaining copyright permission. All of the materials may be duplicated for educational and training purposes. If you need to adapt or modify the materials to tailor them for your audience's needs, go right ahead. We only request that the credit statement found on the copyright page (and on each reproducible page) be retained on all copies. Our liberal copyright policy makes it easy and fast for you to use the materials to do your job. If you intend to reproduce the materials in publications for sale or if you wish to reproduce more than one hundred copies of any one item, please contact us for prior written permission.

If you are a new *Annual* user, welcome! If you like what you see in the 2013 edition, you may want to subscribe to a standing order. By doing so, you are guaranteed to receive your copy each year straight off the press and receive a discount off the cover price. And if you want to go back and have the entire series for your use, then the *Pfeiffer Library—which contains content from the very first edition through the 2007 Annuals*—is available on CD-ROM. You can find information on the *Pfeiffer Library* at www.pfeiffer.com.

I often refer to many of my *Annuals* from the 1980s. They include several classic activities that have become a mainstay in my team-building and strategic planning designs. But most of all, the *Annuals* have been a valuable resource for forty-one years because the materials come from professionals like you who work in the field as trainers, consultants, facilitators, educators, and performance-improvement technologists, whose contributions have been tried and perfected in real-life settings with actual participants and clients to meet real-world needs.

To this end, we encourage you to submit materials to be considered for publication. We are interested in receiving experiential learning activities; inventories, questionnaires, and surveys; and articles and discussion resources. Contact the Pfeiffer Editorial Department at the address listed on the copyright page for copies of our guidelines for contributors or contact me directly at Box 8249, Norfolk, VA 23503, or by email at pfeifferannual@aol.com. We welcome your comments, ideas, and contributions.

Acknowledgments

Kathleen Dolan Davies, Marisa Kelley, Dawn Kilgore, Susan Rachmeler, Rebecca Taff: Every year you produce the number one most valuable resource in the industry, delivering value to our dedicated readers. We all owe you a debt of gratitude for your expert editing and publishing. Thank you to Lorraine Kohart, of ebb associates inc, who pokes, prods, and cajoles our authors into submitting the best for you, the readers. She keeps us all organized, provides submission information, compiles the *Annuals'* content, keeps authors in the loop, and is the go-between communicator for the editing team to ensure all the deadlines are met.

Most importantly, a huge thank you goes to our contributors, who continue to create new and exciting activities and materials so that trainers and consultants everywhere have fresh materials to deliver to their internal and external clients. I invite everyone who is reading this to join these prestigious professionals for our next annual. We are always looking for new authors who have creative yet practical ideas to share with the rest of the profession.

Elaine Biech
Editor
September 2012

The Difference Between Training and Consulting

Which Annual to Use?

Two volumes of the *Pfeiffer Annuals*—training and consulting—are resources for two different but closely related professions. Each *Annual* serves as a collection of tools and support materials used by the professionals in their respective arenas. The volumes include activities, articles, and instruments used by individuals in the training and consulting fields. The training volume is written with the trainer in mind, and the consulting volume is written with the consultant in mind.

How can you differentiate between the two volumes? Let's begin by defining each profession.

A *trainer* can be defined as anyone who is responsible for designing and delivering knowledge to adult learners and may include an internal HRD professional employed by an organization or an external practitioner who contracts with an organization to design and conduct training programs. Generally, the trainer is a subject-matter expert who is expected to transfer knowledge so that the trainee can know or do something new. A *consultant* is someone who provides unique assistance or advice (based on what the consultant knows or has experienced) to someone else, usually known as "the client." The consultant may not necessarily be a subject-matter expert in all situations. Often the consultant is an expert at using specific tools to extract, coordinate, resolve, organize, expedite, or implement an organizational situation.

The lines between the consulting and training professions have blurred in the past few years. First, the names and titles have blurred. For example, some external trainers call themselves "training consultants" as a way of distinguishing themselves from internal trainers. Some organizations now have internal consultants who usually reside in the training department. Second, the roles have blurred. While a consultant has always been expected to deliver measurable results, now trainers are expected to do so as well. Both are expected to improve performance; both are expected to contribute to the bottom line. Facilitation was at one time thought to be a consultant skill; today trainers are expected to use facilitation skills to train. Training one-on-one was a trainer skill; today consultants train executives one-on-one and call it "coaching." The introduction of the "performance technologist," whose role is one of combined trainer and consultant, is a perfect example of a new profession that has evolved due to the need for trainers to use more "consulting" techniques in their work. The "performance consultant" is a new role supported by the American Society for Training and Development (ASTD). ASTD has shifted its focus from training to performance improvement.

As you can see, the roles and goals of training and consulting are not nearly as specific as they once may have been. However, when you step back and examine the two professions from a big-picture perspective, you can more easily differentiate between the two. Maintaining a big-picture focus will also help you determine which *Pfeiffer Annual* to turn to as your first resource.

Both volumes cover the same general topics: communication, teamwork, problem solving, and leadership. However, depending on your requirement and purpose—a training or consulting need—you will use each in different situations. You will select the *Annual* based on *how you will interact with the topic, not on what the topic might be.* Let's take a topic such as teamwork, for example. If you are searching for a lecturette that teaches the advantages of teamwork, a workshop activity that demonstrates the skill of making decisions in a team, or a handout that discusses team stages, look to the Training *Annual*. On the other hand, if you are conducting a team-building session for a dysfunctional team, helping to form a new team, or trying to understand the dynamics of an executive team, you will look to the Consulting *Annual*.

The Training *Annual*

The materials in the Training volume focus on skill building and knowledge enhancement as well as on the professional development of trainers. They generally focus on controlled events: a training program, a conference presentation, a classroom setting. Look to the Training *Annual* to find ways to improve a training session for 10 to 1,000 people and anything else that falls in the human resource development category:

- Specific experiential learning activities that can be built into a training program;

- Techniques to improve training: debriefing exercises, conducting role plays, managing time;

- Topical lecturettes;

- Ideas to improve a boring training program;

- Icebreakers and energizers for a training session;

- Surveys that can be used in a classroom;

- Ideas for moving an organization from training to performance; and

- Ways to improve your skills as a trainer.

The Consulting *Annual*

The materials in the Consulting volume focus on intervention techniques and organizational systems as well as the professional development of consultants. They generally focus on "tools" that you can have available just in case: concepts about organizations and their development (or demise) and about more global situations. Look to the Consulting *Annual* to find ways to improve consulting activities from team building and executive coaching to organization development and strategic planning:

- Skills for working with executives;

- Techniques for solving problems, effecting change, and gathering data;

- Team-building tools, techniques, and tactics;

- Facilitation ideas and methods;

- Processes to examine for improving an organization's effectiveness;

- Surveys that can be used organizationally; and

- Ways to improve your effectiveness as a consultant.

Summary

Even though the professions and the work are closely related and at times interchangeable, there is a difference. Use the following table to help you determine which *Annual* you should scan first for help. Remember, however, there is some blending of the two and either *Annual* may have your answer. It depends . . .

Element	Training	Consulting
Topics	Teams, Communication, Problem Solving	Teams, Communication, Problem Solving
Topic Focus	Individual, Department	Corporate, Global
Purpose	Skill Building, Knowledge Transfer	Coaching, Strategic Planning, Building Teams
Recipient	Individuals, Departments	Usually More Organizational
Organizational Level	All Workforce Members	Usually Closer to the Top
Delivery Profile	Workshops, Presentations	Intervention, Implementation
Atmosphere	Structured	Unstructured
Time Frame	Defined	Undefined
Organizational Cost	Moderate	High
Change Effort	Low to Moderate	Moderate to High
Setting	Usually a Classroom	Anywhere
Professional Experience	Entry Level, Novice	Proficient, Master Level
Risk Level	Low	High
Professional Needs	Activities, Resources	Tools, Theory
Application	Individual Skills	Usually Organizational System

When you get right down to it, we are all trainers and consultants. The skills may cross over. A great trainer is also a skilled consultant. And a great consultant is also a skilled trainer. The topics may be the same, but how you implement them may be vastly different. Which *Annual* to use? Remember to think about your purpose in terms of the big picture: consulting or training.

As you can see, we have both covered.

Introduction

to *The 2013 Pfeiffer Annual: Training*

The 2013 Pfeiffer Annual: Training is a collection of practical and useful materials for professionals in the broad area described as human resource development (HRD). The materials are written by and for professionals, including trainers, organization-development and organization-effectiveness consultants, performance-improvement technologists, facilitators, educators, instructional designers, and others.

Each *Annual* has three main sections: Experiential Learning Activities; Inventories, Questionnaires, and Surveys; and Articles and Discussion Resources. A fourth section, Editor's Choice, has been reserved for those unique contributions that do not fit neatly into one of the three main sections, but are valuable as identified by the editorial staff. Each published submission is classified in one of the following categories: Individual Development, Communication, Problem Solving, Groups, Teams, Consulting, Facilitating, Leadership, and Organizations. Within each category, pieces are further classified into logical subcategories, which are identified in the introductions to the three sections.

The Training *Annual* and the Consulting *Annual* for 2013 have a slightly different focus from past years. Both focus on the theme of preparing leaders for the future, a topic that permeates our organizations and pervades all that we do as professionals in the learning and consulting arena.

The series continues to provide an opportunity for HRD professionals who wish to share their experiences, their viewpoints, and their processes with their colleagues. To that end, Pfeiffer publishes guidelines for potential authors. These guidelines are available from the Pfeiffer Editorial Department at Jossey-Bass, Inc., in San Francisco, California.

Materials are selected for the *Annuals* based on the quality of the ideas, applicability to real-world concerns, relevance to current HRD issues, clarity of presentation, and ability to enhance our readers' professional development. In addition, we choose experiential learning activities that will create a high degree of enthusiasm among the participants and add enjoyment to the learning process. As in the past several years, the contents of each *Annual* span a wide range of subject matter, reflecting the range of interests of our readers.

Our contributor list includes a wide selection of experts in the field: in-house practitioners, consultants, and academically based professionals. A list of contributors to the *Annual* can be found at the end of the volume, including their names, affiliations, addresses, telephone numbers, facsimile numbers, email addresses, and, when available, websites. Readers will find this list useful if they wish to locate the authors of specific pieces for feedback, comments, or questions. Further information on each contributor is presented in a brief biographical sketch that appears at the conclusion of each article. We publish this information to encourage networking, which continues to be a valuable mainstay in the field of human resource development.

We are pleased with the high quality of material that is submitted for publication each year and often regret that we have page limitations. In addition, just as we cannot publish every manuscript we receive, you may find that not all published works are equally useful to you. Therefore, we encourage and invite ideas, materials, and suggestions that will help us to make subsequent *Annuals* as useful as possible to all of our readers.

Introduction
to the Experiential Learning Activities Section

Experiential learning activities ensure that lasting learning occurs. They should be selected with a specific learning objective in mind. These objectives are based on the participants' needs and the facilitator's skills. Although the experiential learning activities presented here all vary in goals, group size, time required, and process, they all incorporate one important element: questions that ensure learning has occurred. This discussion, led by the facilitator, assists participants to process the activity, to internalize the learning, and to relate it to their day-to-day situations. It is this element that creates the unique learning experience and learning opportunity that only an experiential learning activity can bring to the group process.

Readers have used the *Annuals'* experiential learning activities for years to enhance their training and consulting events. Each learning experience is complete and includes all lecturettes, handout content, and other written material necessary to facilitate the activity. All these materials can be found in a downloadable format on the Pfeiffer website using the code provided in this edition. In addition, many include variations of the design that the facilitator might find useful. If the activity does not fit perfectly with your objective, within your time frame, or to your group size, we encourage you to adapt the activity by adding your own variations. You will find additional experiential learning activities listed in the "Experiential Learning Activities Categories" chart that immediately follows this introduction.

The 2013 Pfeiffer Annual: Training includes thirteen activities, including four that are critical to this year's theme of preparing leaders for the future: Are You Ready? Components for Assessing Change Readiness; Pop Goes the Bottom Line! The Impact of Feedback on Performance; The Creative Leader: Measuring Creativity Characteristics; and The Leadership Pyramid: Exploring Skills of Successful Leaders.

The following categories are represented:

Individual Development: Sensory Awareness

The Graham Cracker Challenge: Examining Risk and Reward, by John Goldberg

Individual Development: Life/Career Planning

**Are You Ready? Assessing Change Readiness, by Teri-E Belf

Communication: Feedback

Contradictory Preferences: Role Playing, by Lauri Luoto

Problem Solving: Action Planning

The ADAPT Problem-Solving Model: Using Interviewing, by Jennifer Straub, Nicole Russo, Sarah Eckstein, and Daniel Eckstein

Teams: Feedback

**Pop Goes the Bottom Line! Examining the Impact of Feedback on Performance, by Ken Steiger

Consulting, Training, and Facilitating: Facilitating: Opening

Throwing Kisses: Encouraging Desired Behaviors, by Marilyn Marles

Congratulations! Mixing It Up, by Jan Yuill

Consulting, Training, and Facilitating: Facilitating: Blocks to Learning

†QR Codes for Training: Improving Learning and Performance, by Kella B. Price

Consulting, Training, and Facilitating: Facilitating: Skills

Dialogue: Using Discussions to Facilitate Learning, by Mohandas Nair

Consulting, Training, and Facilitating: Facilitating: Closing

Buzz, Buzz: Increasing Participant Engagement, by Sandra A. Shelton

Leadership: Interviewing/Appraisal

Superpowers: Learning to Improve Performance, by Lisa Strick

**Preparing Leaders for the Future Topic
†Cutting-Edge Topic

Leadership: Styles and Skills

> **The Creative Leader: Measuring Creativity Characteristics, by Shirley Copeland

> **The Leadership Pyramid: Exploring Skills of Successful Leaders, by J. Alexis Mamber

To further assist you in selecting appropriate ELAs, we provide the following grid that summarizes category, time required, group size, and risk factor for each ELA.

Category	ELA Title	Page	Time Required	Group Size	Risk Factor
Individual Development: Sensory Awareness	The Graham Cracker Challenge: Examining Risk and Reward	13	30 minutes	Groups of 4	Low
Individual Development: Life/ Career Planning	Are You Ready? Assessing Change Readiness	17	2 hours	6 to 40	Low
Communication: Feedback	Contradictory Preferences: Role Playing	25	60 to 90 minutes	Groups of 3 managers	Moderate
Problem Solving: Action Planning	The ADAPT Problem- Solving Model: Using Interviewing	35	2 hours	5 groups of 3 to 5	Moderate
Teams: Feedback	Pop Goes the Bottom Line! Examining the Impact of Feedback on Performance	51	20 to 25 minutes	2 teams of 6 to 9	Moderate
Consulting, Training, and Facilitating: Facilitating: Opening	Throwing Kisses: Encouraging Desired Behaviors	57	5 minutes	Best with 8 to 30	Low
Consulting, Training, and Facilitating: Facilitating: Opening	Congratulations! Mixing It Up	61	20 to 30 minutes	Up to 100	Low
Consulting, Training, and Facilitating: Facilitating: Blocks to Learning	QR Codes for Training: Improving Learning and Performance	65	75 to 90 minutes	15 to 25 trainers	Low
Consulting, Training, and Facilitating: Facilitating: Skills	Dialogue: Using Discussions to Facilitate Learning	77	20 to 30 minutes	Any	Moderate
Consulting, Training, and Facilitating: Facilitating: Closing	Buzz, Buzz: Increasing Participant Engagement	81	90 to 120 minutes	10 to 20 in groups of 3 or 4	Moderate
Leadership: Interviewing/ Appraisal	Superpowers: Learning to Improve Performance	87	3 hours	10 to 12 from the same organization	High
Leadership: Styles and Skills	The Creative Leader: Measuring Creativity Characteristics	97	45 to 60 minutes	10 to 20 leaders	Low to Moderate
Leadership: Styles and Skills	The Leadership Pyramid: Exploring Skills of Successful Leaders	103	45 to 55 minutes	10 to 25 lead- ership trainees	Moderate

Experiential Learning Activities Categories

1–24 Volume I, *Handbook*	413–424 1986 *Annual*	605–616 1998 *Annual:* Volume 2, Consulting
25–48 Volume II, *Handbook*	425–436 1987 *Annual*	
49–74 Volume III, *Handbook*	437–448 1988 *Annual*	617–630 1999 *Annual:* Volume 1, Training
75–86 1972 *Annual*	449–460 1989 *Annual*	
87–100 1973 *Annual*	461–472 1990 *Annual*	631–642 1999 *Annual:* Volume 2, Consulting
101–124 Volume IV, *Handbook*	473–484 1991 *Annual*	
125–136 1974 *Annual*	485–496 1992 *Annual*	643–656 2000 *Annual:* Volume 1, Training
137–148 1975 *Annual*	497–508 1993 *Annual*	
149–172 Volume V, *Handbook*	509–520 1994 *Annual*	657–669 2000 *Annual:* Volume 2, Consulting
173–184 1976 *Annual*	521–532 1995 *Annual:* Volume 1, Training	
185–196 1977 *Annual*		670–681 2001 *Annual:* Volume 1, Training
197–220 Volume VI, *Handbook*	533–544 1995 *Annual:* Volume 2, Consulting	
221–232 1978 *Annual*		683–695 2001 *Annual:* Volume 2, Consulting
233–244 1979 *Annual*	545–556 1996 *Annual:* Volume 1, Training	
245–268 Volume VII, *Handbook*		696–709 2002 *Annual:* Volume 1, Training
269–280 1980 *Annual*	557–568 1996 *Annual:* Volume 2, Consulting	
281–292 1981 *Annual*		710–722 2002 *Annual:* Volume 2, Consulting
293–316 Volume VIII, *Handbook*	569–580 1997 *Annual:* Volume 1, Training	
317–328 1982 *Annual*		723–739 2003 *Annual:* Volume 1, Training
329–340 1983 *Annual*	581–592 1997 *Annual:* Volume 2, Consulting	
341–364 Volume IX, *Handbook*		740-752 2003 *Annual:* Volume 2, Consulting
365–376 1984 *Annual*	593–604 1998 *Annual:* Volume 1, Training	
377–388 1985 *Annual*		
389–412 Volume X, *Handbook*		

Note that numbering system was discontinued beginning with the 2004 *Annuals*.

	VOL.	PAGE		VOL.	PAGE		VOL.	PAGE
INDIVIDUAL DEVELOPMENT			What You See (740)	'03-2	11	**Self-Disclosure**		
Sensory Awareness			Highly Leveraged Moments	'04-T	11	Johari Window (13)	I	65
Feelings & Defenses (56)	III	31				Graphics (20)	I	88
Lemons (71)	III	94	Z Fantasy	'04-C	11	Personal Journal (74)	III	109
Growth & Name Fantasy (85)	'72	59	Well-Being	'05-T	11	Make Your Own Bag (90)	'73	13
Group Exploration (119)	IV	92	Picture Yourself	'05-C	11	Growth Cards (109)	IV	30
Relaxation & Perceptual Awareness (136)	'74	84	Presuppositions	'06-C	11	Expressing Anger (122)	IV	104
			The Serendipity Bowl	'07-T	11	Stretching (123)	IV	107
T'ai Chi Chuan (199)	VI	10	Change Partners	'08-T	11	Forced-Choice Identity (129)	'74	20
Roles Impact Feelings (214)	VI	102	Empathy Walk	'08-C	11	Boasting (181)	'76	49
Projections (300)	VIII	30	Encouragement	'09-C	13	The Other You (182)	'76	51
Mastering the Deadline Demon (593)	'98-1	9	One Life, Many Roles	'10-T	13	Praise (306)	VIII	61
			Are You Aware?	'12-T	15	Introjection (321)	'82	29
Learning Shifts (643)	'00-1	11	The Graham Cracker Challenge	'13-T	13	Personality Traits (349)	IX	158
Secret Sponsors (657)	'00-2	11				Understanding the Need for Approval (438)	'88	21
Spirituality at Work (670)	'01-1	11	Mind Your Mind	'13-C	13			

The Graham Cracker Challenge
Examining Risk and Reward

Summary

An experiential activity that allows participants to examine their risk-taking attitudes and behaviors.

Goals

- To take a risk in a safe environment.
- To examine different approaches to risk taking.
- To reflect on a personal experience of risk taking.

Group Size

Several groups of four people.

Time Required

30 minutes.

Materials

- One vertically straight-sided 12-ounce mug or glass or cup, 3 inches in diameter, for each participant.
- Ten ounces of milk per participant.
- Two graham crackers per participant.
- Four prizes of value to participants.

Physical Setting

Participants seated at tables in groups of four per table.

Facilitating Risk Rating

Low.

Process

1. Explain that participants will have the opportunity to take risks and win a prize. Assign four participants per table.

2. Distribute one mug, glass, or cup filled with milk to each participant and one package of graham crackers per table.

3. Ask participants to volunteer to be either an "A" or a "B," ensuring that there are two of each at each table. When they ask what they are volunteering for, simply smile and say it is part of learning about risk.

4. Tell participants that there will be two rounds: first the A round and then the B round. The goal is to keep your graham cracker in the milk longer than anyone else and to put it into your mouth without it falling apart. The winner will win a prize. You may wish to announce the prizes or keep them a secret.

   (5 minutes.)

5. Tell the "A's" that on the count of 3 to put their graham crackers halfway into the milk and leave them as long as they dare before putting them into their mouths. Count to 3. When everyone has finished, announce the "A" winner of Round 1. Then tell the "B's" they will do the same thing. Count to 3 and announce the "B" winner of Round 1.

6. Tell participants to discuss at their tables what they learned that can help them be more successful during the second round.

   (5 to 10 minutes.)

7. Bring the group back together and repeat the process.

8. Debrief the activity with some of the following questions:

   • How comfortable were you with taking a risk?

   • What did you learn about your approach to risk taking?

- What did you notice about other people's risk-taking behavior?

- How are risk and rewards related? Is it possible to eliminate all risk and still have a chance at a reward?

- What could you have done to be more successful in taking a risk in this activity?

- What can you do to be more successful in taking a risk in your work? In your personal life?

- What does this activity suggest that you might want to do when you return to your workplace?

    (15 to 20 minutes.)

9. Summarize for the group.

Variations

- If the activity needs to be shortened, you may wish to use only one round.

- Six or more people can be seated at the same table if needed.

Submitted by John Goldberg.

John Goldberg *is a high-energy, seasoned master trainer with an MBA and more than twenty years of corporate, government, and nonprofit experience focusing on meeting company goals through the development of talent. Specialties include increasing efficiencies, identifying and removing obstacles to performance, motivation, leadership, management, supervision, communication, and teamwork.*

Are You Ready?
Assessing Change Readiness

Activity Summary

An activity that explores eighteen components of readiness using context, internal and external resources, and momentum as criteria.

Goals

- To identify and explore various components of change readiness.

- To assess how ready participants are to change their behavior.

- To learn to assess states of change readiness in others.

Group Size

Six to forty participants.

Time Required

2 hours.

Materials

- Laptop and screen projector or easel with chart paper.

- Masking tape to post flip-chart pages.

- One copy of the Are you Ready? Components for Assessing Readiness sheet for each participant.

- Writing utensils for participants.

Physical Setting

Tables for five to eight people at each. Wall space to post flip-chart pages.

Facilitating Risk Rating

Low.

Preparation

Think about changes you have made in your own life pertinent to the discussion you expect the group to have and be prepared to give real examples when appropriate.

Process

1. Present workshop goals, guidelines, and logistics.

2. Ask participants to take 3 minutes to think about actions they have taken at any point in their lives that involved change. Give some examples such as:

    -   You were ready to drive a car.

    -   You were ready to commit to a relationship.

    -   You were ready to retire.

    -   You were ready to take the turkey out of the oven or vegetables off the grill.

    -   You were ready to commit to your health.

    -   You were ready to submit the final report.

    -   You were ready to change jobs.

3. Provide each participant with a copy of the Are you Ready? Components for Assessing Readiness sheet and a pen or pencil. In small groups at tables, ask participants to spend 20 minutes sharing the changes they select and how they knew they were ready to make that change. Ask each group to select a note-taker and a reporter, which can be the same person.

    (25 minutes.)

4. Ask group reporters to share with the entire group while you write a list of criteria organized into four categories: Context, Internal Resources, External Resources, and Momentum. Create the list on a flip chart or whiteboard, or use a laptop and project it onto a screen. Tell participants to take notes on their handouts.

5. The criteria they come up with will be similar to, and not limited to, the following:

   Context

   - Vision

   - Skills

   - Commitment

   Internal Resources

   - Willing to risk

   - Belief in self

   - Energy

   External Resources

   - Time

   - Money

   - Support network

   Momentum

   - Action step

   - Acknowledgment

   - Learning/feedback

6. Answer questions about what the four categories mean. Spend a few minutes providing some personal examples in each category.

   (15 to 30 minutes.)

7. Lead a discussion about how to use clues such as facial expression, language, and intuition to tell when someone else if ready to take a step or make a change. Ask some of the following questions:

   - What might you see in a person's face that indicates readiness? (Examples might be raised eyebrows; a smile; eyes wider open; relaxed, softer facial muscles, especially around the eyes and jaw.)

   - What auditory clues indicate readiness? (Examples might be speaking more loudly or softly, higher or lower volume, longer or shorter pauses between words, more clear/crisp or muffled diction, emphasis on certain words or phrases, faster or slower tempo.)

- How does your intuition help you assess your own or someone else's readiness?

- In what tense is a person who is ready more likely to speak? Past? Present? Future? (The answer is present and future.)

- What are the differences between ready, willing, and able?

(15 minutes.)

8. Ask participants to jot down on their handouts a key personal or work initiative, project, or developmental goal at the present time.

9. Ask participants to rate themselves according to how ready they feel they are to move ahead with this goal or make progress toward it. Say that a rating of 5 means they are ready, a rating of 1 means they are not at all ready.

10. Ask participants to form dyads, preferably with someone they do not work with on a regular basis.

11. Ask participants to take turns and spend 15 minutes each brainstorming how they can increase their readiness to make the change. Ask the listeners to pay attention to cues that indicate the speaker's readiness. Tell participants to ask for permission from their partners to share with the large group what they noticed, heard, or sensed that indicated a state of readiness. They are not to share any information about the content of anyone's personal goals. Suggest that pairs ask each other questions for those components rated 1, 2, or 3 to enable their partners to increase their readiness. Possible questions appear on the handout and below.

- Whose support do you need?

- What support systems do you already have that you can activate?

- How can you clarify your vision?

- What belief(s) would support you to move ahead?

- What might happen when you succeed?

- What might happen if you do not succeed?

- What training might help you increase your skills or knowledge for this change?

- What would it take for you to commit to the change?

- What resources can you gather that would help you?

- Which of your key values underlie this change?

- Which of your personal qualities can you count on?

- How could you find more time to do this?

(35 minutes.)

12. Ask participants to end their discussions and to take 3 minutes to list actions they will take at home or back on the job to increase their readiness for change.

    (5 minutes.)

13. Ask participants what they learned that will help them assess their own readiness for change and that of others. Ask how the ability to assess readiness can be applied in the workplace or at home. Encourage participants to share ideas with the entire group.

14. Summarize by asking for volunteers to state what they will do as a result of what they have learned by doing this activity.

    (10 minutes.)

Submitted by Teri-E Belf.

Teri-E Belf, *MA, CAGS, BCC, MCC, is a purposeful and inspired coach, coach leader/trainer/mentor, author, speaker, and retreat facilitator. She shares twenty-five years of coaching, eighteen years of HRD management, and twenty-one years of retreat facilitation experience in her retreats, articles, and books, including* Simply Live It Up, Facilitating Life Purpose, Auto Suggestions, *and* Coaching with Spirit.

Are You Ready? Components for Assessing Readiness

Components of Readiness

Clues that indicate someone is ready:

One of my goals:

How ready am I?

           1   2   3   4   5

          not ready   very ready

Why did you rate yourself as you did?

Questions to Help Increase Readiness

- Whose support do you need?

- What support systems do you already have that you can activate?

- How can you clarify your vision?

- What belief(s) would support you to move ahead?

- What might happen when you succeed?

- What might happen if you do not succeed?

- What training might help you increase your skills or knowledge for this change?

- What would it take for you to commit to the change?

- What resources can you gather that would help you?

- Which of your key values underlie this change?

- Which of your personal qualities can you count on?

- How could you find more time to do this?

- Whose support do you need?

- What support systems can you activate that you already have?

My Actions to Increase Readiness

Write some ideas below about how you can apply what you have learned to your work, home life, volunteer activities, and other aspects of your life.

Contradictory Preferences
Role Playing

Activity Summary

A role-play activity that allows participants to practice difficult discussions in a non-threatening environment.

Goals

- To develop skills in managing difficult discussions with subordinates.

- To help participants understand different viewpoints and attitudes.

Group Size

Any number of managers in subgroups of three.

Time Required

60 to 90 minutes.

Materials

- One set of the Contradictory Preferences Role Descriptions for each subgroup. Prepare by copying the sheets onto index stock to create six role cards.

Physical Setting

A large room that will allow the subgroups to role play without disturbing one another.

Facilitating Risk Rating

Moderate.

Process

1. Introduce the activity and the goals.

2. Divide participants into subgroups of three, one "supervisor," one "subordinate," and one observer. Any subgroups with just two members can do the activity without an observer.

3. Distribute the first pair of role description cards so that the supervisors and the subordinates receive their respective cards without seeing each other's. The observer may see both cards.

4. Ask participants to read the cards to themselves and allow the supervisor and the subordinate to spend a few minutes thinking about how to play their roles.

    (5 to 10 minutes.)

5. Instruct the supervisors to begin the role discussion by stating why they have called a meeting with the subordinate. Tell them to follow the roles described on their cards. Tell them they have about 10 minutes.

    (10 minutes.)

6. After 10 minutes, call time and ask the observers to share their observations with the role players.

    (15 minutes.)

7. Reassemble the entire group and lead a discussion by asking these questions:

    *   How did the role players succeed in their roles?

    *   What could the supervisors have done differently?

    *   What optimal solutions to the problem resulted from the discussions?

    *   What universal supervisory skills were highlighted in the role plays?

    (10 minutes.)

8. Have the subgroup members swap roles and repeat Steps 3 through 7 with the second and third cases.

    (45 minutes.)

9. Summarize using some of the following questions:

- How did the role plays progress from the first to the last?

- Did the supervisors do anything differently over the three cases? If so, what?

- What skills are needed in supervisory situations like these?

- How can you continue to gain the skills to provide feedback to your subordinates after this session?

(10 minutes.)

Variation

- More cases can be written by the facilitator or by participants based on real-life experiences.

Submitted by Lauri Luoto.

Lauri Luoto *is an inspiring trainer and innovator of new training concepts. Currently, he is working as a management development consultant at Psycon Corp., one of Finland's leading companies for personal assessments, strategic resourcing, and leadership development. Lauri holds a master's degree in education and is a certified vocational teacher. He has conducted leadership programs and organization-wide development programs for a number of clients, including corporations, government, and nonprofit organizations.*

<u>Contradictory Preferences: Role Description</u>

Case 1: Supervisor

One member in your team does not cooperate with the others. The team member is always—even during coffee breaks—sitting at his/her workstation, and he/she says he/she is too busy to attend staff meetings. Except for this, he/she is doing the job very well. You do not know what the reason is for this kind of behavior, but you think it is undermining the atmosphere of your team. You have invited him/her to your office for a conversation.

Contradictory Preferences: Role Description

Case 1: Subordinate

You have a lot of work to do all of the time, but you do not want to work overtime. For you it is really important to be able to leave the office in time to have dinner with your family and have time for your hobbies. In order to save time, you avoid any meetings that you can. You also eat at your desk while you work. You are proud of your time management skills, but your supervisor tends to point out that you should interact more with your teammates. Your supervisor has invited you to his/her office for a conversation.

<u>Contradictory Preferences: Role Description</u>

Case 2: Supervisor

Your subordinate has started to take regular yoga classes and is very enthusiastic about the new hobby. The subordinate talks constantly about progressing in yoga, and you find this enthusiasm annoying. In your company, you do shift work and now the subordinate has asked whether he/she could avoid being scheduled for any evening shifts. It is impossible for you to accept this proposal, since shift planning is a difficult task anyway and other employees have the right to free evenings as well. You are going to have a talk with this subordinate.

Contradictory Preferences: Role Description

Case 2: Subordinate

You are really interested in yoga and have started to take regular yoga classes. You are convinced that progress in yoga requires lots of practice and dedication. You talk frequently to your colleagues about your new hobby because you are trying to help them see the value. You are doing shift work, and you have asked your supervisor to eliminate evening shifts from your schedule, since you need free evenings for yoga exercise. This is important to you! Your supervisor wants to talk with you about your suggestion.

Contradictory Preferences: Role Description

Case 3: Supervisor

Your subordinate is often late for work in the morning. The delay is usually just 5 minutes, but you think it is still relevant. In your workplace, customers often start calling at 8 a.m. sharp, and it is really embarrassing if there is no one present to answer the call. The situation has remained the same for a long time, so you have scheduled a discussion with the subordinate. Other than the tardiness, you are satisfied with the individual's performance.

<u>Contradictory Preferences: Role Description</u>

Case 3: Subordinate

You live quite far from your workplace and the traffic is often heavy in the mornings. In addition, you have to take your children to school and daycare before going to work, and that takes a lot of time as well. Taking all this into account, you think that you usually get to work at a reasonable time. Sometimes you are late by a couple of minutes, but you do not think it causes any trouble. Now, however, your supervisor wants to talk with you about your arriving late so often.

The ADAPT Problem–Solving Model
Using Interviewing

Activity Summary

A structured activity utilizing the ADAPT problem-solving model for improving workplace conflict-resolution skills.

Goals

- To introduce the ADAPT problem-solving model.

- To highlight the importance of using effective problem-solving tools in the workplace.

- To practice effective interviewing and communication skills.

Group Size

Optimally, five subgroups of three to five members each (more subgroups can be accommodated).

Time Required

2 hours.

Materials

- One copy of ADAPT: Analyze the Gap for the first subgroup.

- One copy of ADAPT: Develop Resources for the second subgroup.

- One copy of ADAPT: Align Goals for the third subgroup.

- One copy of ADAPT: Plan Interventions for the fourth subgroup.

- One copy of ADAPT: Track Implementation for the fifth subgroup.

- One copy of ADAPT Interviewing Tips for each participant.

- One copy of ADAPT Problem-Solving Model for each participant.

- One copy of ADAPT Problem-Solving Model Visual for each participant.

- A pencil and three sheets of paper for each participant.

- A flip chart and a felt-tipped markers (or a whiteboard and markers) for the facilitator.

- Masking tape for posting flip-chart pages.

Physical Setting

A room large enough to permit some privacy for each subgroup to prevent distractions. Writing surfaces and wall space for posting flip-chart pages are required.

Facilitating Risk Rating

Moderate.

Process

1. Review the goals of the session and give an overview of the activity.

2. Obtain a volunteer. This should be someone with a real-life, work-related, interpersonal or systems challenge. He or she will be interviewed by a representative of each of the subgroups, using the ADAPT problem-solving model. As the risk level for this activity is moderate, it might be helpful to use some humor in obtaining a volunteer. For example, you might say, "The issue you've been working on for years in therapy might not be the one you want to explore in front of the entire group."

3. Request that the group members agree to maintain confidentiality about the volunteer and his or her issue. Let your volunteer know that you cannot promise that the agreement will be respected by all group members.

4. Depending on the size of the total group, create at least five subgroups, labeling them 1, 2, 3, 4, and 5. Give the members a few minutes to introduce themselves if they are not already acquainted with one another.

5. Introduce the activity by explaining the ADAPT problem-solving model. Explain the importance of using effective problem-solving tools within the workplace, including effective interviewing and communication skills.

6. Distribute a pencil and three sheets of paper to each participant.

7. Provide each of five subgroups with a different handout from the ADAPT model. If there are more than five groups, repeat by starting over and giving each subgroup one handout.

8. Distribute the Interviewing Tips handout to all participants and review the handout verbally.

   (15 minutes.)

9. Tell the subgroup members that they are to use the Interviewing Tips as a guideline in their forthcoming interviews. Allow 5 minutes for them to discuss this as a group. For Round 1, have two representatives of Group 1 interview the volunteer for 5 to 8 minutes while the other subgroups observe.

10. At the conclusion of the interview, ask all five subgroups to reconvene for 3 minutes. Group 1 is to debrief how its interview went. The volunteer is to make notes on what was helpful and what could have been improved during the interview. The other four groups are to revisit their tasks with the new information.

    (20 minutes.)

11. Have two representatives from each of the remaining four groups interview the volunteer, in turn, while the other groups observe. After each interview, have the subgroups reconvene, as described above.

    (45 minutes.)

12. Interview the volunteer relative to his or her feedback.

    (7 minutes.)

13. Ask each subgroup to take 5 minutes to generate a list of implications/applications relative to the experience. Have each group report their top two ideas.

    (20 minutes.)

14. Distribute an ADAPT Problem-Solving Model handout and an ADAPT Problem-Solving Model Visual to each participant. Allow participants to glance briefly at the handouts. Say: "The ADAPT Problem-Solving Model guides the user through a communicative and mutually respectful collaboration process. It aims to facilitate business partners/teams in uncovering their collective resources, selecting shared goals, and working

together to see these goals transform into progress and prosperity. As the ADAPT model is applied, it is helpful to use techniques outlined in the Interviewing Tips handout."

15. Lead a discussion based on the following questions:

   • What are the implications/applications of the activity to the workplace in general?

   • In what ways can you apply what you have learned about the ADAPT Problem-Solving Model to your workplace?

   (15 minutes.)

Variation

   • Provide each subgroup with a copy of each of the **A, D, A, P,** and **T** handouts and let the groups use the complete model to interview one another.

References

Milliren, A., Milliren, M., & Eckstein, D. (2007). Combining Socratic questions with the "ADAPT" problem-solving model: Implications for couple's conflict resolution. *The Family Journal: Counseling and Therapy for Couples and Families, 15*(4), 415–419.

Sommers-Flannagan, J., & Sommers-Flannagan, R. (2007). *Clinical interviewing* (4th ed.). Hoboken, NJ: John Wiley & Sons.

Submitted by Jennifer Straub, Nicole Russo, Sarah Eckstein, and Daniel Eckstein.

Jennifer Straub *received her master of science degree in mental health counseling from Capella University. She is currently a protective services worker at the Northumberland County Area Agency on Aging and a social worker assistant with Precision Home Health Care, Inc., in Pennsylvania. Her professional work history with a diverse population includes children, adults, and senior citizens. She has co-authored two articles in* The Family Journal: Counseling & Therapy for Couples and Families.

Nicole Russo *obtained a master's degree in mental health counseling from Capella University. Currently, she is counseling individuals with co-occurring conditions at the Willough at Naples. She previously served as a case manager for homeless individuals and veterans with co-occurring conditions. Nicole also has co-authored two articles in* The Family Journal: Counseling & Therapy for Couples and Families.

Sarah Eckstein *earned a bachelor's degree in psychology from the University of Oregon. She is currently a student in a master's program in mental health counseling at Southern Oregon University.*

Daniel Eckstein, Ph.D., *is a professor of medical psychology at the Saba University School of Medicine of the Dutch Caribbean. He is a former senior consultant with University Associates. Daniel is the author of* Leadership by Encouragement, Psychological Fingerprints, Raising Respectful Kids in a Rude World, *and* The Couples Counseling Handbook.

In Memoriam

This page is in honor of Drs. John Jones and Phyliss Cooke. The three of us created the original ADAPT problem-solving model that is the basis of this structured activity.

John Jones, Ph.D.

John Jones earned his doctorate from the University of Alabama, taught at the University of Iowa, and went on to become a co-founder of University Associates. There, and in his later work with a number of people, John Jones was an innovator, a collaborator, and a mentor. He specialized in group and team development, communication skills, and humanizing processes. He also was a well-published writer on a number of subjects. When I was an intern in the Laboratory Education Intern Program, sponsored by University Associates (later Pfeiffer & Company), and during the next decade, when I worked for UA as a senior consultant, John became a valued mentor and colleague. He taught me so much about people, about conducting workshops, about writing, and even more about living in joy.

Phyliss Cooke, Ph.D.

Phyliss Cooke received her Ph.D. from Kent State University. She specialized in group facilitation, organization development, personal development, and management development. At University Associates (later Pfeiffer & Company), she served as a senior consultant and as Dean of the Master's Program in Human Resource Development. Phyliss created the seven themes that were the basis of our encouragement article for couples. They include:

1. Being a positive role model
2. Seeing strengths and abilities in others
3. Support over the long haul (consistency)
4. Seeing people as special
5. Inspiring others
6. Supporting what others are interested in, especially in dark times
7. Helping others make career choices

Phyliss lived these themes as a friend and as a mentor. I am grateful for her friendship, encouragement, and wise advice for over forty years. Phyliss passed away in July 2011.

I miss John and Phyliss, and I hope that all our readers will be blessed with such enduring friendships and such worthy mentors.

Daniel Eckstein

ADAPT: Analyze the Gap

The first step in any growth process is identifying the gap between what you want and what you currently have. Whether it's deciding to give a pay raise to your employees, starting a new business venture, or divvying up everyday tasks around the office, communicating with others to clarify any gaps between what you want and what they want is imperative. Within this step, actively listening to the other person's feelings and thoughts before giving your own opinion sets the mood for mutual understanding, comfort, and forward motion. Without this, it is much more difficult to truly analyze the gap in feelings, actions, and beliefs surrounding any topic.

It is important to keep in mind that we have all risen from the soil of our own gardens and will have a unique perception of the topic.

Sample Scenario

Two companies, Physicians Utilities, Inc., and Doctors Resources International, are merging into one company that will manufacture medical supplies and conduct research about the needs of doctors around the world. In order for a successful merging of these two large companies, the owners of each company need to communicate at length about many factors: distribution of wages, locations of company headquarters, advertising, administrative procedures, etc. Jim Thorton, the owner of Physicians Utilities, Inc., has a very rigid, perfectionist method of management. Hal Goldstein, the owner of Doctors Resources International, highly values diversity of input, communal decision making, and flexibility in his management style. Read on to see how the ADAPT model can be applied to this scenario.

Sample Questions

- What thoughts and feelings do you have now, related to the merging of our companies?

- What thoughts and feelings would we both like to experience about the merger?

- Do differences exist between our expectations?

- What are some key supporting reasons for each person's opinions?

- If you were in my shoes, what do you think I would say to you about the issue of needing to cut back on overtime wages paid to employees?

- On a scale from 1 to 10, how strongly do you feel about having the headquarters in New York City?

- What I've heard you say so far is . . . .

ADAPT: *Develop Resources*

Although facing issues in the workplace can be challenging, a common way to alleviate tension is to seek out resources that will ease the burden. It's highly possible that you or someone you know has solved a similar problem in the past and can offer relief to your anxiety. The "develop resources" step of the ADAPT model involves identifying the skills, knowledge, monetary resources, and ethical values that each person possesses that would help to facilitate a solution to the issue. For example, a resource might be your immense degree of determination in the face of hardship. A brainstorming session can help to facilitate an understanding of some rational means by which the problem can be solved.

Sample Scenario

Jim and Hal begin discussing which resources they can employ in order to bring some relief to this potentially stressful issue. Jim asks his business-savvy father for advice. Hal does extensive research on the subject of international advertising. Hal knows that he can fall back on his well-developed skills of patience, endurance, and compassion in order to work well with Jim. Together, Jim and Hal analyze their budgets to determine that they do have the financial capabilities to go through with their plans and continue to make a profit this year. As long as their communication skills continue to be used, they have hope for a smooth transition.

Sample Questions

- Have you or has anyone you know ever encountered a problem similar to the current one?

- What skills or resources do each of us possess that could help with this merger?

- What additional resources are needed?

ADAPT: Align Goals

Aligning goals within an organization depends on setting goals effectively. Aligning a company's goals in collaboration with employees' needs results in a clearer understanding of performance expectations. Each goal needs to be specific, measurable, attainable, and relevant to the desired outcome. Goal alignment involves focusing on the needs and gaps in regard to the wanted outcome. The involved parties need to find common ground and identify obstacles. Once a goal is set, action must be taken.

Sample Scenario

Jim and Hal developed measurable company goals, based on their visions of the merged company: (1) have at least 90 percent of their positions filled by January 1; (2) design, create, and distribute company-policy handbooks to all international facilities by November 1; and (3) jointly create a new company logo.

Sample Questions

- What do we want to achieve or change?

- What obstacles do we need to overcome?

- What will the end result look like?

ADAPT: *Plan the Intervention*

Once your goals are defined, begin to plan the activities to reach each goal. Just as in using a GPS system, you will need to decide on a definitive destination point in order to reach each goal. Brainstorm different options and activities to help reach a desired goal. Once a list is created, evaluate the options to determine which ones would provide the most assistance in reaching the goal. Then formulate a plan about what specifically will take place. List each step in the order in which it will be implemented to reach the goal. It also helps to list an expected completion date for each step to keep on track.

Sample Scenario

Jim and Hal agree that the plan for the two companies to merge will be completed in six months. They will first focus on outlining company policies and procedures, then on who they will choose as vital staff members, and then on how best to market their new company.

Sample Questions

- What do we need to do to progress from this point?

- Which of these options make the most sense?

- Where do we want to start?

- What other resources do we need to begin and keep moving forward?

ADAPT: *Track Implementation*

Once you develop a plan, set your monitoring strategy. Monitoring each step of your plan allows you to track your progress. Tracking your implementation is a vital component to ensure follow-up and to reach your desired goals. This includes deciding on the specific time frame in which you will reevaluate progress. Together, select a specific date, time, and location for a discussion of your progress. In addition, it is important to determine the criteria for how you will know when you have reached a resolution. This final step of the ADAPT model also involves a reevaluation of how you are doing in reaching your goals at each track-implementation check (Milliren, Milliren, & Eckstein, 2007). Are both of you still aligned with the agreed-on goals? If you and your partner are not aligned, analyze the gap again and repeat the process. If your goals are aligned, return to the intervention plan to select another strategy or the next step to continue working toward the desired goals.

A key element during each check is to interview each other so that each of you has an opportunity to express thoughts and opinions. Remember to use empathic responses and active listening.

Sample Scenario

Jim and Hal have marked their calendars to meet at The Grill restaurant on October 15 at 12:00 p.m. Jim and Hal come to the meeting prepared with updates and notes on their progress toward reaching their desired goals.

Sample Questions

- How will we know when we have reached our desired goals?

- When should we reevaluate our progress?

- Where are we now with our current situation?

- What is the gap between the ideal and the reality?

- What differences of opinion are we presently experiencing?

- What are the areas in which we agree?

- Are we still aligned with the desired goals?

- How do you feel about our progress?

- Are there any new developments?

- How does the development affect progressing toward our goals?

- If the current strategy is not working, what is another intervention strategy we could implement?

- If the current strategy is working, what is the next step and when should we reevaluate?

- What resources do we need to continue working on the plan?

- On a scale of 1 to 10, with 1 meaning that the issue is unresolved and 10 meaning that the issue is resolved, where do you currently lie on that scale?

- What do we need to do differently to reach our desired goals?

ADAPT Interviewing Tips

Listening Responses	Description
Attending Behavior	Encourages communication. Communicates a readiness to respond.
	Eye contact, head nods, facial expressions, and body language.
Empathic Response	Reflects content and feeling. Shows understanding of another's experience.
	"What I hear you saying is. . . ."
Active Listening	Requires the listener to understand, interpret, and evaluate what is heard.
Clarification	In order to obtain additional information. Assists in amending an unclear message or interpretation.
	"Clarify my understanding about. . . ."
Summarizing	Puts together, organizes, and integrates the major aspects of conversation.
	Integrates key ideas or feelings into broad statements.
Paraphrasing	Restates the message heard in one's own words.
Reframing	Broadens restricted responses to promote flexibility in viewing or interpreting situations, thoughts, and actions.

Question Types	Description
Open Versus Closed	Open questions require a response with more than just one word. These questions begin with how, where, what, who, and when.
	"What are your views about merging companies? How are you handling that situation?"
	Closed questions can be answered with one word (yes or no) and can begin with who, do, does, did, is, may, have, and are. They can help to reduce or control how much the other person talks.
	"Do you think you can have the contract prepared by January 1st?"
Why	Refrain from asking "Why?" "Why" questions tend to elicit defensive responses.
Socratic	Broaden our ability to think critically. Challenge us to think accurately and completely while moving us toward our ultimate goal.

	Socratic dialogue includes open questions beginning with how, where, what, who, and when.
	"How do you plan to safeguard our company against the effects of the economic downturn?"
Swing	Can be answered with yes or no, but they produce an elaboration of feelings, thoughts, and issues. These questions start with could, would, can, or will.
	"Will you tell me more about the discussion between you and the operations manager?"
Scaling	Put observations, impressions, and predictions on a scale format, in a range from 0 to 5 or 0 to 10.
	"On a scale of 0 to 10, with 0 representing your being completely against merging the companies and 10 representing your complete agreement to merging the companies, where are you on the scale?"
Language Expression	**Description**
Metaphors	Metaphors enhance mutual understanding and suggest a concept.
	"Level the playing field."
	"It's about the bottom line."
	"We are at a crossroads."
	"I'm on board with that."
Humor	Humor is used to decrease tension.

ADAPT Problem–Solving Model

A	*Analyze the Gap*	Identify the gap between what we want and what we currently have. What emotions, thoughts, and behaviors do you have now related to this topic? What emotions, thoughts, and behaviors would you both like to experience related to this topic?
D	*Develop Resources*	Identify the skills, knowledge, monetary resources, and ethical values that each partner possesses to facilitate a solution for this issue. What skills or resources does each person possess that could help with this merger? What additional resources are needed?
A	*Align Goals*	Each goal needs to be specific, measurable, attainable, and relevant to the desired outcome. Goal alignment involves focusing on the needs and gaps in regard to the wanted outcome. What do we want to achieve or change? What will the result look like?
P	*Plan the Intervention Strategy*	Plan the activities to reach the goals. Develop a list and action steps. Determine who needs to complete each step. Implement the action plan. "What do we need to do to move forward from this point?" "Which of these options makes the most sense in terms of what we are hoping to accomplish?"
T	*Track Implementation*	Track and monitor your progress toward reaching each goal. Mark a specific date, time, and place on a calendar to reevaluate progress.

ADAPT Problem-Solving Model Visual

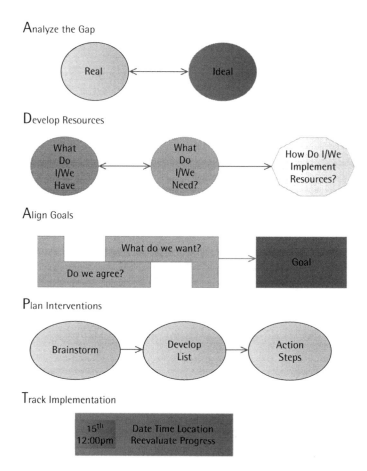

Analyze the Gap

Develop Resources

Align Goals

Plan Interventions

Track Implementation

Developed by Nicole Russo

Pop Goes the Bottom Line!
Examining the Impact of Feedback on Performance

Activity Summary

An energizing activity to demonstrate the power of feedback on motivation and performance.

Goals

- To create a shared experience of the impact of feedback on employees' feelings.

- To examine the impact of feedback on organizational climate, individual motivation, and bottom-line performance.

Group Size

Two teams of approximately six to nine. Larger teams or more teams work, but it is preferable to have an even number of teams.

Time Required

20 to 25 minutes.

Materials

- Six to eight 9-inch balloons per person (approximately one bag of thirty to fifty balloons per team).

- One pushpin per team.

- A flip chart and markers for recording reactions and results.

- The last 3 minutes, when the canon goes off, of Tchaikovsky's "1812 Overture." Remember that music is protected by copyright law, so obtain permission to use the piece.

- A way to play the music.

- (Optional) Small prizes.

Physical Setting

A room large enough for the teams to work without hearing other coach(s) give instructions to their teams.

Facilitating Risk Rating

Moderate.

Facilitator's Note

Be very clear and give good instructions to the two coaches. This is a competitive activity that the participants will quickly engage in, so it's important for the coaches to know exactly what they need to do.

Process

1. Introduce the activity by saying that feedback is critical to individual performance. State that participants are about to experience how feedback can have an impact on them personally.

2. Have participants form two teams at opposite ends of the room. Ask each team to select a coach and come up with a team name. Give each team a bag of balloons.

   (5 minutes.)

3. Have the coaches come forward so that you can give them their instructions privately. Either step outside the room or speak quietly enough not to be overheard. Give each coach a pushpin and explain the following:

   - One coach will be a "good" coach, the other a "bad" coach.

   - Either coach will pop any balloon that does not meet all four of the criteria. A balloon will only be accepted if it is:

     - Fully inflated and tied.

     - Delivered with the left hand.

- A different color than the one just previously accepted.

- Delivered by a different person than the one who delivered the previously accepted balloon.

- Select the good coach and the bad coach. *Note:* If there are more than two teams, either have an equal number of good and bad coaches or have more bad coaches than good.

- Neither coach may give instructions to his or her team before the activity begins.

4. Tell the "good" coach to give specific, behavioral feedback to the team while the team is performing. Comments such as:

- "Thank you. I can accept that balloon because you gave it to me with your left hand."

- "Thanks. That's a perfect balloon because it's fully inflated and knotted."

- {POP!} "Oh, I'm sorry. I can't accept that balloon because I just accepted a blue one from Jenn."

- {POP!} "Wow, Jim, you're really going quickly. Unfortunately, I can't accept this particular balloon from you, since you gave me the last one."

Explain that the team will know exactly what constitutes an acceptable balloon from the feedback, both corrective and reinforcing, all given in a helpful and encouraging manner.

(5 minutes.)

5. Tell the "bad" coach to pop balloons and make critical and cynical remarks (keeping it clean, of course!).

- {POP!} "I can't believe that of all the people I could have had on my team, I've got you losers!"

- {POP!} "Can't you even do a simple task like blow up a balloon?!"

- {POP!} {POP!} "Come on, faster, faster; we're losing!!!!"

The bad coach provides nothing specific about the characteristics of the balloon, just pops balloons and criticizes. (This is the fun role!)

(5 minutes.)

6. Double-check with the coaches to ensure clarity about what constitutes an acceptable balloon and what they're going to do.

(5 minutes.)

7. Return to the main room and have each coach rejoin his or her team. Ask each team to state its team name.

8. Say to the teams, "This is a competitive activity. Your job is to produce as many acceptable balloons as you can in 3 minutes. Your coach will let you know what's acceptable." Don't answer any questions about what constitutes an acceptable balloon.

9. Turn on the last 3 minutes of the "1812 Overture." This serves to energize the room as the popping balloons start to synchronize with the "booms" in the music. It also becomes a timer for the activity!

10. Watch the fun! Be sure the "bad" coach is popping lots of balloons.

(3 minutes.)

11. When the music ends, have participants stay in their teams. Debrief the activity by asking the team members for their reactions. Begin with the team that had the bad coach by asking:

   - How did you feel during the activity?

   - How do you feel about your performance?

   - How do you feel about your coach?

   Next ask the same questions for the team that had the good coach:

   - How did you feel during the activity?

   - How do you feel about your performance?

   - How do you feel about your coach?

12. State that you would now like to discuss performance. Again begin with the team that had the bad coach and ask:

   - How many balloons do you have?

   - What are the criteria for an acceptable balloon? (They may have a few tentative guesses and may have figured out a couple of the criteria. If so, ask, "How hard did you have to work to figure that out?")

13. Now ask the team with the good coach:

    - How many balloons do you have?

    - What are the criteria for an acceptable balloon? (They'll know precisely the criteria set by their coach.)

    (5 to 7 minutes.)

14. Ask everyone to return to their seats. Ask: "What do you think was going on?" Lead a discussion, using the following questions:

    - What was the difference between how the two teams felt?

    - What specifically was happening that caused these feelings and ensured that one team knew what was needed to "win"?

    - What do the results of this activity mean for you as a (supervisor, manager, coach, or leader)?

    - Based on what happened, what do you see as the impact of feedback on individual motivation?

    - What is the impact of feedback on organizational climate and bottom-line performance?

    - What's the one key learning you are taking away from this activity?

    - In what ways can you apply what you have learned to your own department or organization?

    (10 to 15 minutes.)

15. Summarize the key point: Feedback can have a powerful impact on feelings, which impacts morale and motivation, AND it can impact performance and the bottom line.

16. (Optional) Award prizes to both teams (for superior performance for the "good" team and for refraining from physical violence to the people with the "bad" coach.

Submitted by Ken Steiger.

Ken Steiger *has been in the training and consulting field since 1989 and started Steiger Training & Development in 1999, specializing in executive coaching and leadership alignment. He is a regular presenter at Central New York and national ASTD events and served over ten years on the board of the CNY chapter, including three years as president. He was an ASTD National Advisor for Chapters from 2008 to 2011.*

Throwing Kisses
Encouraging Desired Behaviors

Activity Summary

A lively way to encourage participation and engagement during a training session.

Goals

- To increase awareness of others' positive contributions.

- To encourage and reinforce desired behaviors.

Audience

- Any size, but works best with eight to thirty who have easy access to each other.

- Especially useful with intact work teams, groups that have been in conflict and need a light-hearted reminder to look for positives, or groups learning about feedback.

Time Required

5 minutes to introduce; mere seconds throughout a training session.

Materials

- List of Ground Rules or Norms of Behavior for the group.

- Two to three pounds of chocolate kisses, approximately twelve per person.

- (Optional) Small bowls or baskets to hold candy, sufficient to have one for every two or three participants, or if on a table, one large bowl.

Physical Setting

Requires that participants have easy access to an allotment of candies.

Facilitating Risk Rating

Low.

Process

1. Distribute chocolate kisses around the room/area in piles or small containers, either one pile per person or a large pile strategically placed for every two or three participants.

2. Add the phrase "Throw Kisses" as the final bullet on your norms list, whether building it with the participants or predetermined and prepared by you prior to the training session.

3. Create or explain the norms that have been created by the group. When you reach the last one, "Throw Kisses," explain that there are rules associated with the kisses on the table(s) that must be observed throughout the session. These rules include:

   - You cannot give yourself a kiss.

   - You may only give one kiss away, and to only one person at a time.

   - The kiss must be in recognition of another participant's positive behavior, comment, or idea.

   - The process of giving the kiss must include the giver stating aloud to the group: "I am giving this kiss to [recipient] in recognition of [behavior]."

   - If the vocal statement of the kiss is skipped, the kiss must be "re-given" appropriately. (Hopefully, you catch this before it is eaten.)

   - Kisses must be thrown gently and in a safe manner.

   (5 minutes.)

4. Start the process by throwing the first kiss yourself to someone who helped you with setup or participated in creating the norms or other behavior that you desire to have repeated.

5. Be sure to throw a kiss to the first few participants who join in appropriately, and then do so occasionally throughout the session to keep momentum going.

6. Suggestions to ensure success include:

   - Be on the lookout for missed opportunities, e.g., "Gee, was that a comment worthy of a kiss?"

   - Watch for the occasional participant who has not yet been given any kisses; if needed, set him or her up for success by asking an easy question or assigning a simple task (try not to be too obvious, of course).

   - Do not allow vague positives such as "for being such a good team member." Insist on very specific behaviors; they will pick up on this very quickly.

   - Encourage the group to self-monitor for missed opportunities and infractions (eating candy rather than giving it away; forgetting to state aloud what behavior is being recognized; being too vague).

Submitted by Marilyn Marles.

Marilyn Marles *is an organization consultant focused on leveraging organizational and individual strengths to improve performance and productivity. She holds a master's degree from American University/NTL and is a skilled facilitator with strong practical and theoretical background in group dynamics, group process, organization behavior, and results-based performance measurement. She works in the United States and internationally. A recent success involved team development and results-based measures for a federal agency, contributing to a 400 percent increase in department productivity. She proudly owns, and uses, originals of the first eight Pfeiffer & Jones* Handbook of Structured Experiences, *as well as later editions.*

Congratulations!
Mixing It Up

Activity Summary

A simple but effective warm-up and mixer for any group session that reinforces an appreciative approach and the importance of giving recognition.

Goals

- To provide group members a method of introducing themselves to each other in a friendly and non-threatening way.

- To create an atmosphere of appreciation and inquiry.

- To raise the energy level and personal connectedness of a group.

Group Size

Up to one hundred.

Time Required

20 to 30 minutes, depending on group size.

Materials

- One blank congratulations card per person (store-purchased or home-made).

- Pens or pencils.

- The instructions (Steps 4, 5, and 7) on a flip chart (or slide presentation if the group is large).

- Flip chart and markers.

- A container for the cards.
- (Optional) One blank card envelope per person.
- (Optional) Small prizes.

Physical Setting

A writing surface for participants, and a room large enough to move about freely.

Facilitating Risk Rating

Low.

Process

1. Place one congratulations card, standing up as a tent, at each person's place at the table.

2. Introduce the session as a way of "introducing ourselves to each other." Say something like:

   - (For intact teams) "We can always assume that there is someone new to meet or something new to find out about the people we already know. Knowing each other well is critical to our success as a team."

   - (For large groups) "In a large group like this, it would take a great deal of time for all of us to introduce ourselves, even briefly. For eighty people to each give a 3-minute introduction would take over four hours!"

3. Say, "Each of you has a congratulations card at your place. When you sat down, you may have thought of something that you have done recently that would merit a congratulatory note. Maybe you just finished a big report, or finally hired a new assistant, or found out that there's going to be a new baby in the family, or ran the marathon, or reached the age of forty, or finally pruned the apple tree. There are lots of things you could be congratulated for."

4. Ask participants to think of a recent accomplishment. It can be either work-related or of a personal nature, but it should be something specific that they don't mind sharing with others in the room.

5. Ask them to write their accomplishments inside their congratulations cards, phrasing them as "you" statements. For example: "You lost 10 pounds!" They must write legibly and *not* sign their names to the cards.

If you are using envelopes, have participants put their cards into the envelopes before turning them in.

(5 to 10 minutes.)

6. Gather up the cards as they are completed and put them in a bowl, basket, or other large container. Mix them up.

7. Ask each person to draw a card and then find the person whose card he or she has drawn. Once they locate the card's owner, they are to do the following:

   - Introduce themselves if they don't already know each other.

   - Congratulate the other person on the accomplishment.

   - (Optional) Put the card back in the envelope and give it to the person.

8. Allow the party feeling to unfold in the room. People will be mingling, talking, hugging, laughing, as they discover who has accomplished what. As the mingling subsides, invite people to return to their seats.

(10 to 20 minutes.)

9. Ask whether anyone has not found who he or she was looking for. You may allow the group to help them out or, if it is a very large group, tell them that they will have opportunities during breaks to find the person.

10. Once they are settled, ask for any reactions to the activity. Ask who was congratulated for:

    - Something requiring great bravery.

    - The advancement of years (anniversaries or birthdays).

    - A new life (babies, puppies, etc.).

    - A great adventure (e.g., travel).

    - Something learned (from a book, a workshop, a university degree, etc.).

    - Something finished (a report, a decorating project, or a home renovation).

    - A physical accomplishment (ran a race, skied down a mountain).

    - Something that was a big surprise.

11. As people self-identify, congratulate them again. Invite the group members to applaud.

12. Debrief at this point, bringing out comments about:

- Realizing how much more there is to learn about each other.

- Feeling surprised, inspired, and encouraged by others' accomplishments.

- Feeling more connected and uplifted.

(5 minutes.)

Variations

- Debrief using your own categories of accomplishments.

- As you congratulate someone, offer a prize. You may give prizes to both the person whose accomplishment it was and to the person who searched him or her out.

- Base the congratulations cards and prizes on a theme such as a season or upcoming holiday or a color scheme.

Submitted by Jan Yuill.

Jan Yuill *is an organization development consultant, group facilitator, management coach, and interpersonal skills trainer. She provides organizations with simple, yet powerful tools for understanding and balancing complex priorities. For more than twenty years, Jan has partnered with government, private-sector, and nonprofit clients to help create vibrant and remarkable organizations. She is the author of* Organizations Alive! *She has a master of science degree in organization development from Pepperdine University.*

QR Codes for Training
Improving Learning and Performance

Activity Summary

A series of facilitator-led activities that allow trainers to examine how they could integrate QR codes into their work lives.

Goals

- To allow participants to gain a level of comfort in using QR technology.

- To examine current training opportunities for using QR codes.

- To discuss how QR codes improve the effectiveness of learning events.

Group Size

Fifteen to twenty-five trainers.

Time Required

75 to 90 minutes.

Materials

- One Sample Pre-Session Survey for the facilitator.

- One copy of the QR Lecturette for the facilitator.

- One copy of the QR Code Examples for each participant.

- One copy of the QR Code Process Figures.

- Flip chart and markers for recording.

Trainer's Note

You may experience some resistance by those who are technologically averse.

Physical Setting

A room large enough for subgroups to work without disturbing others.

Facilitating Risk Rating

Low.

Preparation

1. Request that trainers bring their smart phones to the session. Note that it is not necessary for all participants to have smart phones.

2. You may wish to preview your audience's awareness and experience with the technology by using a brief survey. Examples of such surveys are located at www.surveymonkey.com/s/TPVZY5F or you can use the example on Sample Pre-Session Survey handout.

3. Test your QR code samples on multiple readers to ensure that they can be read by multiple devices using different applications.

4. (Optional) Post or email information about QR code readers to trainers who will attend before the session.

Process

1. Introduce the session by explaining that participants will be working in small groups to learn how to create and use QR codes in training sessions. Give everyone copies of the handouts. If you have not done so already, explain how QR codes can be used to enhance their work lives. Use the QR Lecturette.

2. Ask participants, "When might you, as training and development professionals, use QR codes?" Responses may include that QR codes may be used to (1) serve a business objective (What is the purpose?), (2) add value for the user (give the end-user a piece of information of value), or (3) provide assistance (take someone to a website, article, or instructions or facilitate a call to action).

3. Divide the trainers into small groups based on level of experience using QR codes and availability of smart phones. Each group must have at least one participant with a smart phone or tablet. One way to create

groups is to use a "living" Likert-type scale. Label four areas across the back of the room:

- I use QR codes all the time.

- I have scanned QR codes.

- I have seen QR codes.

- I know very little about QR codes.

4. Ask each participant to place him- or herself at the location that represents his or her experience with QR codes. Once people have positioned themselves on the scale, form subgroups with one member from each group to ensure experienced users are with those who have never used the technology. Have subgroups find places to work. Give them copies of the two handouts.

(15 minutes.)

5. Tell participants who have smart phones to download one of the free QR code applications, based on the type of phone they have. List the following on the flip chart: Kaywa Reader, QR Reader, BeeTagg, i-nigma, Qrafter, TAPP reader, Bakodo, ATT Code Scanner, and QR Droid. Once everyone has downloaded an application, ask them to open the applications on their phones. Each phone's options will vary slightly, depending on the application that they are using and phone (BlackBerry, Windows 7, iPhone, or Droid). Ask everyone to select the option to "decode from the camera." Ask participants who have smart phones to check their phones to be sure they work with a sample QR code like Example 1 on the handout. Have them hold the camera still to allow it to read the code or to take a photo image of the code, depending on the application. Have the most experienced participants explain to others in their small groups what they are doing. Circulate among the subgroups to ensure each has the level of expertise required to be successful and answer any questions that they may have.

(15 minutes.)

6. Now ask groups to create QR codes using qrcode.kaywa.com. They should go to the website and input information, such as another website. Ask participants to look at Figure 1, where the URL has been selected and the website (www.thepriceconsultinggroup.com) has been entered. Have participants click on "generate" to create their QR codes. A code can be

saved as an image on the phone for future use or cut and pasted into documents.

(15 minutes.)

7. Next, ask the experienced participants to demonstrate to other members of their subgroups how using a link shortener like bit.ly can be used to simplify a QR code. Have them enter www.thepriceconsultinggroup. com on the bit.ly site to create a shorter web address. Have them compare their results with Figure 2. State that the shortener results in fewer characters or less information that needs to be included in the code and therefore a simpler QR code. Tell them to notice ways in which the QR code in Figures 3 and 4 is simpler than the code in Figures 1 and 2, but still directs end-users to the desired website. Let them practice for a while, comparing their results with Example 2.

    (15 minutes.)

8. Explain that shortening the code will make it faster to read and result in less frustration or error when using low-quality phone scanners. This also allows them to track usage of the QR code, as sites like bit.ly capture analytics, such as how many clicks, conversations on Twitter, conversations on Facebook, "Likes," comments, when the link was used, and the country location. Answer any questions participants have.

    (5 minutes.)

9. Bring the large group back together to discuss how QR codes could be used in the training field. One example would be using QR codes for a survey or to facilitate gathering information from end-users. Instead of respondents needing a lengthy link to copy and paste to take a survey, a QR code enables them to quickly access the survey. List other ideas they may have for QR codes on the flip chart. You may wish to add other common uses that were not mentioned, such as:

    *   *Employee satisfaction surveys:* Enable employees to give quick feedback about their jobs, an initiative, or even a training event using their smart phones.

    *   *Exit surveys:* Gather feedback from employees about their experience on the job by including a QR code in their last paycheck.

    *   *Customer survey/performance data:* Include a QR code that directs customers or end-users to provide real-time feedback about their experience.

- *Testing, evaluating, polling:* Use a QR code to direct participants to a website for a test or evaluation during a training session. Participants can also be polled during training by providing a QR code to a polling website to obtain immediate feedback.

- *Name tags:* Include a QR code on employee name badges or business cards to allow customers to obtain contact information.

Note that most of the examples could be created at http://qrcode.kaywa .com/ using one of the options. Youscan.me is another site that allows multiple actions all embedded in one QR code. Ask them to look at Example 5, which shows a QR code that directs the user to follow on Twitter, "like" a Facebook page, or go to a website. Answer any questions.

(15 to 20 minutes.)

10. Tell the trainers that you will show them how QR codes can allow learners to track their progress during a learning event. Display the following questions on a flip-chart page or PowerPoint slide:

- One benefit of using a link shortener is:

- True or False: Mobile barcode (QR code) scanning was up over 4500 percent in 2011 compared with 2010.

- QR codes should:

  - Serve a business objective

  - Add value for the user

  - Provide contextual assistance

  - Be scannable

  - All of the above

11. Tell participants to take 3 minutes to agree on the correct answers to the three posted questions as a group. Once time is up, have the participants scan QR code Example 3 to check their answers. Ask how they did and whether there are any questions. Ask participants for examples of how they might be able to use this feature of QR codes in their training sessions. Some examples of how this could be used in training include:

- Providing a self-check option on handouts or worksheets to have participants assess their understanding of key concepts.

- Providing a link to a quiz (multiple-choice survey using a site like SurveyMonkey) to provide the facilitator feedback on how well the audience understands the content.

- Providing a link to a polling website to obtain audience feedback on a question (safe, anonymous way to gain audience participation).

(10 to 15 minutes.)

12. Ask the trainers how they think QR codes could be used in learning events to distribute information. Some examples include:

- Share articles for reading before or after the session (provide a link to the document).

- Schedule calendar items to change or add learning events to a calendar. These items must be embedded in a webpage first; see directions for Outlook at www.ehow.com/how_8121530_add-calendar-outlook.html. Directions for Gmail at www.google.com/googlecalendar/event_publisher_guide.html.

- Follow up with a copy of a presentation or handout (provide a link to a document on a company website, SlideShare, or blog).

- Providing announcements such as location or time changes or winners of events.

13. Have participants view an announcement at Example 4 on the handout. Have each group create its own QR code announcement. (Note Example 4: Team meeting tomorrow in the break room @ 9am. Join us for doughnuts and coffee. We'll be celebrating someone's service anniversary and the sales contest winner!)

(15 minutes.)

14. After you have completed the activities, lead a final processing discussion asking the following questions. You may wish to use a flip chart to record responses:

- What are the benefits of using a QR code in training?

- What are some of the challenges that you may face in implementing QR codes?

- How can you overcome or address those challenges?

- What ideas do you have to use QR codes in your training?

- How do you intend to integrate QR codes in your future training sessions?

(15 to 20 minutes.)

Variations

- Different activities may be used or added to expand on the basic activities, such as creating a QR code with your personal contact information, creating a QR code link to a video, or identifying opportunities to integrate QR codes within an existing presentation.

- QR codes may be presented in different ways. For example, a PowerPoint slide with QR codes integrated into it may be used.

- Other QR codes may also be presented in hard copy handouts for use following the session.

- Ask participants to share other helpful QR codes or websites they know about with the group.

References

Price, K., & Straining, L. (2011). QR codes: Improving learning and performance. PowerPoint presentation/webinar.

Schottmuller, A. (2011). 10 ways to use QR codes for better conversion rates. Retrieved July 1, 2011, from http://nfcdata.com/blog/2011/07/26/10-ways-to-use-qr-codes-for-better-conversion-rates/#ixzz1cVtePKuT.

———

Submitted by Kella B. Price.

Kella B. Price, DBA, SPHR, CPLP, *CEO of Price Consulting Group, has thirteen years' experience in training and development. Kella has published on social media, diversity, expatriates, and stress. She published an ASTD Info-line on the topic of Twitter that was included in* Road-Tested Activities. *She is adept at using Web 2.0 technologies, including blogging, twitter, bookmarking, and social media networks. She conducts training on how to use technologies as a tool for collaboration and building relationships.*

QR Lecturette

QR code (an abbreviation for *Quick Response Code*) is the trademark for a type of matrix barcode (or two-dimensional code) first designed for the automotive industry. The QR code's fast readability and comparatively large storage capacity has expanded its use to almost every other facet of business. QR codes appear on packaging, signage, and in magazines, but have great utility in the workplace for communication as well as training and development.

The code consists of black modules (square dots) arranged in a square pattern on a white background. The information encoded can be made up of four standardized kinds (modes) of data (numeric, alphanumeric, byte/binary, Kanji), or through supported extensions, virtually any kind of data.

Mobile barcode scanning was up over 4,500 percent from the first quarter of 2010 to the first quarter of 2011, largely because the dissemination of smart phones has put a barcode reader in everyone's pocket. As a result, the QR code has become a focus of advertising strategy, since it provides quick and effortless access to the brand's website. Beyond mere convenience to the consumer, the importance of this capability is that it increases the conversion rate (the chance that contact with the advertisement will convert to a sale), by bringing the viewer to the advertiser's site immediately.

Codes are captured using a QR code decoder, which is a mobile app found on almost all smart phones, or storing a company's information such as address and related information alongside its alpha-numeric text data, as can be seen in the Yellow Pages directory and in-store product labeling. Users may receive text, add a vCard contact to their device, open a uniform resource identifier (URI), or compose an email or text message after scanning QR codes. They can generate and print their own QR codes for others to scan and use by visiting one of several paid or free QR code-generating sites or apps.

QR codes storing addresses and uniform resource locators (URLs) may appear in magazines, on signs, on buses, on business cards, or on almost any object about which users might need information. Users with a camera phone equipped with the correct reader application can scan the image of the QR code to display text, contact information, connect to a wireless network, or open a web page in the telephone's browser.

Sample Pre-Session Survey

1. Which position best describes you?

   ☐ Consultant

   ☐ HR Director

   ☐ Manager

   ☐ Trainer

   ☐ Other

2. I have used QR codes personally.

   ☐ True

   ☐ False

3. I have used QR codes professionally.

   ☐ True

   ☐ False

4. In which areas do you mostly see QR codes being used?

   ☐ Marketing

   ☐ Sales

   ☐ Training

   ☐ Safety

   ☐ Contests

   ☐ Data Collection

   ☐ Data Distribution

5. Please enter your e-mail address.

The 2013 Pfeiffer Annual: Training.
Copyright © 2013 by John Wiley & Sons, Inc. Reprinted by permission of Pfeiffer, an Imprint of Wiley. www.pfeiffer.com

QR Code Examples

QR Code Process Figures

Figure 1. Creating a QR Code

Figure 2. Using a Link-Shortening Website

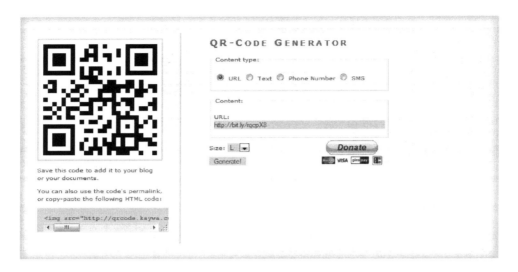

Figure 3. QR Code Using Link Shortener

Figure 4. Differences Between Two QR Codes

Dialogue
Using Discussions to Facilitate Learning

Activity Summary

An activity that assists facilitators to gain buy-in to the benefits of using dialogue as a learning process.

Goals

- To understand how dialogue facilitates better learning.
- To encourage participants to learn through dialogue.

Group Size

Any size.

Time Required

20 to 30 minutes.

Materials

- One copy of the Dialogue handout for each participant.
- Whiteboard or flip chart.
- Markers.
- Paper and pencils for participants.

Physical Setting

Any.

Facilitating Risk

Moderate.

Process

1. Explain that the purpose of the activity is to understand the value of using dialogue during the training session.

2. Use the Dialogue handout as a lecturette to present the benefits of using a dialogue process during a training session. Answer any questions about the technique.

   (10 minutes.)

3. Distribute the handout, paper, and pencils to the participants.

4. Ask them to form small groups of three or four to discuss the topic of dialogue. Suggest issues to consider, such as having a firm mindset or being intolerant of others' ideas. Ensure that all the participants understand the task.

   (5 minutes.)

5. Pull the group back together and bring out major points from their discussions, listing them on the flip chart or whiteboard.

   (15 minutes.)

6. Close with a discussion leading to an agreement from participants to adhere to the dialogue process during the duration of the training program.

   (5 minutes.)

Variation

- The activity could be an entire module in a train-the-trainer program, with participants using chart paper to write their ideas and then having a gallery walk and presentation of those ideas.

Contributed by Mohandas Nair.

Mohandas Nair *is a management educator, teacher, trainer, writer, and a facilitator of learning. He earned a B.Tech. (Mech.) from IIT Kharagpur, India, has a diploma in training and development, and has more than thirty years of experience in industry and consulting in the field of industrial engineering and human resource development. He has published two books, written numerous articles, and facilitated many management development programs.*

Dialogue

When learning, each adult approaches the task in a unique fashion. We all have specific needs and tend to pick up only what *content* we feel is important to our own situations. Depending on what interests us and catches our attention, we pay attention to different aspects of every experience. We may explore some more material out of curiosity, but are likely to do so alone.

We also have our own preferences for *how* to learn. We want flexibility to determine what to explore and what to ignore and the methods to use, such as note-taking, research, discussion, or role playing. Basically, we seek to be independent.

However, when people come together for a learning experience such as this workshop, we learn from each other. This makes us dependent on one another. As your trainer, I must balance your need for independence with the dependency inherent in group learning, which requires sharing and give-and-take. One way to meld these needs is through the process of dialogue.

What is dialogue? It's learning through discussion. For successful dialogue, we all must follow a few simple guidelines. These include:

- Stay on topic.

- Share your thoughts, values, and beliefs on the subject without defensiveness.

- Listen to others' ideas without judgment.

- Listen to understand.

- Display positive body language and provide positive feedback.

- Enquire to clarify what you do not understand.

- Accept others' comments as their thoughts, values, and beliefs, rather than placing your own interpretation on them.

- Remain open to others' ideas.

- Silence for thinking is acceptable.

- Maintain respect for all involved.

Dialogue requires that we listen and respond to others with an open mind. We have to set aside our prejudices and learn from others. In a spirit of dialogue, you and I, as the facilitator, must reach out to understand one another and enrich ourselves.

Dialogue can help us build shared meaning from various perspectives. Dialogue requires that we share our thoughts, values, and beliefs without having to justify them. Dialogue does not have a place for negative feedback. Dialogue requires all of us to seek to understand how we are viewed from others' perspectives. You can increase your own understanding of a topic by hearing others' thoughts on it, even if they are radically different from your own. This give-and-take builds our confidence to handle challenging situations.

Dialogue uses enquiry to dig more deeply into whatever the topic is. Dialogue invites others' assumptions and underlying thinking. We listen more and learn more as a consequence. Listening also communicates respect for others, encouraging them to contribute without fear of being put down. Suspending judgment encourages others to clearly express themselves.

When groups come together in a dialogue, they are learning to think together. The shared understanding that comes out of dialogue leads to a greater whole.

Buzz, Buzz
Increasing Participant Engagement

Activity Summary

A dual outcome training technique that increases participation during and after the learning event and also challenges participants to use the technique in the workplace.

Goals

- To develop an ongoing conversation among training session participants to enhance learning.

- To transfer the concept into the workplace to address lack of engagement and poor communication.

Group Size

Ten to twenty in "buzz groups" of three to four participants. Ideally, participants in each group are from the same organization.

Time Required

90 to 120 minutes or more, depending on the number of buzz group feedback discussions allowed.

Materials

- Paper and pen or pencil for each participant.

- A flip chart and a felt-tipped marker for each buzz group.

- Masking tape for each group to post flip-chart sheets.

Physical Setting

A room large enough for buzz groups to work without disturbing one another.

Facilitating Risk Rating

Moderate.

Process

1. During the opening of a half-day, one-day, or two-day session, explain that participants will practice a learning technique using "buzz groups" that will enhance everyone's learning experience. The "buzz groups" will remain intact throughout the training session and afterward for follow-up. Tell participants that buzz groups are also a viable technique to use in the workplace and ask them to consider ways they can use them back on the job.

2. Explain that the buzz group members should share new perspectives, not rehash or reinforce currently held views. Answer any questions and then ask participants to form buzz groups using the following parameters:

   • Members of a group should not know each other well.

   • Three or four to a group.

   • If possible, members should come from different areas of the organization or even different organizations.

3. Once buzz groups are formed, ask each group to share contact information among group members for a feedback follow-up after the session. Information should include, at a minimum: name, telephone number, physical location (address or room number), and email address. Be sure participants are clear that they will need to follow up after the session; this expectation leads to better comprehension throughout the training session.

   (5 minutes.)

4. Remind them that their "buzz groups" will be used throughout the workshop. Ask each group to:

   • Select a group name and write it at the top of their flip chart, along with all group members' names.

- Choose a spokesperson who will speak for the group more than once during the workshop.

- Ask buzz groups to list three or four things the members are expecting from the training session on their flip charts and to post the sheets on the wall.

State that they have about 20 minutes for this process.

(20 minutes.)

5. Provide a 1-minute warning before the end of the activity (*Note:* This is a good practice to use at other times throughout the session also.)

6. Ask the spokesperson for each buzz group to introduce his or her buzz group and the expectations of members.

(2 minutes per group.)

7. After hearing all the expectations, say, "I see you have some clear expectations; some are similar and some different. One of the key things we will demonstrate today is how to encourage engagement and apply what we learn here to the workplace. What input or questions do you have before we begin?"

(10 minutes.)

8. At predetermined learning or feedback points throughout the training day or as each important "take-away" point is made, have buzz groups debrief what they have just learned. Allow approximately 5 minutes for the buzz group discussions of each learning point or feedback opportunity. Then have the spokespersons present the buzz groups' feedback to the large group, usually as a short summation.

(5 minutes, plus 1 to 2 minutes per group each time.)

9. As the learning day progresses, allow for additional discussions or provide opportunities for the buzz groups to clarify or add information to the group discussion. At times you may assign a topic with directions such as:

- Discuss how this will affect your job, or

- Identify ways to implement this when you get back to the workplace, or

- List roadblocks that prevent you from doing this and what you can do about it.

This allows everyone to become more engaged in the learning and better prepared when returning to the job.

(10 to 15 minutes each time.)

10. Near the end of the day, ask the following questions:

    - What did you experience in your buzz group?

    - What difference did the buzz group make in your learning experience? Did working with your buzz group help you stay better engaged?

    - How did different viewpoints of group members affect your learning?

    - What did you observe about the power of talking things through as the day progressed?

    - How do you anticipate using buzz groups back on the job?

    (10 minutes.)

11. Ask the buzz groups to form one last time to identify what each person will do as a result of the training. Each group should establish a date, time, and location (if possible) for a follow-up meeting to continue to explore the topic and to support each other's goals for using the technique in the future.

    (10 minutes.)

12. Refer to the expectations of the day from the opening activity. Ask each buzz group to articulate whether their expectations were met. Lead a brief discussion about buzz groups.

    - How could the concept of buzz groups be transferred to the workplace?

    - How do you think being a part of a buzz group would impact individual or work group performance?

    - What would it be like in your company if decisions and meetings were handled in the buzz group fashion?

    - What are you going to do as a result of this experience?

    (10 minutes.)

13. Be sure to request feedback about the buzz groups on your evaluation sheet. Remind participants to attend their follow-up buzz group meetings.

Submitted by Sandra A. Shelton.

Sandra A. Shelton *is a leader in workforce engagement, communication, and leadership development. Her perspective includes academic, corporate, and nonprofit leadership and entrepreneurship. Sandra has been making a difference for more than two decades, in fifteen countries, through 2,600 keynotes to hundreds of companies based on StrengthBank®, Communication WorkOuts®, and other unique concepts. Her clear understanding of leadership development relates to every person's service and communication in effective working relationships. Her upcoming book topics include Leadership Revival and Service on Purpose™.*

Superpowers
Learning to Improve Performance

Activity Summary

A superhero character–based activity that allows participants to brainstorm ways to improve their performance.

Goals

- To help participants brainstorm ideas to improve their work performance.

- To help participants translate their ideas into actionable initiatives.

- To create awareness of performance issues and find ways to improve.

Group Size

Ten or twelve people from the same organization, in dyads.

Time Required

3 hours.

Materials

- One Superhero Card per participant, plus four or five additional cards for the facilitator.

- One copy of Superpowers Worksheet 1 for each participant. One copy of Superpowers Worksheet 2 for each participant.

- Paper, Post-it Notes, and a pencil/pen for each participant.

- A flip chart and markers for recording.

- Masking tape for posting flip-chart sheets.

Physical Setting

A room that accommodates up to twelve people and large enough for pairs to work without disturbing others. Privacy is critical, so a room that can be closed off from the regular work space should be used.

Facilitating Risk Rating

High. This is a very personal topic, and employees may feel exposed and need encouragement.

Preparation

1. Create Superhero Cards: select heroes that you feel are the most disparate, inspirational, and even funny. To create your own custom cards, use images or names from the Internet or purchased images. Create cards using cardstock cut to playing card size. See Table 1 for examples of superhero characters.

2. Contact participants before the session and ask them to take out their most recent performance reviews and to select two key areas for improvement. Instruct participants to email you their top two areas for improvement. Reassure participants that their information will remain anonymous.

3. Prior to the session, review all of the responses and prioritize the performance issues based on frequency. Plan to cover the issues relevant to most of the participants. If there are few duplicates, prioritize based on importance to the organization. Take the prioritized list to the session.

Process

1. Start the session by explaining the objective: To help employees transform the areas for improvement from their performance reviews into actionable initiatives.

2. Lead a warm-up exercise to help participants become more comfortable with the topic and to encourage sharing and a few laughs. It will increase participants' familiarity with some of the superheroes and give them practice translating a superhero quality to the workplace.

3. Pass the deck of Superhero Cards, telling participants to each select one as his or her own personal superhero. Explain that they will use their superheroes to introduce themselves. Say that each participant will give the name and powers of his or her chosen superhero and then complete the following statement, written on the flip chart: "If my superhero worked here, his/her job would be _____ and he/she would accomplish it well by doing _____."
    Give them a few minutes to think about the assignment and decide what to say. Answer any questions.

    (10 minutes.)

4. Begin with your own superhero, state his or her powers, and then answer the question on the flip chart. It may be helpful to be a bit amusing with the answer about what your superhero's job would be. Then call on participants in turn until everyone has had a chance to describe his or her superhero.

    (2 minutes per person.)

5. Tell participants that they will next have a chance to determine how superheroes would improve work performance in the organization by using their superpowers. Select one of the superheroes that remains in the deck. Ask all participants to call out the hero's superpowers and how this superhero "saves the day." Capture their comments on the flip chart. When the group has exhausted its responses, offer another superhero and ask them to brainstorm this superhero's powers. Again, list them on the flip chart. Tape the flip-chart sheets to the wall as you fill them. Complete another round or two, depending upon time available.

    (15 to 20 minutes.)

6. Select one of the key performance issues you identified before the session and write it at the top of a new page of the flip chart. Explain that a superhero has been known to exhibit this poor behavior at work. Ask participants to brainstorm: "How might this superhero use his or her powers to improve his or her performance at work?" Allow for silly, crazy, unrealistic, and even illegal ideas to be proposed. Encourage many ideas. When participants have exhausted all ideas, tape the flip-chart pages to the wall.

    (10 minutes.)

7. Select one of the *unrealistic* superpower performance improvements that was brainstormed and write it at the top of a blank flip-chart page. Ask

participants to brainstorm how they might take this silly/unrealistic way to improve performance and make it more realistic. Encourage responses and probe for more realistic ideas and ways to make other ideas more realistic. When their ideas are exhausted, tape the flip-chart pages to the wall.

(5 minutes.)

8. Repeat by brainstorming *realistic* performance improvement ideas, coming up with as many realistic solutions as possible. A total of two more rounds at 5 minutes each is reasonable, but it depends on the priority placed on solving the performance issue. If many people listed a particular performance issue, you may want to devote several rounds to it.

(10 minutes.)

9. Ask participants to walk around the room to review all of the realistic solutions proposed, identify the solutions most likely to help improve performance, and then make checkmarks next to the top four solutions they see. (This is a good time for a short break.)

(5 minutes.)

10. Divide the participants into pairs. Assign each pair two different performance issues from the list you created prior to the session. (You may wish to list all the performance issues on a flip-chart page so that everyone can see all the issues at once, but be sure pairs do not work on the same issues.)

11. Distribute two copies of Superpowers Worksheet 1 to each pair. Have them list the performance issues they were assigned to work on at the top of the worksheets.

12. Review the instructions for each portion of the worksheet and tell them they will have 5 minutes to work together to:

    • Select one of their superheroes for each issue;

    • Discuss the superhero's superpowers and how he or she saves the day; and

    • Write their answers on the worksheets.

    After 5 minutes, call time.

    (5 minutes.)

13. Tell the pairs they now have 10 minutes to brainstorm methods the superheros might use to improve performance at work. Encourage them to be unrealistic, ridiculous, or crazy and to write ideas on Post-it Notes, one

idea per note. When they have finished, they should select their top four ideas. Call time after 10 minutes.

(10 minutes.)

14. Next, have the pairs brainstorm how to make their ideas realistic. Ask, "How might you create more realistic solutions for improving perform- ance?" Tell them to write each idea on a Post-It Note. When they are fin- ished, have them write their top four ideas on Post-it Notes.

(10 minutes.)

15. Have the pairs repeat the steps above for their second performance issue, selecting a different superhero.

(25 minutes.)

16. Instruct pairs to review all of their ideas and to select the top two realistic solutions for each of the two performance issues they have worked on to share with the rest of the group (a total of four solutions).

17. Bring the participants together as a large group. Ask each pair to state the problem and share their top two realistic solutions. As each pair presents, tape completed worksheets onto a wall to create a "wall of performance improvements."

(20 minutes.)

18. Distribute two copies of Superpowers Worksheet 2 to each pair. Tell par- ticipants they will work independently to complete these worksheets. Instruct them to walk to the "wall of performance improvements" to review all of the solutions posted there, paying particular attention to the solutions offered for their own performance issues. Tell partici- pants they should consider how their results can be measured and what next steps should be taken to accomplish each solution. Provide an example based on one of the solutions presented earlier. Give them 20 minutes for this task. Circulate among participants to answer questions and offer suggestions.

(25 minutes.)

19. Bring the workshop to a close by encouraging a few participants to share their initiatives, measures, and next steps. If appropriate, lead applause after each.

(10 minutes.)

20.	Thank everyone for participating and encourage participants to continue to work on their initiatives and next steps. Suggest that participants meet with their supervisors to discuss their plans and to gain support.

Submitted by Lisa Strick.

Lisa Strick *is the chief idea officer of The Idea Bungalow, a boutique marketing and innovation consultancy. A respected trainer, speaker, and author, Lisa has led brainstorming training sessions for creativity professionals at CPSI, licensing executives at Toy Fair, and research professionals at QRCA. Lisa was previously an instructor of creative problem solving at Otis College in Los Angeles. Some of her brainstorming exercises are featured in Arthur Van Gundy's* 101 More Great Games and Activities.

Table 1. Examples of Superhero Characters

Marvel Universe® Characters	DC Comics® Characters	Other Characters
Captain America	Batman	Sabrina, the Teenage Witch (Disney)
Iron Man	Superman	Kim Possible (Disney)
Thor	Wonder Woman	Aladdin (Disney)
Spiderman	The Joker	Peter Pan (Disney)
Fantastic Four	Cat Woman	Popeye (Warner Bros.)
X-Men	Riddler	Harry Potter (Warner Bros.)
Wolverine	Scooby Doo	Speedy Gonzalez (Warner Bros.)
Hulk	Hercules	Kung Fu Panda (DreamWorks)
Invisible Woman	Peacemaker	Shrek (DreamWorks)
Storm		Indiana Jones (Paramount)
Daredevil		James Bond (Columbia Pictures)
		Luke Skywalker (Lucasfilm)
		Hans Solo (Lucasfilm)
		Yoda (Lucasfilm)

Superpowers Worksheet 1

Performance Area to Improve: _____

Superhero Card Selected: _____

Superhero Superpowers/How He or She Saves the Day:

_____

_____

_____

_____

_____

Methods superhero might use to improve performance at work (be unrealistic/ ridiculous/crazy):

1.

2.

3.

4.

Make it realistic: How might you change these and create more realistic solutions to improving your performance?

1.

2.

3.

4.

Superpowers Worksheet 2

Performance Area to Improve: _____

Initiatives	Measures	Next Steps
1.		
2.		
3.		
4.		

The Creative Leader
Measuring Creativity Characteristics

Activity Summary

An activity that highlights the essential behaviors that characterize creative leaders.

Goals

- To identify the roles of a creative leader.

- To assess strengths and weaknesses of being a creative leader.

Group Size

Ten to twenty organizational leaders.

Time Required

45 to 60 minutes.

Materials

- One copy of the Creative Leader Behavior Inventory for each participant.

- Pens or pencils for participants.

- A flip chart and markers.

Physical Setting

A standard training room with chairs and a writing surface.

Facilitating Risk Rating

Low to Moderate.

Process

1. Introduce the topic to the participants, making the following points:

    *   Creative leaders encourage creativity in individuals, teams, and organizations.

    *   A leader's behaviors can hinder or promote creativity in the rest of the organization.

    *   Awareness of one's strengths and weaknesses in the use of creative leadership behaviors can be a starting point for development.

2. Tell participants they will complete an inventory of their own creative leadership behaviors.

3. Distribute copies of the Creative Leader Inventory and a pen or pencil to all participants.

4. Tell participants they will have about 10 minutes to fill out the inventory and score it.

    (15 minutes.)

5. After everyone has finished, lead a discussion using the following questions:

    *   What did you decide your strongest areas are?

    *   In which areas do you need the most improvement?

    *   What can you do to develop your creative abilities as a leader?

    *   What changes can you make within the organization to foster a climate of creativity?

    *   How could you support more creativity for employees and teams?

    *   In what ways could you enhance diversity in teams?

    *   What mechanisms could be put in place to increase collaboration throughout the organization?

    *   What can you do to foster creativity when you return to your job?

    (30 minutes.)

6. End the session by encouraging participants to identify at least three actions they will take within their organizations to demonstrate more effective creative leadership. If time permits, allow them to share what they intend to do with another person.

(10 minutes.)

Submitted by Shirley Copeland.

Shirley Copeland, Ed.D., *is president of the Learning Resource Group, LLC, a management consulting firm she founded in 1993. Her company specializes in leadership development. She has designed and developed award-winning materials and is a frequent contributor to training and development publications.*

Creative Leader Behavior Inventory

Instructions: For each statement below, circle the response that indicates how often you display that behavior.

1. Formulate a clear and compelling vision with clearly articulated goals and objectives.

   Never   Sometimes   Always

2. Foster a climate that rewards failure and risk taking in the attainment of goals.

   Never   Sometimes   Always

3. Allow flexibility in the process of goal attainment.

   Never   Sometimes   Always

4. Establish an environment that is conducive to play, where creativity can thrive.

   Never   Sometimes   Always

5. Encourage others through positive and inspirational feedback and support.

   Never   Sometimes   Always

6. Show a personal passion for creativity.

   Never   Sometimes   Always

7. Seek opportunities to develop personal creativity.

   Never   Sometimes   Always

8. Provide adequate resources and realistic timeframes for projects.

   Never   Sometimes   Always

9. Ensure team composition has diverse perspectives and backgrounds.

   Never   Sometimes   Always

10. Participate in external scanning to improve foresight and to spot opportunities and threats.

    Never   Sometimes   Always

11. Challenge individuals and teams through proper allocation of projects to their capabilities—seek the right balance of stretch.

Never   Sometimes   Always

12. Provide appropriate rewards and recognition for creativity.

Never   Sometimes   Always

13. Seek ways to change the organizational mindset through experimentation and the use of boundary spanning teams.

Never   Sometimes   Always

14. Avoid quick closure to problem framing and problem-solving processes; allow room and time for grappling with uncertainty, ambiguity, and not knowing.

Never   Sometimes   Always

15. Explore "wild card" scenarios for a fresh perspective in strategic thinking.

Never   Sometimes   Always

Rating Your Creative Leader Behaviors

Score your responses as follows:

- For each "never" response, give yourself 1 point.
- For each "sometimes" response, give yourself 2 points.
- For each "always" response, give yourself 3 points.

Total your scores.
Interpret your results by comparing them to the scale below.

40 to 45 = Excellent

34 to 39 = Good

29 to 33 = Fair

If your total score is 28 or below, consider developing an action plan to strengthen your creative leadership behaviors.

The Leadership Pyramid
Exploring Skills of Successful Leaders

Activity Summary

An activity designed to evoke dialogue between participants about skills critical to the success of a leader.

Goals

- To identify skills and traits that successful leaders possess.

- To prioritize the traits that successful leaders demonstrate.

- To compare the skills of a successful leader to one's own skills.

Group Size

Ten to twenty-five participants in a leadership training session.

Time Required

45 to 55 minutes.

Materials

- Ten sticky notes per participant.

- One pen for each participant.

- Extra paper for participants.

- One Leadership Pyramid Worksheet per participant.

- Flip chart and felt-tipped markers for recording.

- Masking tape for posting flip-chart sheets.

Physical Setting

A room with chairs and writing space, large enough to comfortably accommodate the participants.

Facilitating Risk Rating

Moderate.

Process

1. Introduce the activity by leading a discussion on the importance of being successful as a leader.

2. Ask the participants whether they think that successful leaders possess distinctive traits or skills. Have participants call out traits they believe successful leaders possess. Write their responses on the flip chart.

   (10 minutes.)

3. When at least thirty responses have been given, provide ten sticky notes and a pen to each participant.

   (15 minutes.)

4. Have participants individually select the ten traits they believe are most important for a successful leader. Ask them to write one leadership trait or skill per sticky note until they have used all ten. Tell them that they can choose from the list on the flip chart or write others that were not mentioned.

   (5 minutes.)

5. Hand out extra paper and ask participants to create one-dimensional pyramids with their sticky notes. Have them build pyramids with the sticky notes based on what *they* view are the most important. Tell them to start at the top of their pyramids and work left to right in order of importance to fill in the rest of the rows. Improvise a sample on the flip chart to resemble Figure 1.

   (10 minutes.)

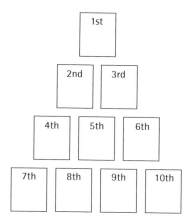

Figure 1. Example of a Leadership Pyramid

6. After all participants have completed their pyramids, give participants copies of the Leadership Pyramid Worksheet and have them capture their information on the worksheet and answer the analysis questions.

   (10 minutes.)

7. Lead a discussion with the group as to which trait/skill they listed as number 10 and why.

   (10 minutes.)

8. Next, lead a discussion with the group as to which trait/skill they listed as number 5 and why.

   (10 minutes.)

9. Finally, lead a discussion with the group about which trait/skill they listed as number 1 and why.

   (10 minutes.)

10. Lead a concluding discussion based on the following questions:

    • Based on the group discussion, do any of you want to change the order of your list? Why or why not?

    • Do you feel that you posses the trait or skill you ranked as number 1? If so, share an example of how you demonstrate that trait or skill.

    • From the list of ten traits and skills, which one do you personally see as an opportunity for growth?

- How can you apply what you learned today back on the job?

- What do you think was the purpose of this activity?

(15 minutes.)

_____

Submitted by J. Alexis Mamber.

J. Alexis Mamber *is a leadership development consultant with Lender Processing Services, where she has worked for the past five years. She holds a bachelor's degree in organizational communication from the University of Central Florida and a master's degree in human resource development from Webster University.*

Leadership Pyramid Worksheet

Instructions: List the leadership traits/skills in order of importance.

1.

2.

3.

4.

5.

6.

7.

8.

9.

10.

Analysis

Was it easy to put the leadership traits/skills in order of importance? Why or why not?

Which trait/skill did you choose to be at the top of the pyramid? Why did you select that particular one?

Do you demonstrate this skill? Think of some examples to share with the group.

Introduction
to the Editor's Choice Section

Unfortunately, in the past we have had to reject exceptional ideas that did not meet the criteria of one of the sections or did not fit into one of our categories. So we created an Editor's Choice Section that allows us to publish unique items that are useful to the profession rather than turn them down. This collection of contributions simply does not fit in one of the other three sections: Experiential Learning Activities; Inventories, Questionnaires, and Surveys; or Articles and Discussion Resources.

Based on the reason for creating this section, it is difficult to predict what you may find. You may anticipate a potpourri of topics, a variety of formats, and an assortment of categories. Some may be directly related to the training and consulting fields, and others may be related tangentially. Some may be obvious additions, and others may not. What you are sure to find is something you may not have expected but that will contribute to your growth and stretch your thinking. Suffice it to say that this section will provide you with a variety of useful ideas, practical strategies, and creative ways to look at the world. The material will add innovation to your training and consulting knowledge and skills. The contributions will challenge you to think differently, consider a new perspective, and add information you may not have considered before. The section will stretch your view of training and consulting topics.

The 2013 Pfeiffer Annual: Training includes three editor's choice selections. Keep in mind the purpose for this section—good ideas that don't fit in the other sections. The submissions by Karl Albrecht, Lily and Peter Cheng, and Lou Russell are perfect examples of items that are valuable to the readers of the Training *Annual*, but simply do not fit in any of the other categories.

Article

The Thinker's Test: A Learning Experience for Thinking More Clearly, Creatively, and Cleverly, by Karl Albrecht

Activities

Build a Better "To Do" List, by Lou Russell

The Cents of It All: Employee Value Simulation, by Lily Cheng and Peter Cheng

The Thinker's Test
A Learning Experience for Thinking More Clearly, Creatively, and Cleverly
Karl Albrecht

Summary

This problem-solving quiz can be used in one-on-one or group settings. It provides participants with an opportunity to hone their problem-solving skills and to assess where their creativity-related strengths and weaknesses lie.

Facilitation Guidelines

This is a versatile training exercise that you can use in a variety of ways, including one-to-one coaching, small-group workshops, and large-group sessions.

Be sure to establish an appropriate learning context for the quiz. Introduce the concept of critical and creative thinking; emphasize its importance in one's work, career, and personal life; and set the tone for a creative, playful learning session.

There are many ways to conduct this quiz. You can simply read out the questions one by one and ask the participants to solve them individually. Or you can arrange the participants in pairs, triads, or other small groups and have them solve the questions by discussion.

If you like, you can reproduce the questions pages and hand them out to the participants. In that case, you also can have them work individually or in pairs or small groups.

You can present all of the questions first—either on paper or by reading them out—and then provide the answers when participants have finished, or you can discuss the answer to each question after they've had time to work on it.

An online, interactive version of this same test is accessible at: www.KarlAlbrecht.com/brainpower/thinkerstest.php

Introduction

> If Tom is shorter than Dick, and Harry is taller than Dick, is Tom taller or shorter than Harry?

Do you find thinking puzzles like this one easy, hard, or somewhere in between? However you find them, they can help you assess and improve your practical thinking skills. If you answered that Tom is shorter than Harry, you've just shown your ability at a skill that psychologists call *sequential thought.*

People who have learned to organize their ideas into sequences or chains of logic can usually reason their way effectively through confused or complicated situations in the business of living.

Are you hungry for mental stimulation? The following Thinker's Test will challenge and exercise a variety of practical thinking skills, so you can identify your strongest ones as well as those that need further development. Before going through the questions, consider these useful strategies: (1) Approach each question with a playful, flexible, and exploratory attitude. (2) Draw thinking diagrams—sketches or "models"—to help organize your thoughts. (3) Think out loud. (4) Put your thoughts into words. (5) Use names, labels, and verbal relationships to clarify and add structure to your thought processes.

You'll find the answers at the end, along with a discussion of the various kinds of thinking skills they call forth. (Don't peek at the answers before you've solved the questions!)

Don't feel discouraged if you haven't managed to answer every question right—most people don't. There is no scoring system, so it's more important to think about thinking—and your relative strengths and learning needs—than to wind up with the "right" answers.

Karl Albrecht, Ph.D., *is a management consultant and author of more than twenty books on professional achievement, organizational performance, and business strategy. He studies cognitive styles and the development of advanced thinking skills. He is the author of many books, including* Social Intelligence: The New Science of Success; Practical Intelligence: The Art and Science of Common Sense; *and the* Mindex Thinking Style Profile. *The Mensa society honored him with its lifetime achievement award for significant contributions by a member to the understanding of intelligence. Originally a physicist, and having served as a military intelligence officer and business executive, he now consults, lectures, and writes about whatever he thinks would be fun.*

The Thinker's Test

1. Bob, Carol, Ted, and Alice are sitting around a table discussing their favorite sports. You have some bits of information about each of the people and their favorite sports. Your task is to figure out what sport each of them prefers.

   Clues:

   a. Bob sits directly across from the jogger.
   b. Carol sits to the right of the racquetball player.
   c. Alice sits across from Ted.
   d. The golfer sits to the left of the tennis player.
   e. A man sits on Ted's right.

2. Find the pattern that governs this familiar sequence, and figure out the next letter:

   "O, T, T, F, F, S, S, E, . . ."

3. If three days ago was the day before Friday, what will the day after tomorrow be? (*Hint:* write the names of the days of the week in a sequence, and use it as a visual aid.)

4. A man needs to transport three items—a wolf, a goat, and a very large cabbage—across a river. His boat is so small that it can only carry him and one of the items across at a time. Clearly, he will have to make a series of crossings. A further restriction is that he must never leave the wolf alone with the goat while he is crossing the river; if he does, the wolf will eat the goat. Also, he must not leave the goat alone with the cabbage, or the goat will eat the cabbage. It is safe to leave the wolf alone with the cabbage. Your task is to figure out: by what series of crossings, and carrying which items, can he get himself and the three items safely to the other side of the river?

5. Six drinking glasses stand in a row, with the first three full of water and the next three empty. By *handling and moving only one glass*, how can you arrange the six glasses so that no full glass stands next to another full one, and no empty glass stands next to another empty one?

6. Excavating in England, an archeologist found a Roman coin dated "44 B.C." and bearing a likeness of Julius Caesar. Another archeologist correctly identified the coin as a fake. How did she know?

7. How can you arrange the numbers from 1 to 9 to form a 3 X 3 square array, such that each row, each column, and the two diagonals will all total exactly 15? (*Hint:* choose the center number first.)

8. In five minutes, write down as many unusual uses as you can for a paper clip.

9. Three playing cards lie face down on the table, in a row. You have some bits of information about the faces and suits of the cards and their positions. Your task is to associate the face and suit of each card with its position.

   We know that:

   a. To the right of the Jack is a Diamond.
   b. To the left of the Diamond is a Club.
   c. To the right of the Heart is a Jack.
   d. To the left of the King is an Ace.

10. Imagine that you put two pieces of typing paper on your desk with a piece of carbon paper between them, as if you wanted to write something in duplicate. Now, imagine that you fold this assembly in half with the crease running left to right, bringing the lower half back up under the top half. If you write your name on the top half of the top sheet, how many copies will you make, where will they appear (front, back, first sheet, second sheet), and how will they be oriented?

Answers to the Thinker's Test

Answer to Number 1

Bob plays tennis, Carol jogs, Ted plays golf, and Alice plays racquetball. This question challenges your skill at *organizing information*, *relational thinking*, and making *logical inferences*.

Answer to Number 2

The next letter is "N," the first letter of the word "Nine." The series consists of the initials of the counting numbers. To answer this one correctly, you had to use your *pattern recognition* skills.

Answer to Number 3

If you answered Tuesday, you have exercised your skill at *sequential thinking*. To solve it, you must "find the end of the rope," first figuring out what today is, and then proceed to establish the day after tomorrow. Drawing a *thinking diagram*, such as a list of the days of the week in sequence, can help here.

Answer to Number 4

It takes seven crossings. First he leaves the wolf and cabbage on the left bank and takes the goat to the other side. He returns with the boat empty. Then he takes the wolf across, leaving the cabbage behind. On the return trip he leaves the wolf on the right bank and brings the goat back (to keep it safe from the wolf). Next he takes the cabbage across, leaving the goat on the left bank. With the wolf and cabbage on the right bank, he returns to get the goat, taking it across on the final trip. This exercise challenges your skills at *sequential thinking* as well as *relational thinking*.

Answer to Number 5

Pick up the middle one of the full glasses and, after pouring its water into the middle empty glass, put it back in its original position. This one helped you to assess your *mental flexibility*. The ability to categorize your options (push, pull, lift, slide, pour, etc.) is also involved here.

Answer to Number 6

The archeologist realized that, since the dating system based on "B.C." and "A.D." originated after the birth of Christ, a coin maker before that time couldn't have known about it, and therefore would not have stamped this date on a coin. If you figured out this answer, you have demonstrated your skill at *critical perception* and *contextual thinking*, which can help give you immunity to propaganda and other forms of ulterior persuasion.

Answer to Number 7

One arrangement of the numbers has 2, 9, and 4 across the first row, 7, 5, and 3 in the second row, and 6, 1, and 8 in the third row. The diagonals become (reading from the left corners) 2, 5, and 8, and 6, 5, and 4.

This puzzle assesses the extent to which you approach problems by *strategic attack*, instead of simple trial-and-error. A careful reasoning process before you start writing down any numbers can reduce the matter to just a few possibilities. For example, we can focus on the number at the center of the matrix, which is added to every other number in some combination or other.

We realize we can't use 9 for the center, because adding it to large numbers like 8 would overshoot the target sum of 15. By the same reasoning process, we can disqualify 8, 7, and 6. We can also eliminate 1, 2, 3, and 4 as too small to make sums of 15 in all directions. When we realize that only 5 will qualify for the center position, we can quickly figure out the rest of them.

This skill is also called *"fencing."*

Answer to Number 8

Count the number of uses you listed. Fewer than ten implies a bit of "mental arthritis." More than twenty suggests you find it easy to think of lots of possibilities and points of view in a situation—a sign of what psychologists consider *creative thinking* or *idea production*.

Answer to Number 9

From left to right, the Ace of Hearts, Jack of Clubs, and King of Diamonds. (The "d" clue does not say "to the immediate left . . . ") Solving this one requires careful *deductive reasoning*.

Answer to Number 10

First, copies can appear only on the face of the second sheet, because, no matter how you fold the package, the ink side of the carbon paper will contact only the second sheet. You will have produced two copies of your name on the front of the second sheet, one of them on the upper half and a mirror-image version on the lower half, with the letters upside down. This puzzle stresses your skill at *fencing*, *visualization*, and *spatial reasoning*.

Build a Better "To Do" List

Activity Summary

This real-world activity helps learners see ways that they contribute to the stress and frustration of their work day.

Goals

- To review a sample to-do list to estimate how much can be accomplished in a day.

- To learn to identify items on a to-do list that are not actually tasks.

- To learn how to prioritize work that can be completed in a day.

Group Size

Unlimited.

Time Required

30 to 45 minutes, depending on discussion and whether the bonus activity is used.

Materials

- One blank sheet of paper and something to write with for each participant.

- One copy of Tasks, Projects, and Processes: What's the Difference? for each participant.

Physical Setting

Enough space for a little privacy and a writing surface for each person.

Facilitating Risk Rating

Moderate.

Trainer's Note

Facilitators must be clear about what the differences are between a task, a project, and a process and should do this activity with one of their own to-do lists before trying to show others how to do it.

Process

1. Provide participants with a blank piece of paper and a writing utensil if they don't already have one.

2. Ask everyone to write his or her to-do list, everything he or she should be doing back in the office. Have them list ten things. Answer any questions Give them about 3 minutes to make their lists.

   (5 minutes.)

3. After approximately 3 minutes (or until at least two-thirds of the group seems to be finishing up. Check to be sure that each participant has at least five things on his or her list. Give them a few more minutes if needed.

   (5 to 7 minutes.)

4. Ask: "How many of you feel happy and productive most days when you leave your office?" [Wait for laughter.] Say to participants: "Your to-do lists may be adding to the frustration you feel at the end of your work day. Maybe it's because we put a lot more than to-do items on our lists. How many of you really like crossing things off a list? This exercise will help you do that."

5. Use the following questions to lead participants through the activity:

   • Look at your lists and see whether there is anything on the list that will take you *less than four uninterrupted hours* to do. Write the letter P next to *all the other items* on your list. In other words, write the letter P next to anything you could not finish if you magically had four hours of uninterrupted time.

   • If you have a "P" next to something, don't even look at it again. Just look at items that are not marked. Do any of these items require help from anyone else to finish, such as a quick email or just letting people know you're finished? Anything on your list that you need someone else's help for, no matter how trivially, put a "P" next to it.

- Look at the remaining items and see whether any of them have been on your list for more than a month. If there are any, put "P's" next to them.

- Finally, and this requires that you be honest with yourself, look at any remaining items and see whether you really have no idea how to finish them. Put another way, are there any that you don't know how to tell when you are finished? If so, add a "P" to them.

(5 minutes.)

6. As you debrief, try to help participants see the differences among tasks, projects, and processes. Provide each participant with a copy of Tasks, Projects, and Processes: What's the Difference? Point out the differences among the three. State that the only thing that belongs on a to-do list is a *task*. Answer any questions.

(5 minutes.)

7. Ask for volunteers to share any items that are still on their lists. For example, someone may say "Complete a review of a new e-learning course." Ask: "What are the steps you would go through to do that?" It's likely the person will rattle off a handful of tasks, which proves it's a *process* and should not be on the to-do list. No matter what a person has on his or her list, a task has to be what is left after items have been eliminated by using the four questions you asked earlier. If a volunteer is confused about why something should *not* be on his or her list, ask the four questions again.

8. Ask for a few more volunteers to share tasks on their list. Then ask someone to share a project that was removed. Clearly differentiate between a project and a process—projects begin and end, but processes do not. Explain that no one wants payroll, which is a process, to end, so it should not be on a to-do list.

9. Encourage participants to help their colleagues differentiate among the three types of items on their lists. If it doesn't come up in this discussion, ask people to raise their hands if "check email" was on his or her list. Ask whether that is a task, a project, or a process. The answer (frustrating as it is) is that it is a process. You can never check it off.

10. Ask participants to offer a way in which a task could morph into a project. Talk a little about how simple things sometimes take days and why that is (usually, you're waiting for someone else, or someone has changed the requirements).

11. Summarize by saying that we set ourselves up for failure by putting projects and processes on our to-do lists, ensuring that many items on our lists stay there for days, months, or even years. Urge them, instead, to use their task list for tasks and keep another list of *projects*. Say that *process* work generally is better on a calendar than on a to-do list.

    (15 to 20 minutes.)

12. Give participants 2 minutes to select which of the things on their individual to-do lists they will have finished by the end of the next day. Then ask them to write next to each of the items selected how much time will go by for them to complete each item, reminding them that they will likely be interrupted if they are in a normal workspace. This is a good place to mention that current research shows that when we are interrupted it takes 20 minutes to completely return to where we were prior to the interruption.

13. Ask participants to now total the time they have planned for the next day. [There may already be groans.] Ask: "How many hours in a normal work day can you work, heads down, in a focused manner on your tasks?" Ask for a show of hands as you ask: "How many think more than five hours? Three? Two? One? Zero?!" Point out that working after hours to get work done is not healthy and it may not be quality work, resulting in rework later on.

14. Ask participants to reflect on the total amount of work they plan to do versus the likely number of hours they'll have to work on it. Point out that we often set ourselves up to fail. Ask people to share ideas about how to improve the quality of their work and the quality of the state of their minds. List their suggestions such as "Do critical tasks before you check email." Remember that it's better to gather ideas from the group than to suggest your own.

Variations

- Use this activity to open a project management workshop or a leadership session.

- This activity is easily translated into an online webinar environment and can also be done as part of an asynchronous e-learning experience.

- Rather than using the handout, you may wish to post the content of Tasks, Projects, and Processes: What's the Difference? on a flip chart or include it in a PowerPoint slide.

Submitted by Lou Russell.

Lou Russell *is the CEO of Russell Martin & Associates, an executive consultant, speaker, and author whose passion is to create growth in companies by guiding the growth of their people. In her speaking, training, and writing, Lou draws on thirty years of experience helping organizations achieve their full potential. Lou is the author of six popular and practical books:* IT Leadership Alchemy; The Accelerated Learning Fieldbook; Training Triage Leadership Training; Project Management for Trainers, *and* 10 Steps to Successful Project Management. *Lou writes for many publications, holds webinars, and is the original queen mother of the local "Wine and Whine" group in Indianapolis.*

Tasks, Projects, and Processes: What's the Difference?

Task	Has a beginning and an end, smallest unit of work, easiest to measure how long it will take to finish, one person can do it. Tasks are combined into projects and processes.	Example: Tie your shoes
Project	Has a beginning and an end, harder to measure how long it will take to finish, multiple temporary people come together to do it. Projects are made up of multiple tasks.	Example: Develop a course.
Process	Has no beginning or end, repeats over and over, often dedicated staff. Processes are made up of multiple tasks.	Example: Payroll, Email

The Cents of It All
Employee Value Simulation

Activity Summary

A lively activity that demonstrates that all employees add value to an organization. It also shows how managers can deploy their human resources to adapt to market demands.

Goals

- To demonstrate that every employee has value.

- To discuss how to proactively manage human resources to satisfy changing market demands.

Group Size

Eight to thirty participants.

Time Required

30 minutes.

Materials

- A flip chart with the six debriefing questions listed on one or two pages.

- Marker for recording.

- Masking tape for posting flip-chart pages.

Physical Setting

An open space for movement for the group.

Facilitating Risk Rating

Moderate.

Process

1. State the goal of the activity.

2. Choose members of the group to represent a minority faction, using observable physical attributes such as wearing a certain color, striped clothing, long hair, short hair, gender, wear glasses, or others.

3. Assign a "market value" of 5 cents each to members of the minority group. Tell the remaining members of the group that they are valued at 10 cents each. Expect to hear complaining.

4. Tell the group members that you require a certain market value, and they will need to form a new group that adds up to the value you state. For example, if you require 50 cents, a group of five 10-cent members should gather and link elbows, confirming that they have formed a value chain that meets your required value of 50 cents. Once participants have formed a group, they should not allow others into the group. Answer any questions.

   (5 minutes.)

5. State that your first market demand is for 25 cents. Pause for them to form groups. Several members will be unable to join any group. Once you see most participants linking elbows and several without a group, stop the action to list their names on the flip chart.

6. Ask the value-chain groups to disband and get ready for the next market-value demand. Repeat this process several times.

7. Lead three or four more rounds, adding names to the flip chart. Some names will probably be repeated. Call a halt to the activity.

   (5 minutes.)

8. Divide the group into subgroups of four to six people to debrief using the following questions:

   • What behaviors did you observe in each round as you responded to the market-value call?

   • What behaviors were helpful in demonstrating that all employees are valuable to the organization?

- What behaviors led to feelings of exclusion and being undervalued by the organization?

- What behaviors demonstrated that employees are at the mercy of market demands?

- What behaviors demonstrated employees who were non-responsive to the market demands?

- What must organizational leaders do to ensure that they effectively deploy human resources to meet market demands?

(20 minutes.)

9. Ask how they will use what they learned back on the job.

10. Summarize and conclude by listing the key learning points of the activity on the flip chart.

Variations

- Tailor the assignment of value to the country of origin in terms of its currency value, e.g. euros, renminbi, pesos.

- The activity can also be focused to demonstrate proactive behaviors in a changing market environment.

Submitted by Lily Cheng and Peter Cheng.

Lily Cheng *is a globally recognized master organization development practitioner. Lily is one of the first two Certified Master Facilitators for The Leadership Challenge® in Asia. She is a Certified Master Coach with the Behavioral Coaching Institute (BCI) and a member of the International Coaching Council (ICC). Lily holds the Advanced Certificate in Training and Assessment (ACTA), is a certified consultant for the People Developer Standard, a Certified Management Consultant (CMC), and a certified Practicing Management Consultant (PMC), conferred by the PMC Certification Board and supported by the Singapore Workforce Development Agency (WDA).*

Peter Cheng *is a highly sought-after leadership coach recognized in the global organization development arena. He is a Certified Management Consultant, Certified Master Coach with the Behavioral Coaching Institute, member of the International Coaching Council, and Pioneer Master Facilitator of The Leadership Challenge® in Asia. Peter now works as executive director of PACE O.D. Consulting, where he facilitates leaders in finding breakthroughs that make a difference in their organizations and in the community.*

Introduction
to the Inventories, Questionnaires, and Surveys Section

Inventories, questionnaires, and surveys are valuable tools for the HRD professional. These feedback tools help respondents take an objective look at themselves and at their organizations. These tools also help to explain how a particular theory applies to them or to their situations.

Inventories, questionnaires, and surveys are useful in a number of training and consulting situations: privately for self-diagnosis; one-on-one to plan individual development; in a small group to open discussion; in a work team to help the team to focus on its highest priorities; or in an organization to gather data to achieve progress. You will find that the use of inventories, questionnaires, and surveys enriches, personalizes, and deepens training, development, and intervention designs. Many can be combined with experiential learning activities or articles in this or other *Annuals* to design an exciting, involving, practical, and well-rounded intervention. Each instrument includes the background necessary for understanding, presenting, and using it. Interpretive information, scales, and scoring sheets are also provided. In addition, we include the reliability and validity data contributed by the authors. If you wish additional information on any of these instruments, contact the authors directly. You will find their addresses and telephone numbers in the "Contributors" listing near the end of this volume.

The 2013 Pfeiffer Annual: Training includes two assessment tools in the following categories:

Consulting, Training, Facilitating

> Measuring Innovators and Adopters for Web 3.0, by Sacip Toker and James L. Moseley

Leadership

The Manager Quality Performance Index (MQPI): Driving Superior People Results Through Measurement, by Allan H. Church, Michael D. Tuller, and Erica I. Desrosiers

Measuring Innovators and Adopters for Web 3.0

Sacip Toker and James L. Moseley

Summary

Measuring Innovators and Adopters for Web 3.0 is a diagnostic tool that helps organizations understand their current employees' perceptions of Web 3.0 skills before planning or beginning initiatives. Two types of skills are defined: cognitive and affective. The instrument, consisting of thirty items, can be used effectively with individuals or with team members from the same organization. While the instrument enjoys content validity, reliability has not been determined. A Scoring Sheet, a Profile Chart, and an Interpretation Chart are provided for easy interpretation and use.

The World Wide Web, like other information systems, is rapidly expanding with the addition of more capabilities and features. Some individuals embrace this new technology, while others are in the dark. Web 3.0 enjoys both advantages and disadvantages. When a new technology is released, the first critical question is whether it is fact or fad. Numerous factors contribute to this perception. However, the reality is that web technologies are created and designed to serve humankind, and humankind adapts to the emerging changes.

Thirty years ago, if someone had proposed a system whereby everyone connects, communicates, and sees other people around the world without physically traveling, most of the population would have been skeptical. However, the Internet and World Wide Web have made new communication modes easy to access and user-friendly. It started with very simple pages on a Netscape browser, which was saying "Hello World!" Then it became Inter-Relay Chat (IRC) or ICQ, which stemmed from the sentence "I seek you." Next, it turned into animations on computer screens. These tools were Web 1.0. Then, wikis and blogs became part of daily life, while discussions of trustworthiness flourished. Tweets began to permeate all aspects of life.

These applications were Web 2.0. Today, iGoogle, mobility with iPhone and Android systems, the semantic web, and more are trendy technology-based buzzwords. Unsurprisingly, they now are called Web 3.0. It sounds really confusing, doesn't it?

Today, many individuals are unsure about the differences among Web 1.0, 2.0, and 3.0 technologies. Agarwal (2009) tabulated these differences in plain English. Web 1.0 is the father of all versions of the web. Web pages are essentially in read-only format; the user can only see and grasp them. Home pages and sites are the widely known locations to store and present useful information. Hypertext mark-up language (HTML) is the main building block for all these pages. When a web page is visited, it is owned by someone. Users' participation is mainly on web forms. Everything is structured as directories, folders, and subfolders defined by taxonomies whereby access is regulated by permission. If the website owner does not provide the user with permission to see some parts of the pages, the information is not retrieved. The most common ways to make money or run a business depend on advertising. Companies and their websites are major consumers, too. Netscape, Geocities, Hotmail, and Britannica Online are the some frequently recalled names when someone is asked about Web 1.0, where users have minimum control.

Web 2.0 added writing to the web technology. Users can both read and write the content. The focus on companies has changed to communities. Therefore, word of mouth is essential. Blogs, wikis, and tweets are the main terms users recall most frequently. Sharing is everything in Web 2.0. The more sharing there is, the more reliable and valid the information becomes. Tagging is the main feature to classify information; it is also called folksonomy. Google, Wikipedia, blogs, and Twitter are the frontrunners. Cost per click is the main way to make money for a business. Extended mark-up language (XML) and really simple syndication (RSS) are the equivalent tools to HTML in Web 1.0.

In Web 3.0, the emphasis is on personalization and mobility for busy individuals. Usually, information is broadcast as lifestreams. The content is dynamic and consolidated. The traditional web is transformed into the semantic web where all web pages are identified and tagged so when a person wants to reach a specific piece of information, computer systems search and show the best matching results, depending on the person's needs. The information includes not only content but also meaning of the content. The meaning components support the smart searching. Search engines know personal behaviors of individuals on the Internet, so they can easily find suitable results. Widgets and drag-drop mash-ups are examples of Web 3.0 tools. Distinct from taxonomy and folksonomy, user behaviors (also known as "me-onomy" are more critical. User engagement is a must for the existence of Web 3.0. iGoogle and NetVibes are the current frontrunners. Users' behaviors and personalized advertisements are the bases for making money as well as running a business.

Web 3.0 is already in place with several initiatives, and it has the attention of the current market. An article published in *The New York Times* by Markoff (2006) and a brief summary of a research study conducted by the American Society for Training and Development (ASTD) about Web 3.0 and its potential in learning and development are important signs of the market's direction. Web 3.0 technologies have a critical role in the future of organizations. Companies are seeking opportunities to utilize Web 3.0's innovative technologies to gain market share and maintain a competitive advantage.

However, these innovative technologies were designed to be implemented very rapidly, without considering their current ability to be adopted. Most have not experienced longevity. Schneider (2009), for example, reports that the first wave of e-commerce business ideas were not as successful as anticipated. All ideas were funded by investors. Eventually, however, the bad ideas led to loss of business, and millions of dollars were wasted in just three years.

In order to prevent this from occurring with Web 3.0 projects, individuals who will use the technology in their daily work need to be sophisticated in their planning, thinking, and usage. Therefore, it is important that potential users' innovation adaptation characteristics be known. Cognitive and affective skills are good places to begin to identify people's innovation categories. Roger's (1995) diffusion of innovation theory, which is explained briefly in the Presentation of Theory section in this discussion, provides a good framework for innovator categories.

The authors developed the Measuring Innovators and Adopters for Web 3.0 instrument to assist organizations in understanding their employees' current skills before thinking about Web 3.0 initiatives. The diagnostic instrument measures the perceptions of employees about their cognitive-level and affective-level skills regarding Web 3.0 and categorizes respondents based on their perceptions of being innovators or adopters. Each of the cognitive and affective skill categories is defined in Figure 1.

We have also published the Cultural Readiness Scale for Web 2.0 (CuReS for Web 2.0; Toker & Moseley, 2012). The main theme of that tool is culture and its change along with Web 2.0 applications. A paradigm shift is a must before Web 2.0

Figure 1. Subculture Categories

Cognitive: The cognitive domain covers mental skills. It usually monitors learning and development of intellectual skills. There are six sub-domains, ranging from simple to complex: (a) knowledge, (b) comprehension, (c) utilization, (d) analysis, (e) synthesis, and (f) evaluation.

Affective: The affective domain is related to feelings and emotions. The major focus is on how individuals feel about a topic when they are learning it. There are five main categories, ranging from simple to complex: (a) receiving, (b) responding, (c) valuing, (d) organization, and (e) internalizing.

applications are fully realized. Compared to Web 2, Web 3.0 is in its infancy. Here we focus on the innovative nature of Web 3.0 and its potential advantages and disadvantages in organizations.

Description of the Instrument

The instrument consists of thirty statements, fifteen for each skill level; a Scoring Sheet; a Profile Chart and an Interpretation Chart. A 6-point modified agreement scale is used, from strongly agree to strongly disagree. The purpose of the instrument is to categorize employees' perceived cognitive and affective skills regarding Web 3.0. The results will help decision-makers initiate projects or applications of Web 3.0. Individual employees in an organization are the intended respondents. Employees are asked to complete the inventory by reading each statement carefully, reflecting on their current skills, and choosing the one response that best describes their beliefs about Web 3.0. The instrument can also be used at the team or divisional level. In this case, averaging scores by designated group or team is suggested.

Administration of the Instrument

This instrument is intended to be used at the tactical, organizational, or strategic level by employees, managers, or executives. It can be administered either individually or organization-wide.

The instrument is scored using a Scoring Sheet, Profile Chart, and Interpretation Sheet. The results can be used for further discussion about Web 3.0 initiatives.

Presentation of Theory

Innovation and Adopter Categories

According to Rogers (1995) the individuals in a social system do not adopt an innovation simultaneously. Rogers identified five adoption categories: (1) innovators or the venturesome, (2) early adopters or respect, (3) early majority or deliberate, (4) late majority or skeptical, and (5) laggards or traditional. He made distinctions between these groups on the basis of the time of adoption. For instance, the innovators are the fastest group to adopt; the laggards are the slowest group; early adopters are slower than the innovators and faster than the early majority. Early majority is faster than the late majority.

Rogers showed that 2.5 percent of individuals in a social system usually are innovators; 13.5 percent are early adopters; 34 percent are early majority; 34 percent are late majority; and 16 percent are laggards. We believe that, when an innovation is diffused in an organization, there should be at least 2.5 percent innovators and 13.5 percent early adopters in order to make the innovation a sustainable part of the business. Otherwise, the diffusion takes longer than expected—and time is money in the business world.

Innovators are the key players in the diffusion process. They are usually obsessed with applying new innovations. They are highly willing to introduce new ideas and challenges into their professional lives and to use them in their daily lives. They also can be critical if they do not see the value of an innovation. They are usually the initiators of an innovation across a social system and are usually isolated from overall society. For this reason, they may not generate respect.

Early adopters are more integrated into the social system of which they are members. They play advisor roles for other potential adopters. They are the driving force that affects how other groups accept the innovation. They are usually well respected by peers and role models for successful adoption of an innovation. They can provide positive testimonials based on experience.

The *early majority* guide other peers. They usually connect upper management and supervisors with the rest of the employees. They take time to deliberate about new ideas before accepting and using them.

The *late majority* is frequently skeptical about innovation. They usually wait for the innovation to be accepted across the organization. They do not like scarce resources and uncertainty stemming from innovation.

The *laggards* focus on the past rather than the future. They usually isolate themselves from new ideas and are reluctant to support them. They are suspicious of innovation and other groups who support it. Because their resources are limited, they guard their use and are cautious about supporting new ideas.

Because of its newness, there is no consensus on a clear and precise definition of Web 3.0. Agarwal (2009) simply explains Web 3.0 as the anthology of semantic web (or the meaning of data), personalization, e.g., iGoogle, intelligent search, and behavioral advertising, among others. Similarly, Green (2011) mentions the semantic web and discusses two additional components: (1) mobile web and (2) immersive Internet. He provides a general definition that ASTD used for a research study to spot trends in the training industry. The mobile web provides the freedom to move information from one device to another and find information from different locations. The immersive Internet covers augmented reality and three-dimensional environments, such as Second Life. Other definitions are consistent with these two.

To help the readers understand Web 3.0 more clearly, we provide a glossary of Web 3.0 terms and tools in Table 1.

Table 1. Glossary of Web 3.0 Terms and Tools

Android	An operating system for mobile devices like smart phones and tablet computers.
Facebook's Beacon	A part of Facebook's advertisement system that sends information to external sites. The purpose is to permit concentrated advertisements and users to share their activities.
Friends of a Friend (FOAF)	Creates a web of machine-readable pages identifying people, the connections between them, and the things they create and do.
Google OpenSocial	Defines a common platform for social applications across multiple websites. With standard web mark-up and programming languages, developers can create applications that access a social network's friends and update feeds.
iGoogle	Provides a customizable start page and web portals. The gadgets are used to support personalization.
iPhone	A line of Internet and multimedia-enabled smart phones produced and marketed by Apple Inc.
Joost	An Internet TV service within which professionals publish their works.
MagPie or PoweMagpie	Supports semantic interpretation in web browsing with less user contribution. It automatically associates the main terms present in the text of the web page to semantic information, dynamically revealed in ontologies accessible on the semantic web.
Metadata	Metadata are data about data. They include detailed information such as the creator, the creation time, the modification time, the basic features of the data, the format of the data, and any other useful information.
NetVibes	The first personalized dashboard publishing platform for the web, including digital life management, widget distribution services, and brand observation rooms.
Ontology Web Language (OWL)	The new version mark-up language format developed to process the content of information regarding web resources.
PowerSet	A semantic search engine using natural language for seeking information targeted to the users' questions, unlike the keyword approach used by traditional search engines.
Resource Description Framework (RDF)	A general framework for describing a website's metadata—or the information about the information on the site. Can provide information to any types of platforms over the web.
Semantic Web	An extension of the current web that provides easier ways to locate, utilize, reuse, and combine data and information. It provides several diverse frameworks to help the computer and information systems understand and filter necessary data and information without spending human effort.

Semantics	The meaning of something, usually used in the computer world to differentiate the meaning of something from its format.
Simple Protocol and RDF Query Language (SPRQL)	A language framework to defines a standard query language and data access protocol for use with the resource description framework (RDF)
Slingbox	A TV streaming device that enables users to remotely view their home's cable, satellite or personal video recorder programming from an Internet-enabled computer with a broadband Internet connection.
Swicki	A custom search portal. It learns from the search behavior of a community of enthusiasts and experts, making it easy for users to quickly find what they are searching for in a particular topic.
Web 3.0	An extension of Web 2.0 that contains collective intelligence and provides the main connection among data, information, applications, and people under one platform.
Widget or Gadget	A small application that can be run on the desktop, in websites, or in mobile devices.
Wink	A search engine that provides all types of information about people, such as phone numbers, addresses, photos, videos, and so forth.

Web 2.0 has enlarged the read-only functionality of Web 1.0 by including the communities and users in the content creation process. The paradigm of Web 1.0 is mostly changed in Web 2.0 (Lassila & Hendler, 2007). Web 3.0 advances Web 2.0 a step forward with the semantic web (Sonntag, Deru, & Bergweiler, 2009). Web 3.0 is strongly tied to the existence of Web 2.0. In other words, it is one of the core components(Wahlster & Dengel, 2006).

Suggested Uses for the Instrument

There are several ways to use this instrument for organizational training:

1. As a needs assessment tool to understand the current or desired perception of any Web 3.0 project being planned or initiated.

2. As a monitoring and evaluation tool for cognitive and affective skill improvement. If an organization begins using Web 3.0 for any business processes and the employees do not feel competent to use it, skill improvements would still be expected.

3. As both a reflection and discussion piece for individuals and team members to make decisions about Web 3.0 projects.

4. More rigorously validated and rendered reliable, it could be used as a potential research tool by scholars in different fields, such as human resources, organization development, information technology, human performance improvement, instructional design, and so forth.

There may be many other uses for the instrument outside the authors' purview. Readers are encouraged to share them with the authors via email.

Validity and Reliability

This instrument was developed on the basis of two skill domains. Each domain was generated by reviewing recent narrative and empirical publications. Then a number of items were suggested and placed on the scale. Items not initially agreed on were revisited and revised. This process especially leveraged the authors' expertise, experiences, and intuitive senses. The process also provided more updated content regarding the topic and instrument.

The instrument has content validity. However, there are neither available empirical data nor any research studies to support reliability issues. The authors encourage researchers and practitioners who use this tool to conduct robust validity and reliability studies.

References

Agarwal, A. (2009, September 30). Web 3.0 concepts explained in plain English (Presentations). Retrieved from www.labnol.org/internet/web-3-concepts-explained /8908/.

Green, M. (2011, April). Better, smarter, faster: Web 3.0 and the future of learning. *T&D, 65*(4), 70–72.

Hendler, J. (2008, January). Web 3.0: Chicken farms on the semantic web. *Computer, 41*(1), 106–108.

Lassila, O., & Hendler, J. (2007). Embracing "web 3. 0." *IEEE Internet Computing, 11*(3), 90–93.

Markoff, J. (2006, November 12). Entrepreneurs see a web guided by commonsense. *The New York Times*, p. 32.

Rogers, E.M. (1995). *Diffusion of innovations* (4th ed.). New York: The Free Press.

Schneider, G.P. (2009). *Electronic commerce* (8th ed.). Boston: Course Technology, Cengage Learning.

Sonntag, D., Deru, M., & Bergweiler, S. (2009). Design and implementation of combined mobile and touchscreen-based multimodal web 3.0 interfaces. In H.R. Arabnia, D. de la Fuente, & J.A. Olivas (Eds.), *Proceedings of the 2009 International Conference on Artificial Intelligence* (pp. 974–979). Las Vegas, NV: CSREA Press.

Toker, S., & Moseley, J.L. (2012). Cultural readiness scale for Web 2.0. In E. Biech (Ed.), *The 2012 annual: Volume 2, consulting*, pp. 151–168. San Francisco: Pfeiffer.

Wahlster W., & Dengel A. (2006, June). Web 3.0: Convergence of Web 2.0 and the semantic web. *Telekom Technology Radar II*, pp. 1–26.

Sacip Toker *is a Ph.D. candidate in instructional technology in the College of Education at Wayne State University, Detroit, Michigan. In his native Turkey, he was involved in several online training programs and provided instructional technology support to the faculties at Middle East Technical University. He also taught information technology and instructional planning courses at Suleyman Demirel University. He is the co-author of book chapters and scholarly articles. He is also a member of ISPI and a presenter at Association for Educational and Communication Technology and International Society for Performance Improvement conferences.*

James L. Moseley, Ed.D., LPC, CHES, CPT, *was an associate professor of instructional technology in the College of Education at Wayne State University, Detroit, Michigan. He taught performance improvement, performance consulting, strategic planning, and program evaluation courses and directed dissertations and projects. He consulted with all levels of management. He was the recipient of teaching awards and service awards and the co-author of seven books, numerous articles, and book chapters. He was a member of both the International Society for Performance Improvement and the American Society for Training and Development. We were saddened to hear of his death earlier this year.*

Measuring Innovators and Adopters for Web 3.0

Sacip Toker and James L. Moseley

Instructions: Read each statement and circle the number that best describes your response to that statement using the following scale. Your immediate response is usually the most accurate.

6 = Very Strongly Agree

5 = Strongly Agree

4 = Agree

3 = Disagree

2 = Strongly Disagree

1 = Very Strongly Disagree

1.	I can explain Web 3.0 to my co-workers.	1	2	3	4	5	6
2.	I appreciate the potential added value of Web 3.0 to my job.	1	2	3	4	5	6
3.	I know the differences among Web 1.0, Web 2.0, and Web 3.0.	1	2	3	4	5	6
4.	I don't resist when Web 3.0 is part of my job's daily routine.	1	2	3	4	5	6
5.	I can use Web 3.0–based services	1	2	3	4	5	6

(typical services and tools include:

- Search Engines: iGoogle, Twine, Swicki, PowerSet

- Social Networking: Wink, Friends of a Friend, Google OpenSocial, Facebook's Beacon

- Entertainment: Joost, Android or iPhone, Slingbox

- Personalization: NetVibes

- Browser: MagPie, PowerMagPie)

6. I give my undivided attention when some-one talks about Web 3.0.   1 2 3 4 5 6

7. I know the basic philosophy behind the semantic web.   1 2 3 4 5 6

8. I do not give up when I have difficulties in conceptualizing Web 3.0.   1 2 3 4 5 6

9. I can explain the semantic web to my co-workers.   1 2 3 4 5 6

10. I willingly use Web 3.0–related products or services.   1 2 3 4 5 6

11. Web 3.0 seems like a personal assistant because it chooses the most appropriate information from the Internet when it is needed.   1 2 3 4 5 6

12. I am willing to share what I know about Web 3.0.   1 2 3 4 5 6

13. I can differentiate Web 3.0 products or services from Web 1.0 and Web 2.0 products or services.   1 2 3 4 5 6

14. I avoid biases in using Web 3.0.   1 2 3 4 5 6

15. I am familiar with the resource description framework (RDF).   1 2 3 4 5 6

16. I can discuss the potential pitfalls of Web 3.0.   1 2 3 4 5 6

17. I can create a resource description framework (RDF).   1 2 3 4 5 6

18. I want to examine the future benefits of Web 3.0.   1 2 3 4 5 6

19. I have had experience with Web 3.0 tools and service such as:

   - Search Engines: iGoogle, Twine, Swicki, PowerSet

   - Social Networking: Wink, Friends of a Friend, Google OpenSocial, Facebook's Beacon

- Entertainment: Joost, Android or iPhone, Slingbox
- Personalization: NetVibes
- Browser: MagPie, PowerMagPie

20.	I anticipate being a big supporter of using Web 3.0 in my job.	1	2	3	4	5	6
21.	I know the relationship between Web 3.0 and widgets.	1	2	3	4	5	6
22.	I accept the reality of Web 3.0 in daily life.	1	2	3	4	5	6
23.	I can inform others about the basics of Web 3.0.	1	2	3	4	5	6
24.	I use of Web 3.0 in daily technology applications.	1	2	3	4	5	6
25.	I know that Web 3.0 and the semantic web are not synonymous concepts.	1	2	3	4	5	6
26.	I support the use of Web 3.0 in business.	1	2	3	4	5	6
27.	Web 3.0 is contextual.	1	2	3	4	5	6
28.	I try to influence others to learn and use Web 3.0.	1	2	3	4	5	6
29.	Web 3.0 provides personalized surfing experiences depending on users' previous behaviors on the Internet.	1	2	3	4	5	6
30.	Learning Web 3.0 is on the top on my priority list.	1	2	3	4	5	6

Measuring Innovators and Adopters Scoring Sheet

Instructions: In each subcategory of the skills chart, find the question numbers from the survey and place your score for that item in the box beneath the item number. Once you have done this for both skill categories, assign the appropriate numerical value to each letter using the following scale:

> 6 = Very Strongly Agree

> 5 = Strongly Agree

> 4 = Agree

> 3 = Disagree

> 2 = Strongly Disagree

> 1 = Very Strongly Disagree

Finally, add the values for each skill together and place the number you obtain in the box below the chart. For example:

Sample Completed Chart

Questions	1	3	5	7	9	11	13	15	17	19	21	23	25	27	29
Value	2	4	1	1	1	5	3	2	2	1	1	4	4	5	1
												Score			37

Cognitive Skills

Questions	1	3	5	7	9	11	13	15	17	19	21	23	25	27	29
Value															
												Score			

Affective Skills

Questions	2	4	6	8	10	12	14	16	18	20	22	24	26	28	30
Value															
												Score			

Measuring Innovators and Adopters Profile Chart

Instructions: If you would like to use this instrument to measure a team's or work group's score, first have all members of the group calculate their scores and then add those scores together and divide by the number of members in the group (rounding applies). This average score can be used as a placement number. Respondents can be directed to the Interpretation Sheet to read the section that is pertinent to the work group's score.

Use the following chart to plot scores for the whole group, if desired.

	Very Strongly Disagree (VSD)	Strongly Disagree (SD)	Disagree (D)	Agree (A)	Strongly Agree (SA)	Very Strongly Agree (VSA)
Cognitive Skills	90 89 88 87 86 85 84 83 82 81 80 79 78 77 76	75 74 73 72 71 70 69 68 67 66 65 64 63 62 61	60 59 58 57 56 55 54 53 52 51 49 48 47 46	45 44 43 42 41 40 39 38 37 36 35 34 33 32 31	30 29 28 27 26 25 24 23 22 21 20 19 18 17 16	15 14 13 12 11 10 9 8 7 6 5 4 3 2 1
Affective Skills	90 89 88 87 86 85 84 83 82 81 80 79 78 77 76	75 74 73 72 71 70 69 68 67 66 65 64 63 62 61	60 59 58 57 56 55 54 53 52 51 49 48 47 46	45 44 43 42 41 40 39 38 37 36 35 34 33 32 31	30 29 28 27 26 25 24 23 22 21 20 19 18 17 16	15 14 13 12 11 10 9 8 7 6 5 4 3 2 1
					Placement Score	

Measuring Innovators and Adopters Interpretation Chart

If a Score Is Between 173 and 180

The employee or work group is an *Innovator* or *Venturesome*. These individuals or groups are usually isolated from other people in terms of accepting new ideas. They are eager to utilize new ideas in their daily lives. They are well-positioned to assist the adoption of the innovation in the organization. However, they are not very respected and thus cannot decrease the uncertainty associated with Web 3.0 applications. They cannot easily communicate the potential pros and cons of the innovation to other people. Their followers tend to be confused about the goals. Innovators can be very critical about the consequences of the innovation.

If you are willing to apply an innovative idea like Web 3.0, at least 2.5 percent of your organization's members should be in this category to assure its acceptance. If you do not have sufficient numbers, it is highly recommended that your organization provide some introductory training or basic performance support tools or job aids around the innovation. Caution is important after introducing Web 3.0 to the organization. Innovators might actually hinder the process. It may be wise for other groups to "carry the ball."

If a Score Is Between 157 and 172

The employee or work group is an *Early Adopter*. These people or groups are more integrated into the organization and command more respect. They need to be assigned to leadership roles for Web 3.0 projects. They probably have already tested Web 3.0 and are convinced of the added value to the business. Their decisions to use new ideas are 99 percent trustworthy. They have better communication channels to spread their experiences regarding Web 3.0, and they are also highly collaborative. They can be the main driving force to increase the use of Web 3.0 applications. For these reasons, they are generally well respected by other members of the organization.

13.5 percent of the organization members should fall into this category. If you do not have sufficient numbers, increasing membership in this group is highly recommended. Provide some introductory training or performance support tools or job aids. Early adopters will be very beneficial for the ongoing performance of the project. They can serve as project managers. They can also monitor the process and troubleshoot the issues when necessary. They can be role models for others. Moreover, Early Adopters can complement Innovators' energy around the change.

If a Score Is Between 106 and 156

The employee or work group is an *Early Majority* or *Deliberate*. These people communicate with other members of the organization; however, they are not inclined to take leadership positions. They are bridges between early and very late adopters. They are a good source to keep everybody connected. They deliberate about Web 3.0 practices, but not as quickly as the first two groups. They neither want to be the first adopter of Web 3.0 nor the last.

Thirty-four percent of the organization members are expected in this category. If you do not have sufficient numbers, provide some introductory training or basic information sheets in the form of job aids. At both the individual and group levels, their main responsibility may be organizational communication. They can be the messengers of Web 3.0 projects and keep everybody informed.

If a Score Is Between 55 and 105

The employee or work group is a *Late Majority* or *Skeptical*. They need some economic necessities or peer pressure to take the first step. They are skeptical about Web 3.0–type projects unless they become a common tool and are integrated into the current rules and norms of the organization. Their main reason to be skeptical is uncertainty, which Web 3.0 brings to the organization. They need extrinsic motivation, especially from their peers.

Like *Early Majority*, *Late Majority* include 34 percent of the organization's members. Because they extend the time to adoption, minimizing their numbers will protect the limited resources of the organization. Their most supportive peers may be *Early Majority* individuals or groups.

If a Score Is Between 30 and 54

The employee or work group is *Laggards* or *Traditional*. They refrain from taking any role during the adoption process. They merely focus on what happened in the past. They usually have limited resources in terms of skills. For this reason, they would like to continue working in ways that were successful for them in the past. They are the main restraining forces for the change needed for Web 3.0. Since they are the sources of resistance and reluctance, they do not take any risks when there are uncertainties.

Usually, 16 percent of an organization's members fall into this category. They need to move to the *Late Adopters* category eventually; otherwise, any Web 3.0 projects will not be successful. The faster groups might coach or supervise them individually to help the adoption progress. Moreover, they can encourage other groups to shift to their level, which could also affect future projects. When there are huge numbers of these people in the organization, caution is advised in initiating the project.

The Manager Quality Performance Index (MQPI)
Driving Superior People Results Through Measurement

Allan H. Church, Michael D. Tuller, and Erica I. Desrosiers

Summary

The Manager Quality Performance Index (MQPI) was developed to provide quantitative and qualitative behavioral information to managers regarding their own level of skill and capability in managing direct reports. The instrument was developed for and deployed in a large multi-national organization as part of a larger performance management agenda. To date it has been used by almost fifteen thousand managers who supervise the work of others, over several annual administrations in more than fifty countries since 2008.

Although this index originated in one organizational setting, the content is universal in nature and can easily be applied to other business, educational, and/or non-profit settings; in short, the index can be used in any situation in which someone manages three or more individuals.

Following an overview of the original business need and theoretical underpinnings of the MQPI, options for survey administration and reporting are described. We then continue with a discussion of key application decisions that need to be made prior to the initial administration of the MQPI (for example, whether the results will be used for developmental or decision-making purposes, or some combination). We include additional suggestions for further enhancement and integration of the tool into existing core HR processes and/or human capital metrics.

Background

While the fields of organizational behavior, workplace learning, and organization development have seen many changes over the last several decades, we know some basic tenets derived from theory and practice to be true. One of these fundamentals is that *people join companies but leave their bosses*. Based on applied research conducted and popularized in the late 1990s and early 2000s during the war for talent frenzied dot.com era (Buckingham & Coffman, 1999; Michaels, Handfield-Jones, & Axelrod, 2001) and reinforced by others since then (Capelli, 2008; Charan, Drotter, & Noel, 2001), having a quality manager has been demonstrated to have a significant and lasting impact on employee engagement and retention. Interestingly enough, this relationship has proven to be consistent (although slightly moderated), even when external environmental factors such as the economy or job market are less than optimal for employees to exit the organization. Moreover, manager quality is equally important for retention purposes, given the changes that have occurred in the employment contract and other factors inherent in the nature of work today (Dibble, 1999; Hankin, 2005; Meister & Willyerd, 2010; Zemke, Raines, & Filipczak, 2000).

Given the importance of having highly effective managers, it is no surprise that many organizations have begun to measure their performance management and development processes against this goal. In 2002, for example, the Corporate Leadership Council published a report on "Closing the Performance Gap" that highlighted a number of examples of performance management trends related to this area. One of these described a new practice at the time that involved discrete ratings of management skill, weighted at 66 percent (business) and 34 percent (people) for managers at PepsiCo (Corporate Executive Board, 2002).

As a result, considerable effort was made to objectively define and measure "people results" for managers across the organization. When the practice was revisited again in 2005 (PepsiCo's Dual Performance Rating Practice), progress had been made and tools had been developed in the implementation process, yet there was still a need to fully operationalize the measurement of management quality. Finally, in 2007 the code was cracked at PepsiCo with the introduction of a new enhanced global Leadership and Individual Effectiveness Model, which included a subset of questions developed to focus exclusively on people managers. In 2008 this survey, the Manager Quality Performance Index (MQPI), was launched as a pilot to targeted groups in the organization, and in 2009 the process was fully rolled out globally as a program to be administered prior to the performance management cycle.

This new survey tool provided senior leaders, managers, and HR professionals with a robust and valid annual measure of management behavior. This new upward feedback process (based on ratings from direct reports only) ultimately provided the impetus for the organization to weigh managers equally (50 percent each) for both business and people results. This was a significant outcome, reinforcing the importance of manager quality in the workplace. To be clear, PepsiCo's people objectives were not about simply being a "nice manager" who was well-liked, but rather how well he or she delivered against annual people objectives.

Theory and Research Behind the Index

The MQPI consists of twelve independent behavioral statements designed to apply to all people managers (supervisors) and reflect a core set of activities that managers are expected to perform to support both individual and organizational outcomes, including:

1. Managing annual performance goals and expectations;

2. Focusing on employee development and talent management planning efforts;

3. Reinforcing a workplace culture of inclusion, empowerment, and recognition; and

4. Acting in a professional manner.

The content of the MQPI was developed in 2006 in parallel with a redesign of the PepsiCo Leadership and Individual Effectiveness model. This extensive effort involved multiple interviews with senior executives; employee focus groups from different functions, levels, businesses, and geographies around with world; and a review of other organizational models and current thinking, research, and literature on leadership competencies. One of the findings was that many "corporate" models of leadership (including the prior version at PepsiCo and those from other benchmarked organizations) often blended and/or even confused the construct of *managing* others with *leading* others. This is an important distinction from both a talent management (organization) and a career progression (individual) perspective, as one could argue based on the leadership pipeline work of Charan, Drotter, and Noel (2001) that people management skills should be honed and cemented long before those abilities that are required to lead larger organizational entities (for example, first-time manager skills occur in their model before leader of managers or leader of leaders).

Thus, following the work of Burke (1986, 2011), Burns (1978) and Zaleznik (1977), among others, regarding the conceptual difference between transformational and transactional leaders (leaders versus managers), a confirmatory factor analysis and an expert item sort were performed on the preexisting leadership competencies and behavioral item set to determine the initial items to be included in the new leadership model. The result was a set of leadership-focused behaviors that were most suitable for 360-degree feedback from direct reports, peers, next-level up or skip-level managers, customers, etc., and a shorter set that was targeted specifically at supervisory roles to be rated by direct reports only for the MQPI. Feedback obtained from the 2008 pilot of the MQPI in the field (targeting samples in both corporate headquarters in the United States and in the field in an international division representing Asia, the Middle East, and Africa) was incorporated into the final process. The findings and recommendations from the pilot test are described below.

Reliability and Validity of the Index

Given the targeted nature of the MQPI on managerial behaviors and performance feedback in the workplace (and not, for example, enduring personality traits or dispositions, which have appropriate uses in other developmental processes), there is limited utility in pursuing a pure test-retest reliability analysis with this measure. That is, if the direct reports are not necessarily the same from administration to administration, only themes in behavioral ratings are relevant, whereas unit score values are less so. That said, and acknowledging the obvious challenges associated with measurement over time of direct reports' aggregate ratings in an ever-changing business environment, a series of analyses was conducted to determine the general psychometric properties of the index over time relative to other available measures of behavior.

First, an inter-item reliability measure was computed for the index, yielding a very high Cronbach alpha of .95. Next, aggregate direct report ratings from the manager sample from 2008 were compared to those obtained in 2009 and 2010. In both instances, the correlations were statistically significant ($p < .001$) and quite strong in nature ($r = .67$ for 2008–2009 and $r = .56$ for 2008–2010), suggesting that, despite the possible changes in direct report team composition and/or behavioral improvement (or decline), the relative ranking of managers across the sample was similar. The fact that the two-year correlation was less than the one-year result was to be expected, given the longer time horizon.

In order to test the level of convergent and discriminant validity of the MQPI, correlations were conducted between the results and those obtained for the same target individuals using the more leadership-focused behaviors from the 360-feedback process over multiple years. Results consistently demonstrated that direct report ratings between the two measures yielded the highest correlations overall

Table 1. Correlations Between Measures 2010–2011 Matched Sample

360-Degree Feedback Dimension Rating	MQPI Overall Rating (Direct Reports)	
Direct Reports	2010	2011
Setting the Agenda	.45	.42
Takings Others with You	.51	.47
Doing It the Right Way	.44	.39
Peers		
Setting the Agenda	.29	.30
Takings Others with You	.28	.30
Doing It the Right Way	.25	.33
Managers		
Setting the Agenda	.07	.10
Takings Others with You	.09	.10
Doing It the Right Way	.05	.03
Matched Sample Size	968	722

(as would be expected, since they are coming from approximately the same rater group), followed by those from peers, and then those from managers (see Table 1).

In addition, patterns between the MQPI and those on the more engagement-oriented dimension of the leadership model (Taking Others with You) were the strongest overall—with ratings on ethics (Doing It the Right Way) yielding the weakest relationships in comparison. We would argue here that, while acting ethically is critically important for managers in general, it represents more of a hygiene factor than a motivator related to perceived manager quality.

In addition, this pattern of results supports the validity of the MQPI, as direct reports ratings within a given year should be the highest among the three rater groups (compared with either peers or managers), however, not so high as to suggest that the behaviors being rated are conceptually the same as those in the 360-feedback measure, which is focused more specifically on leadership (for direct reports, the two measures shared approximately 14 to 26 percent of the variance in ratings overall).

In sum, results from these analyses supported both the relative stability of the MQPI ratings over time and the convergent and discriminant validity of the measure.

While the twelve items may seem like simply measuring the basics of "good management," research and practice have shown that employees often find themselves promoted to people manager roles without having had much formal training or developmental feedback. This phenomenon, which is one form of the Peter

Principle (Peter & Hull, 1969) when applied in this context, is particularly common in organizations in which technical expertise has been the source of initial competitive advantage and/or the organization has seen rapid growth beyond the ability to build managerial skills to support it (see Church & Waclawski, 1998, for a case example). In such instances, the MQPI provides a quick and simple method for measuring manager quality.

Methodological Approach

The twelve behaviors were designed to capture universally expected managerial behaviors, regardless of the job level of the manager—from first-level manager on a plant floor to CEO of a $50 billion business. The behaviors span multiple aspects of people management and supervisory roles, including managing performance goals, developing talent, reinforcing the desired organization culture, and acting with integrity. Fundamentally, these behaviors should be applicable to all managers, and all of a manager's direct reports should be able to rate him or her, regardless of level in the management hierarchy, which is an important distinction between this measure and some 360-degree feedback tools.

Unlike many other types of feedback measures, the MQPI does not require that managers complete a set of self-ratings. While the survey administrator can certainly elect to add this step to the process either prior to administration or after (but before results have been delivered back to the participant), we have found that having ratings collected only from direct reports sends a clear message to the manager and the organization that only direct report feedback matters for this tool. Although gaps in self-awareness are important constructs in most feedback efforts (Church, Walker, & Brockner, 2002), finding them is not the intent of this tool, which is meant to assess manager capability.

Rating Scale Used

The rating scale used is a 5-point unipolar "extent" scale (to no extent, to some extent, to a moderate extent, to a great extent, to a very great extent), as opposed to a typical bipolar scale (strongly disagree to strongly agree) for several reasons.

First, the MQPI measures managerial behaviors, not employee attitudes, whereas the traditional bipolar agreement scale is designed as an attitudinal measure (Church & Waclawski, 1998, 2001). In other words, our intent was to measure the extent to which the twelve behaviors are being demonstrated on a regular basis and not how the employee feels about them per se. An extent scale is better suited for this type of feedback.

In addition, an extent scale allows for a more finite gradation in assessing and reporting, as all scale points express some level of positive expression. (Being "neutral" on a 5-point scale about seeing a behavior exhibited is not particularly meaningful, nor is indicating that someone does not demonstrate that behavior to a strong degree or a very strong degree).

Second, because the MQPI asks direct reports to assess the performance of their managers, political factors (fear of retaliation, etc.) may elicit a bias toward leniency bias, which could in turn lead to a restriction of range if a bipolar scale were used.

In addition to quantitative feedback, raters are given an option to provide qualitative feedback by answering two open-ended questions—what the manager does that is particularly effective and what the manager could do to be more effective. Although the addition of write-in comments can complicate the process and add cost, qualitative feedback provides concrete examples, richness, and clarity and can be useful when creating actionable developmental plans. In our experience, many managers look to the comments for guidance and direction, while they look to the item ratings for comparisons and overall standing.

Administration

The survey can be executed according to the needs of the organization and the relative scope of the process. It can be delivered via a large, highly coordinated and formal effort, a one-off as-needed, or on an ad-hoc basis, or somewhere in between. A large-scale administration allows the organization to tie the results to talent management decisions and hold managers accountable for their managerial quality. Additionally, a large-scale administration can shape the organizational culture by expressing the importance of manager behaviors in the workplace. A large-scale administration also allows for organization-wide "process marketing," communication, and visible senior-level support, along with the obvious economies of scale. Such initiatives, however, do require significant resources, support, and coordination efforts across the organization and a cultural willingness to be open to receiving feedback. See Figure 1 for a sample timeline for a large-scale implementation.

A different method is to use repeated "one-off" survey cycles using the MQPI selecting participants based on their need for diagnostic, confirmatory, or developmental feedback. The simplicity and straightforward nature of the MQPI allow it to be easily used with minimal instructions. The process can be relatively easy to execute with little cost; however, organizational norms and internal benchmarks might be lacking. Individual administration may also allow more personalized attention for respondents, but it is unlikely that any organizational messages about expectations for manager quality will be sent.

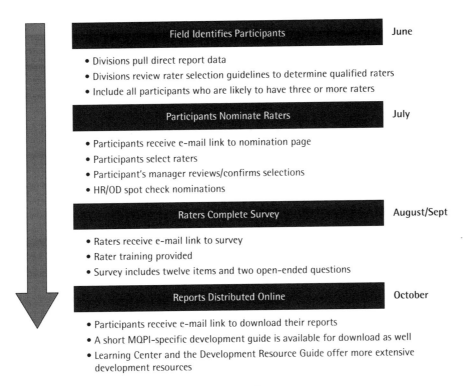

Figure 1. Sample MQPI Process Overview

Considerations may also include potential differences in the mediums raters use to provide feedback. Based on differences in technology, organizations may need to gather the feedback through online, paper, or a mix of reporting approaches. The online approach might be simplest, but requires online access for all raters. The paper process may offer a platform that all associates have access to, but is arduous in terms of distributing, collecting, and scoring responses. Finally, a mixed model might ensure that all respondents have access while minimizing the administrative burden. A majority of our associates complete an online assessment; however, we have a hybrid model to enable front-line associates without computer access to participate in the process.

The Role of Technology

The next consideration is the level of technology required to administer the MQPI. We suggest using a single system or online web or company intranet portal to administer the MQPI, from rater selection to survey distribution and rater completion to report generation and distribution. Without such a system, a manual process is required: creating paper copies of a survey to be distributed or emailed, with ratings completed and aggregated via spreadsheets (we have seen and experienced all forms of administration). In our experience, the planned usage of the tool and the organization's relative size must be considered.

For small- to medium-sized organizations using the tool for one-off purposes, the cost of an automated or high-tech solution may not be worth the investment, although the obvious tradeoff is ease of delivery. However, organizations both large and small that plan to use the tool more broadly (and/or over time) for large-scale administrations would likely benefit from an automated solution. Administration is still required, of course, and participants and raters are still required to use the system, but the manual work of distributing surveys, entering scores, aggregating data, and preparing reports is taken care of. A centralized system allows a single team to design and roll out the process globally with minimal local support. Even large organizations that only plan for ad-hoc use of the tool would likely benefit from implementing a system to help ensure consistency of administration, particularly if additional complexities such as more than one language are involved.

Timing of Administration

One final issue to consider in terms of administration of the MQPI is the timing of the assessment (and the timing of results distribution). Organizations may choose to administer the MQPI as a stand-alone tool or in conjunction with other assessments, which might conserve resources. For example, at PepsiCo the MQPI and 360-degree feedback processes are conducted at the same time so that individuals participating in both processes only need to select a rater list once and raters can complete ratings for both surveys in a single sitting.

The desired usage of the results also impacts the timing. If an organization uses the results as an input for the performance management process, the administration should occur close enough to the performance evaluation process to be meaningful.

Choosing Participants for the Process

The next decision relates to who should receive feedback through the process. If an organization decides to utilize the MQPI in a one-off manner, the direct reports of identified managers can be chosen as needed. However, with large-scale administrations, decisions regarding who should participate become more complex. First, the organization should limit the number of participants based on how many could be reasonably supported, including the ability to provide quality interpretation and follow-up developmental efforts. This is especially important in a manual administration, where the burden is obviously greater. Second, if organizations feel that managers who participate have the resources and support in place to quickly respond to the feedback, more frequent administrations might be beneficial. Conversely, too frequent administrations might be disheartening and demotivating to individuals if they lack sufficient time to respond to the feedback. We have found that an annual administration allows participants ample time to incorporate feedback into their developmental plans, while still remaining linked to the performance management cycle. Some internal groups have experimented with surveying twice a year, however, and have used that quite effectively for immediate remedial action as well. On the other hand, less than once a year is probably too protracted a feedback window to make a different in the level of manager quality.

Protecting Confidentiality

One final point worth mentioning is confidentiality. Organizations may (and probably should) choose to set a minimum threshold of possible raters in order to protect rater confidentiality. Feedback is likely to be more candid and correlate better with actual performance if the results are kept confidential (Eichinger & Lombardo, 2004). In order to protect rater confidentiality at PepsiCo, participants are required to have at least *three* direct reports. However, this threshold can be adjusted based on the organization's stance on confidentiality and presumed need for manager participation (for example, some organizations have been known to set the cutoff at five or more direct reports).

Guidelines for Rater Selection

For the next phase of the process, rater selection, the organization should consider the following points:

First, the organization should provide clear guidelines about who should be raters. At PepsiCo we tell participants they should select the following raters: (1) all direct reports who have worked for that manager for at least four to six months; (2) previous direct reports who recently changed positions (less than three months ago); (3) interns or part-time employees; and (4) dotted-line or matrixed reports. It is important to note that, as an organization, we require that participants include direct reports who are on a performance plan. It is important to give all direct reports a voice and not exclude any individual based on circumstances.

Second, organizations participants should validate their rater lists with either their managers and/or the HR generalist. For a manual administration, these steps can be onerous, especially as the population size increases. By comparison, technology can increase the quality and reduce the burden of the selection process because rater lists can be pre-populated based on existing rater lists from previous administrations or other feedback processes (such as 360-degree feedback) or hierarchical relationships identified in an HRIS data feed.

Third, quality checks can be built into the process to validate the raters selected. At PepsiCo all submitted rater lists, regardless of how the raters will complete the assessment, are sent to next-level managers for approval, after which they are approved or returned to the participant with suggested changes. There is a short time slot for HR review of rater lists as well. A final factor here that may be assumed, but is worth mentioning, is that rater participation should be voluntary. Raters should have the ability to decline without fear of penalty or reprisal.

Interpretation

Once the data has been collected, the next step is interpretation of the results. Here, the presentation format is important, as it impacts the manager's understanding of the results. The results can be reported both at the item level and at the construct level. Although several descriptive statistics can be used to express the results, we suggest that the mean and range are the simplest and most beneficial to present. Based on a total of results from more than 6,500 managers, we have a grand mean score to date of 3.94 on the MQPI.

While some practitioners argue against using range in any type of feedback measure because of the potential for violating individual confidentiality (or at least perceived confidentiality), the inclusion of the range is valuable from our perspective because, as suggested by Graen and Uhl-Bien (1995), managers do not interact with all direct reports equally, which is likely to be expressed in rating variation. Although we recommend using the range, in order to protect rater confidentiality, the report should only include the endpoints of the range and not include every rating point. Table 2 demonstrates one method for providing this type of data, using scores that represent the 25th and 75th percentile for one large population of raters using the MQPI.

The results can also be compared relative to different standards to increase their meaningfulness. For example, current MQPI results can be compared against previous MQPI results for the same individual (year over year or biannually, recognizing the caveats involved with measurement over time on these types of measures). This allows the organization to see how the manager has changed since the previous administration.

The individual results can also be compared against a previously selected peer group if the organization has a large enough sample. This type of comparison allows the manager and the organization to see relative standing and provide context to a specific score. For example, an average score of a 4.1 on a 5-point scale might sound high, but as an organization we find that item scores tend to range from 3.5 to 4.5. The comparison can be displayed in two primary ways (norm score and percentile) for each item and for the overall score. Providing both values

Table 2. Sample MQPI Ratings Distribution

Behavioral Items	25th Percentile Score	75th Percentile Score
1. Keeps people focused on the right priorities.	3.67	4.40
2. Sets challenging but attainable performance goals.	3.67	4.33
3. Constructively addresses performance issues.	3.57	4.33
4. Balances a concern for results with a concern for the needs of individuals in his/her group.	3.67	4.40
5. Effectively manages and works with people who are different from him- or herself.	3.67	4.42
6. Provides timely and direct feedback to others regarding performance or workplace issues.	3.60	4.33
7. Engages in candid discussions with others regarding their career opportunities.	3.50	4.28
8. Provides others with challenging assignments and training experiences to promote their development.	3.57	4.28
9. Recognizes and celebrates the significant achievement of others.	3.67	4.40
10. Effectively uses different rewards and incentives to drive performance.	3.20	4.00
11. Gives others full credit for their ideas and contributions.	3.80	4.50
12. Treats others' concerns and issues fairly and with sensitivity and confidentiality.	3.83	4.57
Manager Quality Performance Index	3.68	4.29

gives critical information about where the norm group falls, while also showing the individual's relative standing.

The next decision is determining the correct norm group. In a small organization, the norm group might be every MQPI participant. However, for larger organizations, the decision might be more complex. Is the best norm one that is level-based, function-based, or geographically based? PepsiCo creates norm groups based on hierarchical level and organizational structure, but other factors may be considered, such as function or even work shift. As part of our process, senior-level executives are compared with their peers across the organization, and lower executives and managers are compared against others at their level in their own business sectors.

The final issue relates to the presentation of the open-ended comments. Organizations can choose to identify which rater provided the open-ended comments (which would not be a confidential or anonymous process) or leave them unidentified. This links back to rater confidentiality. PepsiCo emphasizes confidentiality, so the open-ended comments are presented collectively. In fact, the comments are presented in alphabetical order based on the first word of the statement, so comments from a single rater may not be listed the same way for both questions.

When working with the results from the MQPI, it is helpful to walk through the basics of interpretation and action planning with the individual, his or her manager, and/or the HR generalist. The MQPI Interpretation Sheet has been used extensively in our own company. It covers both the positives and opportunity areas in the results and focuses on next steps.

Applications of the MQPI

The purpose of the MQPI is to measure the extent to which twelve specific behaviors related to managerial quality are demonstrated on a regular basis for a given people manager and to provide an absolute score (the index) based on the average set of observations from three or more direct reports' ratings. While the original design and intent of the MQPI was to feed the "People Results" ratings in PepsiCo's performance management process as well as support managers' quality development agendas, the tool can be used for many applications at three distinct levels in an organization.

1. At the *individual level* the MQPI results are extremely helpful in determining the overall level of manager quality of a given individual (and to the extent that normative and/or comparative data are available, where the individual ranks relative to peers), as well as provide targeted feedback on specific areas for improvement. Thus, the total score and the individual behaviors yield valid and actionable information.

2. At the *group level*, aggregate MQPI scores can be used to determine areas of strength and opportunities for capability building within a given team, function, geography, or business unit. For example, if all 150 managers in a given location score below a certain threshold (such as 3.5) on the survey and that is being driven largely by scores regarding clarity of performance feedback, the organization development team can implement a targeted intervention to build skills in this area.

3. At the highest level of *systems thinking*, MQPI scores for an entire operation, business sector, or organization reflect a broader cultural context that can be helpful in determining key barriers and/or levers for change with respect to other initiatives (for example, what type of culture does a given organization have?). Here results from measure like this take on a decidedly broader

OD perspective and are similar in a way to the themes obtained from an employee culture or engagement survey (Church, Walker, & Brockner, 2002). Thus, before deciding to implement a process like the MQPI, it is useful to have an understanding of the broader application of the results.

Perhaps the most important decision point, however, is at the individual level and whether the survey results are to be used for (1) development only, (2) personnel decision making only, or (3) some combination of the two. Many other authors have discussed the pros and cons of these approaches with respect to 360-degree or multi-rater feedback, so the reader is directed elsewhere for more detail (e.g., Bracken, Timmreck, & Church, 2001; London, 2001). From our perspective, however, it is most important to note three things:

1. Communication of the intended usage of the measure is critical during all phases of implementation, but particularly if the MQPI is being delivered for the first time in a team, work group, or organizational setting. Moreover, if the results are going to be used as input into a decision-making process (either performance management or internal staffing decisions), we recommend that participants be given a trial run or first pass through the process without it having an impact so that they have a chance to level set their behaviors and performance plans.

2. Regardless of the intended usage of the results, the timing of the administration and the feedback process should be linked to an existing performance and/or development cycle and with appropriate resources offered so employees can maximize the value of the tool.

3. Although the specific behavior-based items detailed here are appropriate for all types of managerial situations and reflect the concept being measured broadly, we recognize that there may be situations in which the addition of a few more behaviors might be needed to supplement the MQPI to drive improvement in key areas of manager quality. These can easily be derived and added to the MQPI through targeted focus group and pilot interventions.

References

Bracken, D.W., Timmreck, C.W., & Church, A.H. (Eds.). (2001). *The handbook of multi-source feedback: The comprehensive resource for designing and implementing MSF processes.* San Francisco: Jossey-Bass.

Buckingham, M., & Coffman, C. (1999). *First, break all the rules: What the world's greatest managers do differently.* New York; Simon & Schuster.

Burke, W.W. (1986). Leadership as empowering others. In S. Srivastva (Ed.), *Executive power* (pp. 51–77). San Francisco: Jossey-Bass.

Burke, W.W. (2011). *Organization change: Theory and practice* (3rd ed.). Thousand Oaks, CA: Sage.

Burke, W.W., & Litwin, G.H. (1992). A causal model of organizational performance and change. *Journal of Management, 18,* 523–545.

Burns, J.M. (1978). *Leadership.* New York: Harper & Row.

Charan, R., Drotter, S., & Noel, J. (2001). *The leadership pipeline: How to build the leadership powered company.* San Francisco: Jossey-Bass.

Capelli, P. (2008). *Talent on demand: Managing talent in an age of uncertainty.* Boston: Harvard Business School Press.

Church, A.H., & Waclawski, J. (1998). The vendor mind-set: The devolution from organizational consultant to street peddler. *Consulting Psychology Journal: Practice & Research, 5*(2), 87–100.

Church, A.H., & Waclawski, J. (2001). *Designing and using organizational surveys: A seven step approach.* San Francisco: Jossey-Bass.

Church, A.H., Walker, A.G., & Brockner, J. (2002). Multisource feedback for organization development and change. In J. Waclawski & A.H. Church (Eds.), *Organization development: A data-driven approach to organizational change* (pp. 27–54). San Francisco: Jossey-Bass.

Corporate Leadership Council. (2002). *Closing the performance gap: Driving business results through performance management.* Washington, DC: Corporate Executive Board.

Corporate Leadership Council. (2005). *PepsiCo's dual performance rating practice: An overview of the practice and a conversation with Allan Church, VP organization & management development.* Washington, DC: Corporate Executive Board.

Dibble, S. (1999). *Keeping your valuable employees: Retention strategies for your organization's most important resource.* Hoboken, NJ: John Wiley & Sons.

Eichinger, R., & Lombardo, M. (2004). Patterns of rater accuracy in 360-degree feedback. *Human Resource Planning, 27*(4), 23–25.

Graen, G.B., & Uhl-Bien, M. (1995). The relationship-based approach to leadership: Development of LMX theory of leadership over 25 years: Applying a multi-level, multi-domain perspective. *Leadership Quarterly, 6*(2), 219–247.

Hankin, H. (2005). *The new workforce: Five sweeping trends that will shape your company's future,* New York: AMACOM.

London, M. (2001). The great debate: Should 360 be used for administration or development only? In D.W. Bracken, C.W. Timmreck, & A.H. Church (Eds.), *The handbook of multisource feedback* (pp. 368–385), San Francisco: Jossey-Bass.

Meister, J.C., & Willyerd, K. (2010). *The 2010 workplace: How innovative companies attract, develop, and keep tomorrow's employees today.* New York: HarperCollins.

Michaels, E., Handfield-Jones, H., & Axelrod, B. (2001). *The war for talent.* Boston: Harvard Business School Press.

Peter, L.J.,& Hull, R. (1969). *The Peter principle: Why things always go wrong.* New York: William Morrow and Company.

Zaleznik, A. (1977). Managers and leaders: Are they different? *Harvard Business Review,* 55(3), 67–78.

Zemke, R., Raines, C., & Filipczak, B. (2000). *Generations at work: Managing the clash of veterans, boomers, Xers, and nexters in your workplace.* New York: American Management Association.

Allan H. Church, Ph.D., *is vice president of global talent development for PepsiCo, where he is responsible for leading the global talent management and people development agenda. He has also worked for IBM and Warner Burke Associates and has been affiliated with Columbia University, Benedictine University, the Mayflower Group, and the Council of Talent Management Executives. He received his Ph.D. from Columbia University and is a SIOP, APA, and APS Fellow.*

Michael D. Tuller, Ph.D., *is a manager at PepsiCo with the enterprise organization and management development team. He plays a key role in the execution and management of the organization's 360-degree feedback processes as well as several other organizational feedback processes, including the MQPI, Hogan Personality Inventory, and a targeted development "check-in" tool. He received his Ph.D. from the University of Connecticut and is a member of the Society for Industrial and Organizational Psychology (SIOP).*

Erica I. Desrosiers, Ph.D., *is senior director, global talent development, for PepsiCo. Erica's primary focus is executive talent development and coaching, and she leads the organization's 360-degree feedback and upward feedback processes. Erica received her Ph.D. in industrial and organizational psychology from Purdue University. She is a member of the Society for Industrial and Organizational Psychology and is on the board of the Mayflower Group, as well as the executive committee of the Conference Board Council on Executive Coaching.*

Manager Quality Performance Index (MQPI)

Allan H. Church, Michael D. Tuller, and Erica I. Desrosiers

Instructions: Your manager has been selected to participate in the MQPI feedback process. Please answer the following questions as candidly as possible using the response scale provided.

1 = To no extent

2 = To a limited extent

3 = To some extent

4 = To a moderate extent

5 = To a great extent

_____ 1. Keeps people focused on the right priorities.

_____ 2. Sets challenging but attainable performance goals.

_____ 3. Constructively addresses performance issues.

_____ 4. Balances a concern for results with a concern for the needs of individuals in his/her group.

_____ 5. Effectively manages and works with people who are different from him- or herself.

_____ 6. Provides timely and direct feedback to others regarding performance or workplace issues.

_____ 7. Engages in candid discussions with others regarding their career opportunities.

_____ 8. Provides others with challenging assignments and training experiences to promote their development.

_____ 9. Recognizes and celebrates the significant achievements of others.

_____10. Effectively uses different rewards and incentives to drive performance.

_____11. Gives others full credit for their ideas and contributions.

_____12. Treats others' concerns and issues fairly and with sensitivity and confidentiality.

Open-Ended Questions

13. What are some of the things your manager does that are very effective?

14. What could your manager do to be even more effective?

MQPI Interpretation Sheet

Purpose of This Document

This worksheet provides useful questions for MQPI participants and their managers to contemplate prior to their action planning meetings. In addition, managers may want to fill out and bring this worksheet to calibration meetings where they will discuss their direct report's people manager behaviors.

Questions for MQPI Participants and Their Managers

What is your overall reaction to the results?

What surprised you about the results?

What was consistent? What did you expect to see?

What strengths were identified that should continue to be built upon?

What developmental next steps can be taken to address identified areas of opportunity?

What questions still exist for you? What information is needed to answer them?

How do you intend to incorporate the results into the People Results rating?

Introduction

to the Articles and Discussion Resources Section

The Articles and Discussion Resources Section is a collection of materials useful to every facilitator. The theories, background information, models, and methods will challenge facilitators' thinking, enrich their professional development, and assist their internal and external clients with productive change. These articles may be used as a basis for lecturettes, as handouts in training sessions, or as background reading material. This section will provide you with a variety of useful ideas, theoretical opinions, teachable models, practical strategies, and proven intervention methods. The articles will add richness and depth to your training and consulting knowledge and skills. They will challenge you to think differently, explore new concepts, and experiment with new interventions. The articles will continue to add a fresh perspective to your work.

The 2013 Pfeiffer Annual: Training features twelve articles, including seven that focus on this year's theme of preparing leaders for the future.

The following categories are represented:

Individual Development: Developing Awareness and Understanding

**Self-Reflection: A Key Leadership Competency, by Deb Pastors

Individual Development: Life/Career Planning

**Considering the "Soft" Aspects of Decision Making, by Erwin Rausch and Charles Anderson

Communication: Coaching and Encouraging

The Supervisor's Motivational Tool Kit, by Deborah Spring Laurel

---

**Preparing Leaders for the Future Topic

Communication: Technology

†A Positive Vision for 2020: The Confluence of Information Technology with T&D, by Phillip E. Nelson and Teri-E Belf

Groups and Teams: Group Development

**Toward a Healthy World: Meeting the Leadership Challenges of the 21st Century, by Sherene Zolno

Consulting/Training: Organizations: Their Characteristics and How They Function

Keeping Training Alive in a Recovering Economy, by Kurt Iskrzycki, Susan Cain, and Tim Buividas

Consulting/Training: Strategies and Techniques

What Makes Up the Most Beloved Activities? Framework for Rapid Training Activity Creation, by Lauri Luoto

Planning, Not Playing: Training Through Simulation Design, by Noam Ebner and Daniel Druckman

Facilitating: Evaluation

**Leadership and Accountability Lecturette, by Phil Van Horn

Leadership: Theories and Models

**Developing Values-Based Leaders, by Homer H. Johnson

Leadership: Strategies and Techniques

**I Have Seen the Future and It's Not What It Was Cracked Up to Be, by Leonard D. Goodstein

Leadership: Top-Management Issues/Concerns

**Connecting the Dots: Developing Leaders Who See the Big Picture, by Catherine J. Rezak

---

†Cutting-Edge Topic

As with previous *Annuals*, this volume covers a wide variety of topics. The range of articles presented encourages thought-provoking discussion about the present and future of HRD. We have done our best to categorize the articles for easy reference; however, many of the articles encompass a range of topics, disciplines, and applications. If you do not find what you are looking for under one category, check a related category. In some cases we may place an article in the "Training" *Annual* that also has implications for "Consulting" and vice versa. As the field of HRD continues to grow and develop, there is more and more crossover between training and consulting. Explore all the contents of both volumes of the *Annual* in order to realize the full potential for learning and development that each offers.

Self-Reflection
A Key Leadership Competency
Deb Pastors

Summary

A review of leadership competencies written about over the last decade or so reveals a host of requirements—the ability to form and communicate a vision, think strategically, develop others, manage change, foster collaboration—the list is extensive. But there is a key leadership ability that you'll rarely find in a leadership competency model—self-reflection. Without the ability to self-reflect, leaders risk undermining themselves and their organizations.

At its core, self-reflection is simply asking oneself key questions on a given topic, listening to the responses from within, and learning and taking action from those responses. The questions may be about our values, relationships, or decisions. While it may not be something we consider consciously, all learning requires reflection. Without reflection, we risk making the same mistakes over and over.

Self-reflection should not be confused with self-awareness. Leaders must know their strengths and weaknesses, how they are perceived by others, what their tendencies and preferences are. However, many rely on *external* sources to provide these data—personality/style assessments, 360 surveys, performance appraisals, direct feedback. Self-reflection is a critical component of self-awareness, but also of the numerous other leadership competencies.

Leaders may balk and say that there is simply no time to stop to reflect. Amid the many demands on them, taking time out of the day to reflect may seem an egregious waste of time. Yet we live in a time of constant data bombardment, rapid technological progress, increasing complexity. Urgency is the name of the game. Leaders can seldom take all the time they might like to make a decision. However, leaders must also be able to learn *and unlearn* quickly. They must be able to question what's working, what's not, and why. They must be able to make adjustments quickly, distill good data from bad, identify which influencers should be considered, which discarded. Just as "the unexamined life is not worth living," the unexamined daily work life may have serious consequences for leaders, their followers, and their organizations. Without an ability to slow down and reflect, leaders may miss key details or opportunities that are instrumental for both their individual success and that of their organizations.

Developing and Practicing Self-Reflection

So how does a leader go about "doing" self-reflection? And what can workplace learning professionals do to help leaders develop this competency?

While it may seem that self-reflection is best carried out in solitude, with endless unscheduled time, beside a peaceful stream with blue sky and puffy white clouds above (cue the dramatic music), in reality it can be accomplished in small increments of time and in almost any environment. This is easier to do if the leader can find a balanced, "centered" state. Technically speaking, the center of the body is the spot on which the entire body can be balanced. The physical center is located approximately two inches below the navel. Those who are unfamiliar with "being centered" can start by standing with feet a comfortable distance apart, lengthening the spine, relaxing the shoulders, and breathing slowly—not from the chest, but from the abdomen, or center. This will help relax the body and focus the mind. Individuals who learn to find a centered state will soon be able to access that state at any time.

From this centered state, leaders can begin to reflect on questions that are key for *them*. It is not necessary to reflect on everything at once; they can pick an area or two to reflect on for a few minutes at a time over the course of several days. These are questions a leader might consider:

- Think about a critical decision that you've recently made. How did you make that decision? What factors did you consider? How do you know that you used good data? Whom did you involve? *How* did you involve them?

- How are you developing your subordinates? Are you involving them in decisions that will enable their development? Are you coaching or mentoring them? Is there someone on your staff who's ripe for a challenging project? Are you preparing someone on your team to take over your job?

- How do you fill your day? Is your time spent on busywork or key priorities? Are you attending some meetings by habit or necessity? Can you attend fewer meetings? Can you call fewer meetings?

- Are you thinking about your work strategically? Is your work aligned with the organization's priorities? Is your work aligned with your priorities and values?

- Are you satisfied with the balance of your work and non-work life? Are you eating properly, getting enough rest, exercising regularly? Are you happy with the amount of time you get to spend with your family?

It is not necessary to spend a great deal of time on reflection—ten to fifteen minutes at a time can provide great insight. Leaders may choose to spend more time reflecting as they become comfortable with the practice. Nor is it necessary to have a specific location in which to reflect. A brief walk at lunchtime, the train ride home, before falling asleep—any time and place at which the leader is uninterrupted is ideal for reflection.

While reflecting on the answers to the questions, leaders should also pay attention to how their physical bodies are responding. For example, is your jaw clenched? Is there a knot in your stomach? Is your body tensing? Our bodies also have wisdom, and we can learn a great deal from them if we are attentive. Any physical tension in response to reflection is a signal that the topic may require exploration.

Leaders may find it useful to write down both their questions and their reflections. In this way they can refer to their learning at later times. They may also benefit from discussing both their questions and learning with a respected confidant.

Self-Reflection as Part of a Leadership Development Program

Learning professionals charged with leadership development can incorporate self-reflection into their leadership development programs:

- Ask learners to develop questions on which they would like to reflect. Have them share the questions with others in the program. Begin a "master list" of reflection questions.

- Assign one question for reflection. Ask all learners to reflect on that question each day for a week. Have them record their answers in a notebook. At the conclusion of the week, ask learners to share their insights with others in the program.

- Ask mentors to share their own questions for reflection—and what they have learned—with learners.

- Teach learners how to find a "centered state." This is a useful skill, not just for preparing for reflection, but for reducing physical tension and focusing throughout the day.

- Solicit reflection questions from senior leaders around *each* of the leadership competencies in your organization's leadership model. Encourage senior leaders to self-reflect, and share what they learn with each other and subordinate leaders.

Conclusion

Self-reflection may never show up on an organization's leadership competency model. Yet the ability to reflect, learn, and stay or change course may be just as important for success as the ability to plan strategically or manage change. And as the world seems to spin faster, this ability may just be what gives an organization a competitive edge.

Deb Pastors, MSMOB, *is president of Education Development Growth Enterprises Inc. and a consultant and trainer with more than twenty-five years of experience in human resources, workplace learning and performance, and organization development. She is a past president of the Chicagoland Chapter of ASTD and currently serves on the ASTD Chapter Recognition Committee. Deb is also a black belt in the martial art of aikido and uses her experiences "on the mat" to bring a unique perspective to her work.*

Considering the "Soft" Aspects of Decision Making

Erwin Rausch and Charles Anderson

Summary

This article discusses the importance of including the "soft" aspects of decision making in leadership education and development programs. After presenting the argument for why these aspects are worth considering, two brief scenarios are provided to help illustrate the relevant issues. Finally, the authors provide a foundational set of guidelines for considering soft aspects of decision making.

Sound decisions in all human endeavors have become even more important in the 21st century. The increasing complexity of decisions caused by the revolution in electronic media, the impact of globalization on management and leadership practices, and the increasing nexus between private and public organizations demand that decisions be better aligned with expectations. Specifically, it is important to reduce the incidence of undesirable, unexpected consequences. That requires that all issues be brought up when decisions are being made and that no issues are ignored.

To satisfy this requirement, attention has to be devoted not only to the technical aspects of decisions, but also to the soft aspects, where problems are more likely to originate.

The Two Facets of Decisions

Both the *technical* and the *soft* aspects are important to optimal decisions (see Figure 1). However, most decision-makers consider only the technical aspects that center on issues addressed. Professionals are comfortable in the domains of their discipline; they have extensive backgrounds gained from education, interest, and on-the-job experience; and they are confident that they understand the options available to them and their likely consequences.

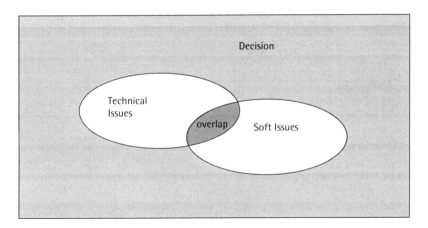

Figure 1. The Two Facets of Decisions

The soft issues such as communication, level of participation, competence, and satisfaction apply universally, and yet often are not covered in training and professional development programs, in part because they are not well defined and do not have empirically tested conceptual foundations. They are also often mistakenly considered to be obvious or fully understood. Soft issues should not only be considered when making decisions, but they should be emphasized. Just as formulae and rules need to be followed when making technical decisions, soft aspects require guidelines to help decision-makers organize their thinking.

As Figure 1 shows, there is no sharp delineation between the technical and the soft aspects of a decision. Some primarily technical issues, such as setting learning goals, are soft. Similarly, competence development requires both a knowledge of technical aspects and of soft issues.

Primary Guidelines for the Soft Aspects of Decisions

As long as they are consistent and comprehensive, guidelines are possible for making soft decisions. Universally applicable guidelines could include the following:

- *Communication:* What should be communicated, by whom, to whom, and when?

- *Participation:* Who should be invited to participate in the decision, be consulted, be asked for comments, or just be informed because they may be affected?

- *Competence:* What knowledge and skills are needed for implementation of the decision, whether they are already available and, if not, how any deficiencies should be corrected, by when?

- *Satisfaction:* What will the reaction of stakeholders be? What can be done to ensure the best possible reaction?

These issues are not independent; there is overlap—especially with communication. None of the others is possible without communication. Also, competence and satisfaction require consideration of participation. Less immediately apparent links also exist.

Combined with the technical considerations for making decisions, the guidelines for the soft aspects bring some measure of assurance that as many relevant issues as possible will be considered, preventing undesirable consequences.

Dissatisfaction with managers who have supervisory responsibilities rests mostly on the soft side. Employee dissatisfaction tends to be less if managers are taught to pay more attention to at least some of the soft issues. Interesting discussions of these problems can be found in Bennis and O'Toole (2005), Russo and Schoemaker (1990), and Vroom and Yetton (1973).

Developing Good Decision-Making Habits

Forming the habit of using the soft decision-making guidelines is not easy. Fortunately, managers can be taught to make decisions in stages, remembering the key words of the guidelines, thus ensuring that each guideline receives at least some thought. For instance, the word "communications" could remind him or her to give timely notification when cancelling a meeting.

The next level beyond knowing key words would be the next few words in the guideline; for "communications," it is the *what, by whom, to whom,* and *when.* Still more detail comes from the meaning of those words. The guidelines do not address skills, but some users may be reminded of the need to actively listen and to seek or offer feedback—key communications skills.

Leadership research provides a limited empirical foundation for the guidelines offered here. However, too many issues are involved to permit a comprehensive study, as Victor Vroom's extensive work on participation demonstrates (Vroom & Jago, 1988; Vroom & Yetton, 1973). Other shortcomings of research on the issue thus far include:

- It is primarily descriptive and not prescriptive, which would be necessary for practical application of any guideline.

- It is not comprehensive enough to cover all possible decisions.

- It is not as practical as necessary to ensure that little is overlooked when making decisions.

Guidelines for the soft side of decisions, then, must become second-nature to decision-makers so that no relevant issues are forgotten and there are no unintended consequences. The four guidelines listed earlier, as well as four less frequently applied ones (discussed later) are demonstrated next with the help of two scenarios—one from a work environment and one from a personal situation.

Illustrative Scenarios

Scenario 1

Joan is an executive in charge of MIS program development at ABC, a medium-sized wholesaler of consumer products. The company has recently acquired a smaller company with a different product line that sells partly in the same market and partly in a market not previously served by ABC. To simplify the transition to a unified company, a computer program was developed to replace the incompatible programs of the two companies. A pilot test was conducted with a few sales representatives from each sales force. The program ran smoothly for all possible situations when used by the developers—no programming changes were necessary. However, it became clear that extensive sales representative training would be necessary so that the reps could use the program efficiently.

What should Joan consider under the four guidelines listed above as she moves toward a decision on full-scale implementation with the combined sales force? There are no technical aspects to consider, since the program runs fine. With respect to the soft issues, how would the four primary guidelines apply? For example:

- Might consultations with a few or with all representatives help with selecting the best alternative?

- Would joint meetings of training and program design staff members with selected representatives be useful to identify best approaches?

- Should an outside consultant be considered?

- What should be communicated to management and when?

- What should be communicated to sales—management, field managers, representatives?

- What training, if any, should be given to programming staff involved with any redesign?

- What psychological rewards can be provided to ensure greatest enthusiasm by all those involved?

Scenario 2

Joan also has a personal issue requiring a decision. She and her husband recently purchased a home, having lived in an apartment since their marriage. As their first child was five years old and another was planned, time had come to buy a house. The kitchen in the house they purchased needs major renovation. Joan and her husband have separate assets (bank and small stockbroker accounts) and a joint account for daily living expenses, mortgage payments, property taxes and insurance, and for special needs such as income taxes to which they both contribute regularly. Their parents are alive. His parents, who are in a better financial situation than hers are, gave them the money they needed at a lower rate than offered by the bank.

The same distinction between technical and soft types of issues pertains in this scenario, although there is likely to be less prior experience with the technical ones—only greater comfort, possibly, in addressing them.

The technical issues center on the timing, quality, and costs of kitchen renovation, including appliances and services and, second, on assessing the effect of renovation on the long-term appreciation of the residence.

Prospective soft issues under the four primary guidelines include:

- Whose "satisfaction" should receive priority in decisions on the various aspects of renovation design and selection/purchase of appliances?

- How should the kitchen renovation be financed, and which partner should bear the greater burden of the financing costs? If monies are to be borrowed, should additional funds be solicited from parents and on what terms?

- How best to conduct a market search for contractors. Of what value are friends, neighbors, and relatives in addressing this matter?

- How should conflicts between Joan and her husband be resolved? These conflicts center on aesthetics, debt, future values, and uses.

Additional Guidelines

Four secondary soft guidelines are worth considering when making decisions and possibly for the two scenarios. These are

- What can be done to achieve the highest level of coordination as well as cooperation by all those involved?

- What goals should be set, and how, for and with teams and individuals?

- What organizational and individual norms (including those that pertain to ethics, diversity, and organizational justice) are involved in the decision and how can alignment be promoted?

- What performance evaluations are applicable in the situation, and how?

These are often less relevant and less frequently applicable in non-organizational settings where supervisory responsibilities are not involved. In the two scenarios:

- Setting and working toward achievement of goals, if it applies at all, would not be formal. Subsidiary issues such as who should set the goal and the respective responsibilities are not likely to be relevant.

- Ensuring the highest possible level of coordination and cooperation would apply only if a number of people were involved.

- Working with norms, including those that pertain to ethics, diversity, and organizational justice, may deserve consideration.

- Ensuring fair and comprehensive project and performance reviews would apply only in Scenario 1 and there only if performance is evaluated formally. In Scenario 1 it would also involve how it would be affected by the changes, including the integration of the two companies.

Perspectives on the Guidelines

The eight guidelines are intended to promote awareness of the types of things that should be considered. They help the decision-maker avoid overlooking anything relevant when defining desired outcomes, selecting alternatives, and determining the specifics of the final decision.

They do not represent the only way to look at decisions. They can be modified or replaced with others that would achieve the same objective—a decision that considers all relevant issues. Whether these or others, some type of guidelines are highly recommended for addressing the relevance of leadership and management education and development.

While most writing on management leaves it up to the reader to interpret the theory, the guidelines discussed here are prescriptive, giving specific suggestions on which areas to consider. Of course, they are not specific with respect to which ones are to be applied, or how, but they can help to ensure that nothing relevant is overlooked.

Using the Guidelines

Using the eight guidelines for each decision may seem overwhelming and require too much time. But rarely do all of the issues have to be considered. Some, such as those pertaining to competence, goals, coordination and cooperation, norms, and performance reviews, do not have to be considered each time if they were recently used. They can be given only a brief glance to determine whether they are still relevant.

Also, many of the guidelines overlap, such as those in communications, participation, and satisfaction; they could therefore be considered at the same time.

Habits are essential for successful use of the guidelines. Habits greatly simplify seemingly complex tasks, as can be seen from the speed with which we can type, compared to the chore of selecting the proper key when we were learning to type. Habits also play a big part in a more complex environment, such as that of the chess master who intuitively applies the appropriate strategies while playing against several or many opponents. So too for these guidelines. They become instinctual with practice.

Further Explanation of the Eight Guidelines

Now that our arguments supporting the use of the guidelines have been presented, we provide a more complete discussion of all eight.

1. Communications

This guideline suggests that when making any decision the experienced user consider the following:

- What to communicate and to whom. Certainly anything a person needs to know to help with making the decision is covered under these two aspects of the communications guideline. There is a great need to provide all necessary and relevant information to stakeholders (individually and/or in groups), so they can effectively perform any task that the decision requires of them, or that they should be aware of for competence or satisfaction reasons.

- By whom is often overlooked; it is likely to be decided intuitively without adequate thought since it usually seems obvious.

- How (what methods/media to use) has become considerably more complicated in light of the proliferation of electronic media. Speed, accuracy, avoidance of misunderstanding, and effort required are all relevant considerations for this guideline

- When, if not considered in time, can lead to all kinds of delays in making the decision and in implementing it.

In addition to the these considerations are oral and written communications skills, which are essential. These include all aspects of listening, open and closed questions, and techniques related to seeking and volunteering feedback.

In light of the vast literature on all aspects of communication, no specific titles are mentioned here. Proof of its importance for making decisions can be found from higher education texts on communication, education, and management. There the issues and skills are discussed and the underlying empirical evidence is presented.

2. Participation

Every manager, and every decision-maker, is aware that "two heads are better than one." Still, few decision-makers appreciate that there can be a vast difference between participation and *appropriate* participation. Who should do the selecting and who should be selected? How are individuals or teams to be selected? What is the authority of the chosen participants?

Extensive research has been conducted on levels of participation. The first comprehensive study was conducted by Tannenbaum and Schmidt (1958). The authors proposed an "Autocratic-Democratic Continuum," from no participation (merely being informed) to almost full authority to make a decision. Victor Vroom, both alone and with Jago (1988) refined the continuum adding points such as the extent to which the "leader" (the person or team with the primary responsibility for the decision) has the needed information, how acceptable a specific solution would be to the participants, the likelihood of conflict and disputes, and so forth. Norman Maier (1967) and Hersey and Blanchard (1969) expanded on the participation issue by including the characteristics of participants. Blake and Mouton (1964) contributed their thoughts about the impact of participation on organizational climate and success. A rather amusing incident occurred in a class where this issue was discussed. When students were asked to list participants for Scenario 2 above, no one suggested the wife's in-laws as possible participants. The instructor asked, "What about the husband's parents?" one class member immediately replied, "Over my dead body should my mother-in-law become involved." That student clearly overlooked one of the participation selection criteria—the impact on the continuing relationship between decision-maker and prospective participant.

3. Competence Assessment and Development

Using this guideline helps to assess the competence of everyone who will be involved in making the decision and implementing it. Taking these steps ensures that adequate competence exists. In an organizational environment using the guideline identifies weaknesses as well as strengths of individuals selected. The conceptual foundation for this guideline comes from the vast education and training literature. The best overview can be found in higher education texts on learning, education, and training.

4. Ensuring Adequate Satisfaction

This can be considered the most important guideline. It, together with the participation guideline that supports it, represents the foundation for motivation strategies. If participants gain satisfaction from decisions, they are likely to support whatever needs to be done. Avoiding poor perceptions about a decision will keep people from being dissatisfied about their jobs. Considering employees' satisfaction leads to their feeling empowered. Appropriate intangible and tangible rewards for staff members assures more satisfaction. The major theoretical foundations for this guideline can be found in many studies on motivation, almost all in one way or another building on Maslow (1954) and Herzberg (1968). Writing on what is important to employees, Nelson (1997, 2002, & 2005), and Rausch and Washbush (1997) deserve attention also.

5. Setting and Working Toward Goals

Not all organizations set formal goals at all levels, although management as well as all levels of staff usually have informal goals. This is true at all major career and personal stages.

Issues for this guideline pertain to the organizational processes for deciding what is to be achieved. These issues refer to the processes that should be used in setting and working toward goals. They include the respective responsibilities of staff members and of the managers to whom they report, and how clearly and measurably the outcomes are expressed and communicated. They do not refer to the specifics of the goals, which are more likely to be technical rather than soft issues. There is considerable coverage of these topics in the literature of the second half of the 20th century, particularly in House (1971), Hughes (1965), and Locke and Latham (1990); there is also an in-depth discussion in Rausch (1978).

6. Ensuring Coordination and Stimulating Cooperation

This guideline concerns ways to achieve coordination and to stimulate cooperation, while anticipating, preventing, and managing damaging conflict. In light of the many issues, their complexity and interrelationships, an inordinately long list of references would have to be cited. A thorough overview can be found in Rausch and Washbush (1997) and Rausch (2003, 2008). The literature on conflict is somewhat more focused. In addition to the ongoing publications of the Harvard Negotiation Research Project and related Harvard programs, issues on conflict are explored in Fisher and Ury (2001), Ury (1991), and Whetten and Cameron (1993, 1995).

7. Working with Norms, Including Those Pertaining to Ethics, Diversity, and Organizational Justice

This guideline has become increasingly significant in the past few years. The issues have become more important as workplace diversity increases and businesses expand globally. Effectively identifying norms and aligning them so there are fewer disputes inside organizations (or between family members and friends) are the topics on which the guideline centers. Here there is less information in the literature, as the thinking about these issues is in a state of flux, with new ideas emerging continuously. We therefore refer decision-makers to the Internet for guidance on what to consider when making such decisions.

8. Fair and Comprehensive Project and Performance Reviews

The issues for the last guideline pertain to the effectiveness of project and performance reviews and the need to conduct such reviews. Most organizations have to address the need for fairness in performance evaluations, a very complex issue that is not widely understood, and this guideline reminds evaluators of that fact. Literature in support of the issues in this guideline can be found in Armstrong (2003), Fear (1984), and Rausch (1985).

Conclusion

In summary, the following points were made in this article:

1. Enhancing decisions is synonymous with achieving greater quality and thereby avoiding unexpected, often undesirable consequences.

2. The quality of decisions, as with everything else, depends on thoroughness. That means attention to detail, considering all relevant issues, and not overlooking anything important.

3. Attention to detail requires awareness of both the technical and the soft aspects of every decision, and the details of both.

4. Having guidelines structures and simplifies the decision-making task, ensuring that nothing is overlooked.

5. To make better decisions requires that we develop the habit of at least skimming a set of guidelines.

6. Developing the habit of quickly reviewing the guidelines when making any significant decision is the key to better decisions.

There are undoubtedly other methods that can be used for making decisions, but mastering any method depends on learning the details and making them a habit. In fact, the foundation for better decision making can be laid in grades K-12 and then be expanded in almost any professional higher education program. Thereafter, those in a position to make organizational decisions become self-motivated to solve the issues, thus strengthening their ability to become better decision-makers.

References*

Armstrong, B.A. (2003). Collegiate leadership programs. Claremont, CA: Claremont Graduate University, Department of Education. Unpublished paper.

Bennis, W.G., & O'Toole, J. (2005, May). How business schools lost their way. *Harvard Business Review*.

Blake, R.R., & Mouton, J. (1964). *The managerial grid*. Houston, TX: Gulf.

Fear, R.A. (1984). *The evaluation interview* (3rd ed.). New York: McGraw-Hill.

Fisher, R., & Ury, W. (2001). *Getting to yes*. Boston: Houghton Mifflin.

Hersey, P., & Blanchard, K.H. (1969, May). Life cycle theory of leadership. *Training and Development Journal, 23*(2).

Herzberg, F. (1968, Jan/Feb). One more time: How do you motivate employees? *Harvard Business Review, 68,* 108.

House, R.J. (1971, September). A path-goal theory of leader effectiveness. *Administrative Science Quarterly, 16,* 321–338.

Hughes, C.L. (1965). *Goal setting: Key to individual and organizational effectiveness*. New York: American Management Association.

Locke, E.A., & Latham, G.P. (1990). *A theory of goal setting and task performance*. Englewood Cliffs, NJ: Prentice Hall.

Maier, N.R.F. (1967). Assets and liabilities in group problem solving: The need for an integrative junction. *Psychological Review, 74*(4), 240–241.

Maslow, A.H. (1954). *Motivation and personality*. New York: Harper and Row.

Nelson, B. (1997). *1001 ways to energize employees*. New York: Workman.

Nelson, B. (2002). *1001 rewards and recognition fieldbook*. New York: Workman.

Nelson, B. (2005). *1001 ways to reward employees* (2nd ed.). New York: Workman.

Rausch, E. (1978). *Balancing needs of people and organizations: The linking elements concept*. Washington, DC: Bureau of National Affairs.

Rausch, E. (1985). *Win-win performance management/appraisal*. Hoboken, NJ: John Wiley & Sons.

---

*Some readers may object to the use of dated references. They are used here because most of the research on these issues originated in the 20th century. The latest thinking is not needed here; the original or foundation thoughts are discussed by the authors referenced here. Later work contributed mainly refinements and amplifications.

Rausch, E. (2003). *Guidelines for management and leadership decisions*. Bradford, UK: Management Decision.

Rausch, E. (2008). *Planning, common sense, and superior performance*. Charlotte, NC: Information Age Publishing.

Rausch, E.R., & Washbush, J.B. (1997). *High quality leadership: Practical guidelines to becoming a more effective manager*. Milwaukee, WI: Quality Press.

Russo, E.J., & Schoemaker, P.J.H. (1990). *Decision traps: Ten barriers to brilliant decision making and how to overcome them*. New York: Fireside Books.

Tannenbaum, R., & Schmidt, W.H. (1958, March/April). How to choose a leadership pattern. *Harvard Business Review*, p. 96 (revisited May/June 1973).

Ury, W. (1991). *Getting past no*. New York: Bantam Books.

Vroom, V., & Yetton, P.W. (1973). *Leadership and decision making*. Pittsburgh, PA: University of Pittsburgh Press.

Vroom, V.H., & Jago, A.G. (1988). *The new leadership: Managing participation in organizations*. Englewood Cliffs, NJ: Prentice Hall.

Whetten, D.A., & Cameron, K.S. (1993). *Developing management skills: Managing conflict*. New York: HarperCollins.

Whetten, D.A., & Cameron, K.S. (1995). *Developing management skills* (3rd ed.). New York: HarperCollins.

Erwin Rausch *is adjunct at Kean University and retired president of Didactic Systems, Inc., Cranford, New Jersey, publishers and consultants in training and development. He also taught evening courses at Rutgers University. He is the author, lead author, or editor of eight books, many articles/papers, and numerous simulation/games and self-coaching guides.*

Dr. Charles Anderson *is currently a professor of economics and coordinator of the economics program at Kean University, Elizabeth, New Jersey. He was also the founding dean of the College of Business and Public Administration at Kean University. Dr. Anderson earned a doctorate in economics from Stanford University.*

The Supervisor's Motivational Tool Kit

Deborah Spring Laurel

Summary

One of the age-old questions for supervisors is "How do I motivate my employees?" This article offers seven factors that are critical to ensure a high level of employee motivation. When done right, motivation isn't something extra that a supervisor does; it happens naturally from being a good supervisor.

Seven factors have high potential for increasing employee motivation. If a supervisor sets employees up for success and provides feedback so that the employees know when they are successful, that will increase employees' confidence in their abilities.

In addition, when a supervisor relates desired job performance to specific employee interests, keeps employee concerns at a reasonable level, and maintains a positive environment in the workplace, that supervisor can help employees view job performance as its own reward rather than as a means to an end.

1. Extrinsic–Intrinsic Motivation

When employees work in order to gain something else, they are operating from an extrinsic motivation. For example, employees may first come to a job simply to earn a paycheck (an extrinsic reason).

However, if the employees feel valued, have sufficient challenge, and are successful in their jobs, they may start to come to work because they feel good about the jobs themselves (an intrinsic reason). Employees have intrinsic motivation when they receive satisfaction from the work itself.

Converting extrinsic employee motivation to intrinsic motivation is the key to creating a self-directed workforce. In order to accomplish this, a supervisor can employ any of the remaining six motivational factors.

2. Success

Human beings prefer tasks that they can perform successfully, rather than tasks at which they are unsuccessful. According to W. Edwards Deming (2000), the quality management guru who is credited for Japan's economic recovery after World War II, 94 percent of an employee's ability to perform successfully on the job depends on the system.

By "the system," he meant the company structure, its policies and procedures, its culture, as well as its management style. A supervisor can set employees up to be successful by giving complete instructions, sufficient resources, necessary training, and constructive feedback.

3. Feedback

Employees know whether they are performing successfully when they receive feedback. This feedback, which may be oral or written, can come from their supervisors, peers, or customers. However, employees can also determine their own success if they have specific, observable, and measurable standards against which to evaluate their own performance.

Employees need specific feedback about what they are doing well so that they can continue to repeat that effective performance. Supervisors should also provide specific, constructive feedback that will help employees clearly understand what they need to do to improve their performance, when necessary.

When employees know that they have been successful, based on the feedback they receive, the result is a boost to their self-confidence.

4. Confidence

Employees are more likely to be confident about achieving success when they believe that success is within their control. A supervisor can set employees up for success by clarifying what performance level is expected, ensuring sufficient training and resources to achieve that performance, and providing ongoing specific and constructive feedback about that performance.

Successful job performance that is validated by feedback will result in increased employee confidence in their ability to perform. Employee confidence can reinforce their interest in assuming additional and possibly greater responsibilities.

5. Interest

Employees will be more motivated to perform well if what they are asked to do is directly related to something that interests them. These compelling interests and needs will obviously vary depending on the individual employee. Supervisors who do not already know what interests their employees will have to ask them. Gaining increased visibility, input into decision making, experience necessary for promotion, or the opportunity to help others might be attractive to some employees and not to others.

A supervisor has to be careful not to misread employees' interests in order to avoid unduly raising employees' concern. For example, some employees may appreciate a more challenging assignment, while other employees might feel anxious and overwhelmed by such an assignment.

6. Concern

Employees need to have a moderate level of concern in order to expend sufficient effort to perform satisfactorily. If they do not care about performing well, their supervisor may need to raise their level of concern by pointing out the consequences of continued unacceptable performance.

On the other hand, if employees are highly anxious, due to real or perceived risks involved, they will not be able to perform effectively until the level of concern is reduced. For example, if employees are highly concerned about changes on the job, a supervisor might lower their level of concern by giving them some control over the change process.

7. Work Environment

If employees have a comfortable and supportive work situation, they will be more inclined to put forth effort to perform. For this reason, it is important for a supervisor to create and maintain a work atmosphere in which employees feel valued for their abilities, supported in their actions, and respected by their peers.

Summary

Employees who have been set up for success, know they are successful based on the feedback they have received, feel confident in their abilities, recognize that their performance satisfies a compelling need, and have an appropriate level of concern will have a good feeling about their work. All of these factors will increase the probability of intrinsic employee motivation. Employees' performance of the job will be satisfying in itself, rather than just a means to an end.

Reference

Deming, W.E. (2000). *The new economics for industry, government, education* (2nd ed.). Cambridge, MA: MIT Press.

Deborah Spring Laurel *has been a trainer and a consultant in the areas of workplace learning and performance improvement for more than thirty years. She is the president of Laurel and Associates, Ltd., which specializes in enhancing interpersonal dynamics within organizations. Deborah teaches management and supervisory topics for the Executive Management Institute and the Small Business Development Center at the University of Wisconsin–Madison. She has her master's degree from the University of Wisconsin–Madison.*

A Positive Vision for 2020
The Confluence of Information Technology with T&D

Phillip E. Nelson and Teri-E Belf

Summary

This article presents an optimistic vision of humankind emerging in the year 2016 and progressing to the year 2020 and beyond. With the Global Megacrisis coming, simultaneous enhancements of information technology (IT) will assist us to acclimate and thrive during the process. Through technological advancements via the Internet and in training and allied professions, we are evolving into a global brain network. The outcome is a global heart and spirit. This positive vision is based on projections and speculations by renowned futurists and the authors' familiarity with the field of training and development (T&D).

Global Megacrisis—Danger and Opportunity

The coming Global Megacrisis presents us with danger and opportunity. According to Halal and Marien (2009), megacrisis happens when several crises converge and cascade, causing additional stressors. At this time we are faced with financial implosions, environmental degradation, and accelerating global warming. Scarcity of resources tends to cause wars. Environmental disasters have caused migration of major populations. Akin to a chain of falling dominoes, humankind, unfamiliar with how to deal with and cope with these challenges, tends to blunder and collapse. Do we have the ability to act wisely at this time?

Fortunately, exponentially accelerating IT will evolve just in time to enable us to resolve the projected megacrisis and rapidly evolve beyond it. By 2020, we could see a collaborative, synergistic global economy; transformed institutions; and evolving new sources of wisdom, solutions, and energy. We predict that, about 2015, an IT-driven, accelerating global economic boom will start to evolve in the global economy. After that, our global culture will proceed with surprising alacrity, eventually creating something like a unified global brain, heart, and spirit.

Ray Kurzweil (2005) estimates that exponentially accelerating IT will catalyze the acceleration of most other technologies. Whereas it once required a lead time of two hundred years for an idea to go into widespread use, it now takes five years or less. Clearly, keeping up with technological advances is essential.

TechCast (www.techcast.org), one of the top technology forecasting systems on the Internet, forecasts that by 2020, thirty specific major new technologies will be in widespread global use. In order to navigate new products, technologies, and markets, organizations must include technology forecasts in their strategic planning processes.

The synergy of these breakthrough technologies will trigger the evolution of an advanced global economy and civilization with collaborative tools and shared intelligence to address the Global Megacrisis. Our prophecy is optimistic.

Technological Changes

Intriguing technological inventions will increase in availability and use, and new ones will appear. By 2015, global access, virtual education, and holographic video conferencing will be the norm in industrialized nations. By 2016, we will have technological assistants that can scan our environment, perform routine tasks, and, upon our command, negotiate win-win solutions. Welcome your digital assistant.

Another technological breakthrough will be available to utilize the capabilities of the digital assistant. This digital helper will contain software and processes to gather information about your business, other businesses, and the entire business world. Welcome your digital self.

By 2016 we will be better informed, better forewarned, and better prepared because we will have our digital helpers.

In the same year, the intelligent interface (conversational interface) will automatically translate and thereby dissolve cultural barriers. Creative individuals around the world will be more easily able to collaborate to find and create solutions without a language barrier. Natural communities of interest will temporarily override cultural differences. Major companies like Apple, Intel, Google, and Microsoft already have intelligent interfaces and digital assistants in queue. The race to market has begun.

Digital Assistants and Digital Selves: Technological Allies

Digital Assistants

Your digital assistant will be in perpetual scanning mode to retrieve information about technological advances and market shifts that might impact your organization's performance and your personal career direction. For example, scans might search training and career ladder databases in your organization. Additionally, your digital assistant will have the capability to access the organization's long-range plans, goals and strategies, annual initiatives, up-to-date vacancies, and salaries. The knowledge base of your digital assistant will include your organization's standards of performance and methods of monitoring and evaluation.

The digital assistant's job description will include the following—and more:

- Collect relevant data and organize it according to how an individual, group, team, or organization chooses to receive and process information. You will be able to retrieve information in ways meaningful to you.

- Provide information from market scans, projections, and databases both inside and outside the organization, including worldwide economic trends.

- Scan to retrieve information about technological advances that impact an organization's direction.

- House an organized collection of best practices.

Digital Selves

John Smart (2010), the futurist who predicts the emergence of the digital self, describes a digital self as "a mirror of you," created from the intersection of artificial intelligence, natural language processing, and business intelligence (BI). BI, now mainly in the hands of corporations, will be available to individuals. This technological mirror will house information about you (programmed by you), such as mission in life, values, key beliefs, learning style, skills, interests, wishes, plans, dreams, and desires. Smart asserts that it will serve as your mentor, planner, advocate, and negotiator. Later in this article you will read how your digital self can access and use the best "just in time" training tailored to your individual learning style.

Business intelligence will provide the digital self with information on business inputs, processing, and outputs. Examples of BI that the digital self will find useful include:

- Suppliers: supply chain, responsiveness, and quality measures.

- Customers: evolving needs and demands.

- Competition: forecasts, products, and plans.

- Internal organizational characteristics: processing, capabilities, resilience, and plans.

The digital self's job description will include at least the following:

- Maintain a record of your life purpose, values, career plans, key qualities, competencies, strengths and interests, opportunities congruent with your visions, and so on.

- Maintain an executive dashboard that can earmark patterns of problems and opportunities using BI.

- Advise on career choices and best options.

- Negotiate on your behalf (only if you so delegate) with other employees, your supervisor, team members, suppliers, customers, prospective employers, human resources, and all other stakeholders in your life. Negotiation might even happen with the digital selves of others.

- Determine the best fit for you, in career advancement or career stability.

- Take the initiative to keep your supervisor or team leader or colleagues informed, in the mode in which you inform it that they want to receive information.

- Alert you to strategic changes in your company's direction that may impact your position.

- Offer options for communication with others while preserving your values and honoring theirs as well.

Jump into the Future

The year is 2016 and certain technological advances are in full swing. Digital helpers abound and the following example sheds light on how you use them.

You have been experiencing stress on your job lately and wonder whether a career move or perhaps another position might be a wise choice. Even though you have achieved a leadership position, you are still not experiencing the feelings of satisfaction you had hoped for when you accepted the position about eighteen months ago. Your mid-year performance evaluation is coming up and you want to be prepared with questions and a game plan.

You ask your digital self how you can improve performance and regain a sense of meaningfulness from your job so that stress would decrease. Your self suggests training in leadership communication skills. This seems like a good approach. Your digital self asks your digital assistant to research whether these sorts of programs have been approved, and you receive an instant positive report. Your supervisor hinted this would be useful at a staff meeting a few months ago, although it was not formally mandated on your last review.

Your digital self scans your learning preference style, values, background, former courses you have taken, long-term career goals, performance reviews (including prior positions), and the amount of funding still available to you in this fiscal year. At the same time your digital assistant researches what programs are available within the next two months. Your digital self checks your calendar and stores information about viable possibilities.

Three recommendations surface, and your digital self does an analysis and informs you of the best match for you and your needs, taking into account your lifestyle. For example, you (1) are a strongly dominant visual learner, (2) like to use concepts and metaphors, (3) are a mother of three who needs to stay within one hour's driving distance of home, and (4) need to be available when your partner is away on an upcoming business trip.

You delay action because you want your digital self to provide you with more specific information about your communication behavior patterns.

During the next two weeks, your digital assistant lights up when certain challenges arise that affect you. Your digital self, alerted to your training request, begins to see a pattern emerging that specifically pinpoints your issue as one that involves how you give feedback to employees. Your assertive style is inconsistent with the styles of others in leadership positions. Your style is overly directive, almost dictatorial, and your vocal volume too loud. You give the impression of being angry, even when giving staff neutral feedback for improvement. It appears you are falling below the required minimum organizational standard on selected communication skills, in this case giving feedback.

Now you have enough data to take the initiative to sign up for a training program. In the meantime, your digital self has updated your digital assistant about the shift in the focus for training, i.e., giving feedback instead of communication in general. A new search ensues. With new options, you make your selection and ask your digital assistant to sign you up, inform accounting to budget for the event, and let your supervisor know.

You know that the training program you selected will be tailored to your learning style and preferences.

By 2015, any training package can be automatically and easily adapted to one's learning style and preferences. Your digital self will know you well, as you have already answered questions and demonstrated your preferred learning behaviors such as whether you:

- Prefer learning in a group or individually

- Like to experience something or hear about it first before practicing

- Use visualization techniques

- Learn by seeing similarities in patterns or the differences

- Want to be acknowledged for successes along the way or at the end

Training Programs Must Keep Changing

External technological advancements will require organizations to review their business plans more frequently. This impacts training plans and directives. Whereas a training department may have shifting priorities and schedules, individualized training is still possible due to individualized, just-in-time, online training and virtual training. Evaluation and feedback from program participants, along with the pros and cons of a particular program, will be continually added to the T&D database, so each employee's digital assistant can use this updated information.

As new technology emerges, new customers, suppliers, and stakeholders will emerge. With new data, your digital self will generate new career roadmaps.

Training curriculum developers will use automated programs to accelerate release of new training programs to handle rapid adaptations to technological and organizational change. Curriculum developers in T&D will access these programs and submit them to HR and T&D for inclusion in training databases. As needed, updated training options will be made available to digital assistants so that digital selves can have current information.

By 2016 choices for training will require only a manager's oversight. Your digital self will have negotiated with your manager's digital self to obtain approval. You may also delegate to your digital self to take the initiative to keep your manager informed.

By 2016 digital assistants will replace 30 percent of routine monotonous chores. Surely few people will long for the good old days of monotonous, routine work.

Conclusion

In summary, what do we gain? By 2020, the accelerating rate of change will require organizations to be very agile and choose the most advanced, tested, reliable IT alongside training to keep them on the leading edge.

On an individual level, agility and responsiveness are also mandatory. Our gifts, strengths, expertise, and talents will have an exciting environment in which to thrive. We will have the time and freedom to (1) be more creative, (2) more frequently access intuition and inner wisdom, (3) experience deeper more meaningful connections with people, and (4) just be.

Our vision encompasses people living more of their human potential with greater fulfillment. We hold this vision and invite you to share it with us.

References

Halal, W. & Marien, M. (2009, December). Global megacrisis survey: Four scenarios on a pessimism-optimism axis analysis. www.techcast.org/hot-issues-global-warming .aspx?

Halal, W. (1995–2011). TechCast: Information technology. www.techcast.org/Trategic Analysis2.aspx?FieldID=22

Kurzweil, R. (2005). *The singularity is near: When humans transcend biology.* New York: Viking Penguin.

Smart, J. (2010, March). Dice NextTech. (Slides) The digital self: When social media get personal. http://accelerating.org/slides.html

Smart, J. (2004–2008). Human performance enhancement in 2032: A scenario for military planners. Section B2, personality capture/digital twin/cybertwin. www.acceler ating.org/articles/hpe2032army.html#pcdt

Phillip E. Nelson, Ph.D., *a member of Mensa and graduate of West Point, has more than fifteen years of experience in federal service as a management trainer and organization development consultant focusing on IT-driven change and sociotechnical work system design. He enjoys co-creating focused synergy and fun while facilitating creative project teams. As a long-time member of the World Future Society, he applies his futurist interests when writing articles and serving as one of the TechCast experts.*

Teri-E Belf *is a purposeful and inspiring coaching leader, trainer, mentor and coach with twenty-six years in the coaching field and eighteen years of HRD and T&D management experience. Her current passions include directing Success Unlimited Network®, which has a worldwide ICF-accredited coach training program including annual coaching education retreats and offering workshops to empower and retreats to support women through Wrinkle Wisdom, weaving women into the fabric of world wisdom and honoring women as sages.*

Toward a Healthy World
Meeting the Leadership Challenges of the 21st Century*
Sherene Zolno

Summary

Participating in an educational simulation teaches the next generation of leaders and executive coaches and consultants how to engage as learners, partners and catalysts in today's complex organizations. As CEOs and managers, they seek to lead from the core identified in the Leadership for a Healthy World model, ensuring a sense of self-worth, hope, and capability in themselves and their followers.

"We must build a sense of self-worth, hope, and capability to meet the challenges of the next millennium."

Sixty-five students and seven members of the faculty were gathered in the room on that Friday after lunch. Tensions were high; excitement and anxious chatter echoed off the walls as we convened. Marketplace was about to begin.

The simulation that is not a simulation—that is the Marketplace. Conceived of as a capstone event during which second-year students could demonstrate their leadership skills as CEOs, managers, and supervisors of companies, and where first-year students had their final opportunity to demonstrate who they were and what they had learned about systems before their first assessment, Marketplace had come to be the crucible within which one's sense of self might be forever changed.

*The author wishes to acknowledge the theoretical contributions of David Cooperrider, Paul Rebillot, Robert Dilts, and Frank Barrett to the Leadership for a Healthy World model, as well as Jeananne Oliphant, Research and Design Team Co-Leaders, and The Leading Clinic's R & D team members, including Geoffrey Bellman, Diana Whitney, Dell Drake, Stephanie Hemingway, Sheila Kelly, Kim Krisco, J. Loux, Marge Schiller, Jane Seiling, and Robert Woodruff, who participated in the early research.

We say that Marketplace is not "pretending to be something you are not"; it is "being as much of who you are as you can be." Over the years Marketplace has shifted and grown.

What Is Marketplace?

From its humble origins as an educational process within which to experience how hierarchical systems can have a profound impact on an individual, Marketplace has become a fast-paced, learning-intensive opportunity to explore new and critical questions facing people in organizations: How can we survive and thrive as a business offering our creative products and services, yet contribute positively to our community, the environment, and our members' health and well-being? And how do we need to show up as leaders to make this possible?

The question of how to add value in the new global village will be a particularly challenging one for organizations and their leaders in the upcoming decades. Changes in societies, markets, customers, competition, and technology around the globe are forcing us to clarify our values, develop new strategies, and learn new ways of operating. In this environment, the role of the leader is changing. Being a leader today involves having the courage to face a new reality of complexity, uncertainty, and, yes, tremendous possibility—while helping the people around you to face this reality as well.

Marketplace is a microcosm of that challenge. The paradoxes of competition versus collaboration, of leading versus sharing leadership, of satisfying personal needs in the moment versus contributing to a team, company, community and healthy world, the here and now versus taking the long view—all are present. Add them up, toss in some interesting power dynamics, and, oh, don't forget self-management and self-awareness issues, and you know that participants will have learned much more than they imagined.

Two Models of Leadership

With the intention of designing a program to develop leaders responsive to these complex challenges, several years ago The Leading Clinic of Vashon, Washington, sponsored the coming together of a team of researchers to examine what could be learned from the experiences of effective leaders, from the writings of leadership experts, and from innovative thinkers in other related fields, such as psychology and psychotherapy, the new sciences, and the study of communication. The integrated view of leadership that resulted from their effort was named Leadership for a Healthy World.

At the heart of Leadership for a Healthy World are two models that were developed to guide our research team's thinking about the kind of leadership that could be possible for any level of system: individual, team, organization, community, or world. These models illustrate the most significant finding of our research—that when leaders, and the people who live and work with them, feel worthy, hopeful, and capable, there exists the potential for exceptional accomplishment.

The first model pictures the research team's thinking of how a strong sense of self-worth, hope, and capability would act like a pebble thrown into a pond. The impact of having this empowered sense of self expands from the healthy core of the individual, causing overlapping and widening circles to ripple outward, touching everything in their wake.

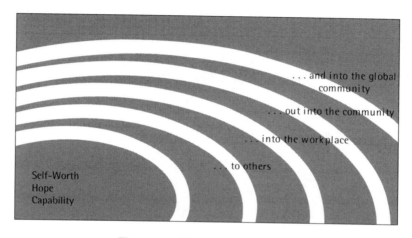

Figure 1. The Ripple Model

Building self-worth, hope, and capability in oneself and in others allows people, organizations and communities to flourish and, we hypothesized, would eventually be the key to global wellbeing.

As shown in Figure 2, the research team began to recognize how essential a sense of self-worth, hope and capability were in creating healthy, high functioning communities, and through them, the world. The Leadership for a Healthy World model focuses on how individuals, teams, organizations, and communities who experience this sense of self-worth, hope, and capability, as contrasted with those experiencing worthlessness, hopelessness, and helplessness, seemed to be able to focus on their possibilities rather than on their limitations.

Whole System Health Begins with Health at the Core

At the center of the Leadership for a Healthy World model (see the central ring in Figure 2) is self-worth, hope, and capability that leaders need to build within

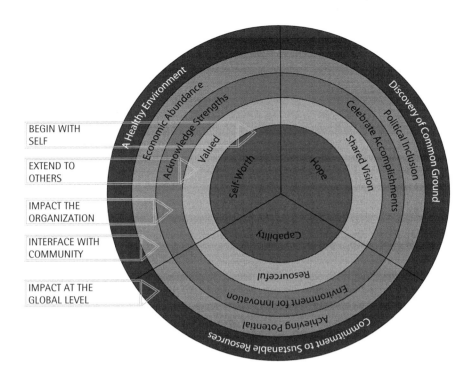

Figure 2. Leadership for a Healthy World

themselves. Our research clearly demonstrated that a solid core of self-worth, hope, and capability had a profound impact on every experience leaders had, affecting how capable they were in dealing with others, to what heights they aspired, and ultimately, what they were able to accomplish within organizations.

For example, Abraham Zaleznik (1965), from the Harvard Business School, discovered in his research that leaders with low self-worth apparently begin to think of themselves as having fewer choices, even when others saw many options yet available. Richard Skillman (2000), former hospital system CEO and executive director of several major medical organizations, referring to the high turnover among executives in the tumultuous healthcare industry, said, "It's hopelessness that causes us to abandon initiatives in midstream, and to give up on ourselves and our employees."

In the model, the second ring out from the center indicates the leader's role in maximizing the potential for others to contribute to the success of the system: from their direct contact with the leader, people would feel valued, resourceful, and engaged in creating a shared vision.

Jim Kouzes and Barry Posner (1987), in their book *The Leadership Challenge*, refer to this as "enabling others to act." In their research and interviews with leaders across the country, they found that exemplary leaders made others feel capable and, when they did, extraordinary things happened.

Nathaniel Branden (1994), clinician and researcher, compared the need for self-worth, hope, and capability to the need for calcium in the diet—if people lacked it, they didn't necessarily die, but rather became impaired in their ability to function. He demonstrated that high self-esteem subjects in research experiments actually persisted at a task significantly longer than low self-esteem subjects.

Two examples of leaders who understood this were Edwin Land, who, in the early days of Polaroid, convinced his managers that they couldn't fail, and Coach John Robinson of the Los Angeles Rams, who once reported that he never critiqued his players until they were convinced of his unconditional confidence in their abilities.

The Ripple Effect

Via the contributions the leader and individuals in contact with the leader make, system effectiveness is impacted. From systems filled with confident, capable, and hopeful people, an effective community begins to develop. And, finally, healthy well-functioning communities contribute to global well-being. This ripple effect is possible when leaders understand their role in building personal and system-wide self-worth, hope, and capability.

As Chunliang Al Huang and Jerry Lynch (1995) say in their book, *Mentoring: The Tao of Giving and Receiving Wisdom*, "By cultivating the powerful 'self' we begin to offer the possibility of change to those in our world; change comes from the individual heart and fans outward, creating a unified, interconnected community."

In the Leadership for a Healthy World training program, based on the two models presented in this article, participants initiate the process of transforming their sense of themselves by challenging their own limiting beliefs, becoming *inquirers* and *learners*. Then, to impact others, leaders develop the skills of *coaching*. In the program, coaching is differentiated from other leader-follower interactions and is defined as "a passionate, responsible relationship for creating an opening for action and engagement."

Next, as a *partner*, leaders collaborate in developing the organization's potential for high performance. The key to this is how the leader acknowledges the system's strengths and celebrates its accomplishments (what David Cooperrider [1990] refers to as the "life giving forces of the organization"), while creating a resilient environment for embracing change.

For many long-term employees, this acknowledgment is the key to retaining a sense of their worthiness and maintaining a sense of hope during times of chaotic change. With the failed mergers of the past decade still smarting, some of our nation's top leaders claim they learned this the hard way, having seen the plunging morale from poorly planned and led transitions completely incapacitate their organizations.

Ultimately, when change is on the horizon, it is each employee's sense of resourcefulness that enables an organization to be flexible, responsive, and open to new requirements.

Moving from the center to the outer rings of the Leadership for a Healthy World model, leaders enhance the relationships between their organizations and the outside community by learning to view their communities as sources of economic abundance, political inclusion, and support for achieving each community member's potential. In this way, being hopeful and believing themselves and their organizations to be worthy and capable, leaders serve as *catalysts* for creating inter-relationships within the community that support the organization's success.

In doing that, leaders, as learners, coaches, partners, and catalysts, can create a harmonious world with a healthy environment, a focus on common ground, and a commitment to sustainable resources.

Health in the Marketplace

This year, equipped with an understanding of the Leadership for a Healthy World model, second-year student-leaders in four different companies engaged their "employees" (first-year students) in identifying the values that would drive their Marketplace choices: what products and/or services they would offer and what processes they would use in creating and then selling them. Unlike the global marketplace, however, our Marketplace is made up of thirty-minute "days," and there are only eight of them and a somewhat sleep-deprived night available to form, storm, norm, and perform as a company! Yet, because of their shared commitment to creating healthy systems, important time was taken from the rush of this one-and-a-half-day experiential curriculum to reflect, to journal, and to step back long enough to notice their own contributions to creating health in the system, while acknowledging the challenge each leader and member had taken on to *live* the Leadership for a Healthy World model.

In today's business climate there is a compelling belief that how leaders lead is the link to how competently organizations run. The information derived from the investigations of The Leading Clinic's research team indicate that organizations filled with and led by worthy, hopeful, and capable individuals will thrive in the climate of this century.

As faculty, in sharing the Leadership for a Healthy World model with the students, we are hopeful that they will go forward into careers that contribute to the health of our world—from the inside out.

References

Barrett, F. (1995). Creating appreciative learning cultures. *Organization Dynamics*.

Branden, N. (1994). *The six pillars of self-esteem*. New York: Bantam Books.

Chunliang, A., & Lynch, J. (1995). *Mentoring: The Tao of giving and receiving wisdom*. San Francisco: Harper.

Cooperrider, D.L. (1990). Positive image, positive action: The affirmative basis of organizing. In S. Srivastva & D.L. Cooperrider (Eds.), *Appreciative management and leadership*. San Francisco: Jossey-Bass.

Kouzes, J.M., & Posner, B.Z. (1987). *The leadership challenge* (1st ed.). San Francisco: Jossey-Bass.

Skillman, R. (2000). Personal conversation.

Zaleznick, A. (1965, May/June). The dynamics of subordinancy. *Harvard Business Review*.

Sherene Zolno, MS, *RODC, Certified Master Coach, is a learning and development consultant and executive director of The Leading Clinic. Her expertise includes working with leaders, teams, and organizations in identifying strategic intentions, improving operations, and transforming culture. She has made significant contributions to the field of management and leadership education and is an internationally known leadership researcher and seasoned business coach. Sherene served on ASTD's OD Professional Practice Area board. Her writing has been published in ASTD's* Research Monograph *and OD Network's* OD Practitioner, *and VisionAction journals, and in the Pfeiffer Annuals. The research-based* Leadership for a Healthy World *model serves as an important foundation for her work in whole system positive-core change. You can read more about it at www.proactionassociates.com.*

Keeping Training Alive in a Recovering Economy

Kurt Iskrzycki, Susan Cain, and Tim Buividas

Summary

In this article, the authors review the impact that the latest recession has had on corporate training, describe a survey conducted to find out how organizations and training departments are coping during the economic downturn, and offer some recommendations that all organizations can implement to maintain leader and team development training and achieve their current training goals.

The recent economic recession has impacted the world's economy in ways unfelt for decades. Infrastructures have been torn apart, and unemployment rates have risen to shocking heights.

Organizational leaders and professionals know all too well that when a dip in the economic cycle occurs, pressure from both outside and inside a business forces cost-cutting and reductions (Paradise & Mosley, 2009). Management balances budgets by eliminating performance development programs and training initiatives that they feel are either unneeded or of no significant value (Minton-Eversole, 2008). While this may be seen as short-term thinking, training and development professionals are accustomed to being the first in line for the chopping block (Coleman, 2009; Phillips, 2009).

As reverberations of the recent recession continue to trickle down, organizations now face a daunting set of challenges to pick up the fallen pieces. At no time in recent years have leaders been placed under more pressure to aid in this reformation than now (Coleman, 2009). Survival (or a bailout) isn't a certainty anymore, and organizational leaders are being sent to the front lines to lead businesses toward an unknown future.

As early as 2007, when signs of impending doom were being broadcast throughout the world, organizational training and development cuts, including team building and leadership training, felt the notches of the "belt tightening" (Taylor, 2010). Thoughts of future leaders and learning initiatives gave way to keeping one's head above water.

With this most recent recession, author Lynn Taylor detailed the important need to maintain employee training, even in tough economic times. In her article, "Put Leadership Training on the Front Burner," she cites a 2008 study conducted by Expertus, a learning service firm, where 48 percent of the eighty-four corporate and government training professionals who were surveyed indicated 2009 training budgets were going to be decreased significantly. Those figures rose from 41 percent from the previous year (Taylor, 2010). As we see from these results, organizations haven't been afraid to cut learning and development budgets. Those actions have repercussions that are both short- and long-term. Nearing 2011, those organizations that drastically trimmed T&D budgets may now be second-guessing themselves.

It appears that some organizations realize the impact of reducing or eliminating training throughout their organization. The Boston Consulting Group led a global executive survey that focused on the significant role that leadership development plays within organizations. Executives surveyed within the United States indicated that leadership development was the second-most-critical human resource issue they faced (Hansen, 2008).

Impact on Leadership Development and Productivity

Adding insult to injury, it can be seen that eliminating or even reducing leadership development training has secondary casualties. In any organization, developing leaders must be given adequate opportunities for development, and the slashing of learning initiatives lowers morale and reduces skill acquisition and employee engagement. In addition, reduced or eliminated training opportunities drain organizational productivity (Taylor, 2010). The snail-like progression of growth, coupled with deficient leadership development, produces a waiting state within organizations (Parks, 2009). This complacency and frame-by-frame movement fails to place businesses in positions to be proactive and combat the difficulties within this post-recession economy and breeds reactivity (Coleman, 2009). Given the real need that organizations have to cut spending and the impact this has on developing an adequate performance pipeline, the question becomes one of considering the next strategic step to serve both purposes.

A Possible Turnaround

Where budget cuts and lost jobs have been the norm since 2007, signs of strength within the economy are slowly but steadily becoming apparent. We now have more opportunities to revitalize leadership training in organizations (Taylor, 2010). Organizations can become proactive once again through learning and development initiatives on a fiscally conscientious basis. Even though budgets are still decreased, organizations can review their strategies and select those needed training and development options as smart investments (Minton-Eversole, 2008; Taylor, 2010). Engagement, morale, motivation, and performance increase through reinvigorated training and development opportunities and help companies make money (Coleman, 2009; Minton-Eversole, 2008).

What lies ahead for organizational training initiatives? Whether or not current management sees the need to invest in learning to instill the competencies and knowledge needed within the next generation of leadership is yet to be seen (Burns, Bingham, & Galagan, 2010; Johnson, 2009). What is readily evident, though, is the fact that a new generation of leaders is emerging and, with leadership development training, these individuals stand a greater chance of positively influencing an organization's long-term goals (George, 2009). Mercer CEO Michele Burns states it best: "There are times when you have to invest in learning, even at the worst of times, because it will make the difference between success and failure" (Burns, Bingham, & Galagan, 2010).

The CLI Client Survey*

The Corporate Learning Institute distributed a survey to a client base of twelve hundred organizations, asking clients about their leadership and team development practices in the recent economic recession. It was our null hypothesis, and assumption, that the economy had affected our client organizations adversely, causing a decrease in available training funds and development opportunities available for employees and the organization, compared with pre-2007 conditions. Our assumptions were that, if development had been suspended, it would weaken motivation and/or growth, which in turn would hinder organizational performance and/or profitability. From the results gathered, we offer the following feedback:

1. Our client organizations have felt the pressure from the recession and have taken actions such as recruiting talent internally, cutting outside consulting work, and strategically evaluating the efficiency of both training and selection processes.

---

*The authors thank those CLI clients who responded to the survey and allowed a better understanding of how to help organizations achieve their current training goals.

2. Leadership and team development training is still being instituted within a majority of our client organizations, yet the breadth and level of opportunity have been decreased due to recession and economic effects.

3. Even though changes have had to be made concerning training and development initiatives within our client organizations, strides are being taken to provide employees and leaders with continued opportunities for training and development.

Conclusion and CLI Recommendations

In a recovering economy, it is important to provide training and support services in a budget-friendly manner. Not only is training a motivational and engagement tool, but it is also necessary for developing the leadership pipeline in an organization. We believe there are steps organizations can take to offer development opportunities despite the down economy and offer three vital recommendations:

1. There are many options for organizations wishing to offer cost-effective training solutions. One is to use web-based training programs or inexpensive seminars such as those offered by SkillPath. We advised one organization to create a "Leadership Academy" with a series of cost-effective training opportunities for attendees to complete.

2. Prioritize your training needs and spend your available budget money where you see the greatest need. Perhaps conducting a SWOT analysis would be a useful way to determine the training needs that you have.

3. Work with training firms and consultants who will adapt their training services to meet your budget needs. It never hurts to ask, and most professionals should be invested in your needs. When clients ask us to negotiate fees or training services, we collaborate to find training alternatives that fit within the framework of their fiscal and time limitations.

If you have some good ideas or thought-provoking suggestions for keeping training alive in a recovering economy, contact Dr. Susan Cain at scain@corplearning.com.

References

Burns, M., Bingham, T., & Galagan, P. (2010). Trial by fire. *T+D, 64*(9), 36.
Coleman, A. (2009). Follow the leader. *Director, 62*(8), 59.
George, B. (2009). The economic crisis will shape new leaders. *BusinessWeek Online, 31*.
Hansen, F. (2008). Bracing for the second half. *Workforce Management, 87*(12), 20.

Johnson, R. (2009). The sky isn't falling. *Supply House Times, 52*(2), 44–46.

Minton-Eversole, T. (2008). Developing leaders: First—or last—to cut during recession? *HR Magazine, 53*, 39.

Paradise, A., & Mosley, J. (2009). Learning in a down economy. *T+D, 63*(4), 44.

Parks, D. (2009). Leading recovery. *Leadership Excellence, 26*(12), 19.

Phillips, L. (2009). Firms get savvy with training in downturn. *People Management, 15*(9), 7.

Taylor, L. (2010). Put leadership training on the front burner. *BusinessWeek.com, 3.*

Kurt Iskrzycki *received a B.S. in psychology from Western Illinois University in 2009 and an M.A. in industrial/organizational psychology from Elmhurst College in 2011. He is currently employed by CareerBuilder as a workforce analytics analyst and resides in the Chicago area.*

Susan Cain, Ed.D., *is co-founder and partner of The Corporate Learning Institute and a founding partner of the Black River Center for Management Enhancement. Susan is an expert in the field of corporate training and development. She is a valued consultant and coach to numerous Fortune 500 companies crossing all industry sectors worldwide. She has a proven record of accomplishment of collaborating with teams from top-tier companies to maximize their return on strategic and human capital investments.*

Tim Buividas, Ed.D., *is a partner at the Corporate Learning Institute. Tim provides services that focus on managing change, leadership and management development, team building, and personal style assessment for organizations that are ready to create positive change throughout their organizations. He is certified in experiential education, Meyers-Briggs, DiSC Personal Profile Systems, and Situational Leadership. Tim received his doctorate in organizational leadership. He received his graduate and undergraduate degrees from Benedictine University. He holds a master of science degree in management and organizational behavior, with a focus in organization development and a bachelor of science degree. Tim is a member of many organizations, including the Organization Development Institute, Organization Development Network, Association of Experiential Education, American Society for Training & Development, SHRM, TEC, Experiential Training and Development Alliance, and the Association of Psychological Type. Tim is on the boards of directors of the Experiential Training and Development Alliance and the Career Advancement Network. His goal is to create provocative learning experiences that change people's lives.*

What Makes Up the Most Beloved Activities?
Framework for Rapid Training Activity Creation
Lauri Luoto

Summary

Increasingly, training customers are demanding services that are tailored to meet their particular needs. This includes customized training games and other activities. The aim of this article is to provide a framework for creating new tailored activities based on the lessons learned from successful existing activities. Having analyzed some 1,500 activities, the author concludes that the most popular techniques applied in training activities can be classified into five categories—sorting, summarizing, metaphors, role taking, and structured sharing. The author describes and provides several examples of each type.

Anyone familiar with training games or other activities knows that there are plenty of effective and fun activities, but they are spread across different books and manuals, each of which is organized in its own unique way. Finding an idea for a new, relevant activity is far from easy.

The aim of this article is to make this process more manageable by presenting the results of an analysis of more than 1,500 activities from various books, manuals, and fellow trainers. The material was gathered from both the United States and Europe, and the activities covered are often "frame games," that is, they are not associated with any specific context or training topic but rather can be used as a frame for any content. The idea was to find common patterns or mechanisms. Presumably, training professionals have found that some activities work well, and so they generate more similar activities. In fact, many activities are mere variations of certain basic ideas—factors that make activities work, provoke thoughts, and give energy to training sessions. Five classes of activities have been identified, many of which are so generic that they could have an unlimited number of variations, especially in fields such as leadership and communication. Many of the mechanisms are not only used in training but have also been applied in board games and problem-solving methods. The categories are as follows: sorting, summarizing, metaphors, role taking, and structured sharing.

This study is purely empirical, so the types of activities that would be of use from a theoretical or practical point of view are not discussed. The categories have been created based on similarities among documented activities. Within a category, the activities share a learning mechanism but differ in appearance, thus allowing sufficient adaptability for different needs.

The classes differ from each other in terms of how information is processed and how participants interact or cooperate during the activity. Additionally, they motivate people in different ways. Christopher and Smith argue that everyone is capable of being motivated by a combination of need for power, people, and problem solving, and games include these three elements (1987, p. 24). The activity categories take into consideration different amounts of power (the possibility to influence, make choices, and compete), people (the possibility of interacting and working together), and problem solving. By knowing the aims for a training session, the classification system presented here helps trainers to choose the right category and to start designing relevant activities.

Open-Ended vs. Closed Activities

In addition to the five categories, there seems to be another important distinction between activities. Some are closed, that is, the trainer provides most of the input for the process and the main duty of the participants is to process this input according to certain rules. Open-ended activities are more creative, because the trainer only sets the rules and the content comes mostly from the participants. Drawing a picture would be an example of an open-ended activity, whereas analyzing a picture is a closed activity. In all of the five categories, there are examples of both closed and open-ended activities. Closed activities are more relevant for learning factual knowledge or disseminating values or behavioral patterns. Open-ended activities are far more difficult for a trainer to steer because one does not know beforehand where they might go. At the same time, they are more relevant for processing participants' own experiences and creating commitment.

The Five Categories

The categories are described in detail in the following material, along with real-life examples of both open-ended and closed activities—classics that can be found from many sources.

Sorting

It would be a relatively easy task to list a dozen important characteristics of, say, leadership. However, listing two or three of the most important would not be that easy. Many activities are based on the energizing effect that occurs when things have to be put in an order. Closed activities often involve either putting things into subgroups, putting them in order, or picking a few items from a larger collection. Examples of such activities could be (1) choose the three most important tasks from a list of tasks; (2) sort the given list of habits that take place in a workplace into two groups based on whether they support or prevent good time management; or (3) decide who, within your group, best meets a given criteria. On the other hand, an open-ended activity could be to: Name the three most important characteristics of a good leader.

Sorting activities can take a variety of forms, including auctioning, bargaining, and card games. In fact, many boxed management games are based, in one way or another, on the idea of sorting.

Summarizing

In school, we were often asked to write summaries in order to learn the major points of a written work. Summarizing is also one of the most relevant mechanisms in training activities, although not always in written form. In some cases, the end-product is what we are seeking in a summarizing activity. For example, this is the case when defining the vision of an organization. Also, at times the process is valuable on its own and the result is not of so much interest.

In a summarizing activity, the trainer creates an assignment for the participants with very limited time or space. An open summarizing activity could, for example, have some of the following forms: (1) crystallize your team's development idea into a slogan that could be printed on a t-shirt ad or bumper sticker or (2) design a job advertisement describing the qualifications and skills a manager in your organization should hold. A closed assignment could be as follows: plan and perform a short mime expressing a given topic (such as one of the values of your organization) and let the other participants guess which it is. In the latter case, it is not the writing space or the number of words that is limited but rather the time and ways of expression allowed. In either case, a limitation of sorts is a key characteristic for a summarizing activity and establishes the dynamics and goal for the activity.

Metaphors

Even in Biblical times, metaphors were seen as an efficient tool for learning. Today, many delicate and ambiguous topics are easier to discuss through metaphors than directly.

In metaphor activities, the participants create connections between real-life situations or feelings and different objects, gestures, or pictures. When doing a closed activity, the trainer provides material, or the target, for metaphors, as seen in following: (1) participants are provided with stuffed animals and are asked to choose the one that reacts to threat in a way similar to their own reaction to threat or (2) participants choose a picture and explain to the group in which respect it represents their ways of acting as leaders. Open assignments may involve creating metaphorical objects, as in the following example: build a mobile representing the balancing of the units or key processes of your organization.

Role Taking

Taking another viewpoint on a topic is often very thought-provoking. Many activities provide the participants with an opportunity for taking on the role of another person or a representative of another profession or adopting thoughts or goals other than their own. Debate, in which people have to defend views other than what they might believe, was used as an efficient training method by Socrates and his successors. Another closed activity is a role discussion conducted as part of a management training program, where a real-life situation between a subordinate and a manager is reenacted by managers with the help of role description cards.

An open activity could take on the form of a group exercise in which participants are working as a team on a given project, but everyone has a (secret or shared) role or goal to follow while working. A "role" can mean anything from a profession to a way of thinking and everything in between. The "Six Thinking Hats" method by Edward de Bono is a good example of a method whereby the "roles" are quite intangible, like "bad points judgment" or "creativity."

Structured Sharing

Quite often, someone states that a coffee break was one of the most valuable parts of a training session because it provided an opportunity to share thoughts and experiences with other participants. Sharing is a vital element in learning, and many activities are made to intensify and give structure to sharing.

Open activities are often quite simple because, basically, all the participants need is a topic and forum for sharing. The activity can be as simple as having half of the participants appointed as consultants and another half as customers. Then the consultants solve professional problems set by the customers. Sometimes an open activity can lead to results quite far from the initial topic of the session. Thus, when there is a need for efficiency, a closed activity might be more useful: In "Participant Bingo," the participants wander a room seeking others who hold a skill or experience, using a form of a bingo card.

How to Use the Framework

When there is a need for rapid training activity creation, the first thing to do is to define the learning objective. Once the objective is clear, choose, with the help of Table 1, either an open-ended or a closed approach and then the most suitable of the five categories. In some cases, the activity can also be a combination of two categories.

When designing the activity, the following questions should be addressed:

- *Is the activity based on symmetric or asymmetric information between partici-pants?* Most of the board and card games apply asymmetric information. Every participant only sees his or her own cards or—as is the case in detective games like Clue—has some snippets of information needed to solve the game. The same activity is very different if it is based on symmetric or asymmetric information. Think, for example, of solving a puzzle in a

Table 1. Selecting an Appropriate Activity Category

Method	Typical Uses	
	Open-Ended	Closed
Sorting	Generate ideas for further discussion. Generate target-oriented discussion on given topic.	Evaluate training material against participants' own experiences. Assessment learning. Take a stance on given topics.
Summarizing	Converge discussion or ideas toward a shared end.	Clarify core content or practical applications of the topic.
Metaphors	Promote and ease group discussion on a difficult topic.	Help different views and feelings on the topic to emerge.
Role Taking	Help understanding of different viewpoints or roles.	Apply behavioral models in practice.
Structured Sharing	Reflect on the training topic with fellow participants.	Get to know something about everyone for further discussion in a short period of time.

group when all the pieces are on the board versus when the pieces are in the hands of the participants and everyone only sees his or her own pieces.

- *Are the participants divided into large or small groups?* Small groups promote intensive cooperation and discussion, while large groups allow for more material for sharing experiences.

- *Is the time allowed limited or unlimited?* Time pressure makes the activity flow more smoothly and puts group dynamics and leadership to the test. If your learning goal involves in-depth discussions and creative solutions, the time limit should not, however, be too tight.

- *Is the activity based on competition or cooperation?* Competition gives energy to power-motivated people, while cooperation motivates people persons. Often, some kind of combination is the best option to keep everyone active.

Conclusion

The five categories are, of course, not exhaustive. Not all activities can be put in one of these categories, and many efficient and popular activities are based on different mechanisms than those described in this article. Nevertheless, the five categories seem to represent the most popular and adaptable frames for successful activity creation. This framework has proven to be very useful when there is a need for rapid training activity creation for a tailored need. Moreover, the framework illustrates how training activities energize people by satisfying human needs for power, people, and problem solving.

Reference

Christoper, E., & Smith, L. (1987). *Leadership training through gaming.* London: Kogan Page.

Lauri Luoto *is an inspiring trainer and innovator of new training concepts. Currently, he is working as a management development consultant at Psycon Corp, one of Finland's leading companies for personal assessments, strategic resourcing, and leadership development. Mr. Luoto holds a master of education degree and is a certified vocational teacher. He has conducted leadership programs and organization-wide development programs for a number of client organizations, including corporations, government, and non-profit organizations.*

Planning, Not Playing
Training Through Simulation Design
Noam Ebner and Daniel Druckman

Summary

New research into use of simulations for educational purposes shows that, as beneficial as this method is for participants, people designing these simulations learn more than the role players themselves do.

This article introduces trainers to the benefits of simulation design as well as providing a guide to how these advantages might be harnessed for training purposes. Sample instructions are provided for conducting simulation-design exercises as part of a workshop, training, or course.

Is there any training activity more commonly employed than role plays and simulations? Indeed, these methods enjoy wide popularity among educators in the social sciences in academia—and they are particularly popular among trainers conducting workshops on management skills, negotiation, communication, and other topics relating to interpersonal or interaction skills. The popularity of this training method might be best demonstrated, in the context of this publication, by referring readers to previous editions of the Pfeiffer *Annuals*, where the ubiquity of such activities stands out among the range of training tools offered.

Educational simulations (see Inbar and Stoll's [1972] distinctions among modes of simulation) are intended primarily to enhance learning benefits for the role players participating in them. Training objectives are thought to be accomplished by providing realistic, but controlled, environments in which participants are guided only by implicit rules.

In the literature on using educational simulations, two themes stand out:

1. Simulation is a highly effective teaching method providing multiple benefits in terms of skills transfer, concept learning, and motivation.

2. Simulation design, or creating the learning environment in which partici-
    pants will enjoy these benefits, is a task best left to the experts (the teacher
    or trainer managing the class) with regard both to the content of the sim-
    ulation and the learning process.

We will explore the relationship between these two themes in greater detail below.

Benefits Associated with Simulation

Cathy Stein Greenblat (1981), a leading writer on the subject of simulations,
captured and categorized the many claims made about simulation by its propo-
nents and enthusiasts. She broke the inventory of claims down into six categories.
Simulations and games:

1. Enhance participant motivation and interest (in the activity itself and in
    the topic being learned);

2. Promote cognitive learning (of factual information, procedural sequences,
    general principles, real-life structures, best practices, etc.), decision-making
    skills and systematic analysis;

3. Make changes in the character of future participant work in the course/
    training (more meaningful participation, more sophisticated and relevant
    inquiry and greater participation);

4. Trigger affective learning toward the subject matter (changed perspectives
    and orientations, increased empathy with others);

5. Enhance affective elements of learning (increased self-awareness and self-
    confidence); and

6. Promote changes in classroom structure and relations (better participant-
    trainer relations, greater freedom to express and explore ideas, higher degree
    of participant autonomy, greater degree of participant peer acceptance).

Does Simulation Deliver the Goods?

Many trainers using simulations vouch for the benefits noted by Greenblat.
However, as Greenblat herself comments, most assertions made regarding the
value of role play tend to be anecdotal rather than grounded in empirical research.
Indeed, as we have noted in an earlier article, some of these assertions have never

been properly researched—and some of those assertions that have been examined have been found to be overreaching, if not actually mistaken (Druckman & Ebner, 2008). A meta-review of the research comparing simulation to other teaching methods demonstrates that the technique's only proven advantages lie in the realm of the first claim, namely, that simulations enhance participant interest and motivation (an early comparative study was reported by Cherryholmes, 1966). All other claims, including claims regarding advantages in the realms of content learning and skills transfer to real-life situations, might seem reasonable if not intuitively compelling, but they have not been borne out by the research (Druckman & Ebner, 2008).

Indeed, fields in which simulations have long been a central training tool, such as peace and conflict studies and negotiation (Druckman & Ebner, in press) have recently been reassessing the centrality awarded to this method along their pedagogical spectrums (see Ebner & Kovach, 2010) due to an apparent lack of clear educational benefits as well as other issues concerning cultural suitability and classroom challenges (see Alexander & LeBaron, 2009).

Training Participants as Simulation Designers

In this article, we suggest a new way to use simulation that enables trainers to achieve more of the benefits associated with simulation, namely, by tweaking the second trend in the literature noted earlier: Instead of the top-down, trainer-designed approach to role play, we suggest engaging training participants in designing role plays themselves.

In a series of experiments we conducted with students in negotiation courses, we compared students who engaged in simulations as role players with students who had designed and prepared the simulation exercises for other students. We discovered that the design process enjoys many advantages over role playing: Students designing simulations learned more about the negotiation concepts they applied, retained that understanding better over time, and understood relationships between discrete concepts to a higher degree than students who participated as role players in simulations. In addition, simulation design was shown to be a highly motivating exercise, showing more motivation for the designers than for the role players. In other words, not only was designing found to be more effective than role playing in terms of content learning, but it trounced role play at its one proven forte—motivating students and engaging their interest and investment (see Druckman & Ebner, 2008, 2010).

As noted, our own experimentation was conducted in the context of negotiation teaching—a field of learning incorporating both theoretical "ground laying" and practical skills training. We would expect this approach to be equally effective in other fields that bridge these two elements, in particular in the fields of management and organizational training. Indeed, since we began our research, teachers and trainers from other fields who have discussed it with us have used the method in their work in a variety of contexts and frameworks, including the fields of social work, management, urban planning, and communication skills. As a result, we feel confident in making suggestions for incorporating simulation-design exercises in a wide variety of training settings, encouraging trainers in different areas of practice to use and improve on our own experiences with the method as well as to perform experiments similar to those that we have conducted.

Simulation Design as a Training Method

Designing exercises could find their way into the training room in many ways. In the following sections, we provide trainers what they need to start: suggestions for different kinds of design exercises, sample instructions to give participants, and a list of considerations to keep in mind while employing the method. Many of our examples describe negotiation skills as the material being taught, based on our own experience, but this is in no way meant to limit the range of topics that might benefit from this method.

Sequencing Design with Other Learning Activities

We should stress that we have used this method as an activity that follows more direct teaching, such as lectures and/or participant reading; it is an *application* exercise, not an *introductory* exercise. In other words, in contrast to simulations in which some trainers prefer what might be called an experience/learn approach—engaging participants in the simulation and using the debriefing to introduce new concepts by naming elements and interactions that emerged during the simulations—simulation design requires what might be dubbed a teach/apply approach in which participants learn concepts and then apply them in their designs. We are not suggesting assigning participants the task of writing simulations in which they weave in elements that have not been fully described and explained in class as a method for introducing them to these new elements.

We have also had experience in conducting design exercises at a distance. Trainers might consider saving in-class time by assigning participants a design exercise to be conducted and submitted electronically between training sessions. Such an exercise could also enhance relational development among members of the group, allowing them to function more smoothly in class (Bhappu, Ebner, Kaufman, & Welch, 2009).

Finally, if role playing is a method employed in the training, we recommend assigning design exercises after participants have participated in at least one role play so that they have a sense for how such texts are scripted and structured.

Scope of Training

This method has been used to teach at varying levels of complexity, including:

- Teaching individual concepts;

- Teaching sets of concepts;

- Teaching/comparing entire models; and

- Integrating the material of entire workshops and courses.

We will detail each of these, discussing the benefits of each and making suggestions for conducting the exercise.

Teaching Individual Concepts

Using design to teach one element at a time is simple and can be done in a relatively short time frame. One benefit of using this method early in training is that it prepares participants to design more complex simulations later. Our experience with this dual purpose (concept learning and design practice) exercise has led to suggestions for procedures that enhance its implementation.

After explaining the selected negotiation concept, have participants imagine how the concept comes to life in an actual situation. Instruct them to write a brief story about a negotiator who is considering that element. For example, if you have taught participants to choose between conducting the current negotiation or abandoning it in favor of another prospective deal, you might ask them to write a brief story about a person negotiating for a used car in which this deliberation comes into play. Next, you might ask them to write the scenario a second time, this time placing the role player in the story (in other words, instead of "Mr. Jones is a plumber who needs to buy a new van," write "You are John Jones, plumber extraordinaire. You are expanding your business, and you have decided it is time for a new van"). It would be interesting to observe changes in the type of information given. Encourage a few participants to read their stories out loud, so as to make sure that the concept of alternative negotiations (in this case, the plumber's ability to negotiate with another car dealer) is embedded in them and perhaps to make design-focused comments along the way. Finally, suggest that they write the opposite's role (in this case, a used car salesperson with a van on his or her lot) incorporating the concept of alternatives, such as other clients interested in purchasing the van. Ask a few other participants to read their pieces and, once again, give alternatives and design-related feedback.

Another activity for designing single elements involves participants in the task of altering *existing* scenarios. For example, after teaching the concept of alternatives, ask participants to retrieve their copy of a role play conducted in a previous training and add two sentences, referring to alternatives that they think would have changed the negotiation dynamics substantially. (In order to do this, of course, you need to remember to ask participants to save their role information and to bring it to subsequent sessions or prepare extra copies yourself). Next, you can request that participants work with the person who was their opposite during that negotiation, adding two sentences to each role related to alternatives that they think would have led the process toward a resolution or two sentences that would have, in their opinion, led the process down the path of impasse.

The first, step-by-step, party-by-party design exercise can be completed in half an hour, whereas the scenario-alteration exercises can each be completed in less than ten minutes. This would seem to be a good investment of time if more extensive design is planned as an activity later in the training sessions.

Teaching Sets of Concepts

Most areas of training really are less about discrete elements than about encouraging participants to first understand and then manage the tensions that exist between various elements and the interplay of influences among them through time. Teaching participants about *relationships between individual elements* and how to take them into consideration is an important aim of any training. In negotiation training, for example, participants need to understand the notion of alternative deals, but they also need to understand how *alternatives* influence the flow of *power* in a negotiation, how power affects *communication*, how communication patterns affect *trust*, and so on.

Simulation design is a particularly powerful method for teaching about relationships between concepts. The method achieves better results in this regard than just participating in a lecture on the topic and better results than participating as role players in simulations (Druckman & Ebner, 2008). It is even more effective when participants are primed to take these relationships into account throughout the design process and to create situations in which each element affects and is affected by other elements.

Exhibit 1 provides sample instructions that we have used in an exercise aimed at applying knowledge about three important negotiation concepts: alternatives, time pressure, and power. The instructions are applicable, with very few changes, for concepts at the heart of virtually any field of study.

Exhibit 1. Instructions for Simulation Design

Designing Scenarios Exercise

During this stage of the session, we are asking you to prepare a scenario that can be used as a role-playing simulation. The aim is to facilitate learning the three negotiation concepts we discussed. The scenario should highlight relationships among the ideas of *alternatives, time pressure,* and *power* in a bilateral (two-party) negotiation. Assume that you are writing a simulation that might later be used in the group with other participants being asked to perform as negotiators enacting your script. Working on your own, use the guidelines below, which can be regarded as a rough ordering of tasks:

1. Choose a negotiation situation that you think might be suitable for the exercise. Any type/topic of negotiation is suitable, provided that it allows for a bilateral negotiation, in which three or four issues are on the table.
2. Define the role of each party (such as employer or employee, tenant and landlord, parent and child, union or management representative, defendant and prosecutor, spokesperson for each of two opposing political parties or ethnic groups, student and teacher, representatives of two companies contemplating a merger, and so on).
3. Define the issues indicating the initial positions on each issue for each party. You may want to arrange some of the issues on a scale with starting positions and various possible compromise positions in between. Other issues may be better left open-ended.
4. Draft a summary of relevant background on the history of the problem leading up to these talks.
5. Briefly describe the current situation and the consequences of reaching agreements or deadlocking on the issues.
6. Incorporate each of the three concepts into the simulation. For example, alternatives refer to terms available outside the negotiation; time pressure may refer to costs (including transaction costs) incurred while negotiating or to a deadline that can either be imposed or negotiated by the role players; and power can refer to resources brought to the table by the two parties. The scenario you

create might be one in which parties are symmetrical (equal) in power or asymmetrical (unequal) in varying degrees. *Please give this task special attention.*

7. While considering how to incorporate the three concepts into your scenario, *consider the relationships among them.* This is particularly important. For example, a negotiator's power or lack thereof might link to the attractiveness of his or her alternatives. Facing time pressure, a negotiator might not be able to consider or create alternatives. A negotiator with all the time in the world might be at an advantage with an opposite who is pressed for time. *Consider how you might craft your scenario such that these relationships could emerge and influence the way the simulation develops during role play. Please make this a priority in your design.* A good simulation, for the purposes of this simulation-writing exercise, will be one that helps role players to understand the interplay among the three ideas. Their actions should be affected by this interplay.

8. The total amount of time for the negotiation, when this scenario will be played out by other participants, is thirty-five minutes, preceded by a twenty-minute reading and planning session during which negotiators become familiar with the context and issues that you have devised and develop negotiating strategies.

9. You can prepare joint, shared information for the two parties and/or different sheets with confidential facts for the two parties.

10. Incorporate any other elements that you would like to include (but not highlight) as part of the setting. Although you are being asked to focus on three concepts, you may want to mention such elements as aspects of the groups being represented by the negotiators, third-party involvement, negotiating experience, and longer-term relationships between the negotiators or their groups.

11. Try to keep your scenario simple so that your fellow participants who will role play your scenarios do not have to struggle to understand the instructions.

Remember that the main purposes of this exercise are to learn the relationships among three concepts and to ensure that role players of your scenario also learn the way that these ideas are related. We will NOT use your scenarios to evaluate your negotiating or literary skills.

Have fun!

Teaching/Comparing Entire Models

The simulation design method can be applied on a larger scale. For example, we have used it, with instructions similar to those in Exhibit 1, to allow participants to apply a full "elements" model of negotiation, such as the ten element model developed by Ebner and Efron (2013), as well as the comparable, well-known Harvard model delineating seven elements (see Patton, 2005). Such an exercise is preceded by considerable learning of the model and usually involves participants in the development of more extensive role information. Having such a wide range of elements available enables trainers to highlight three or four of them, asking participants to stress the relationships among these particular concepts in their designs.

A colleague who teaches a graduate course on the theory of social work practice, after reading the Druckman and Ebner (2008) article, decided to take this type of exercise in a different direction, applying it on an even larger scale.*

She uses it as a vehicle for comparison *between* theoretical models. In the second semester of her year-long class, students are asked to choose two out of the five central theories of social work practice studied in the previous semester. They are then tasked with designing a simulation in which elements related to both models are embedded such that they are likely to be called into play in a therapeutic situation. The simulation story line takes into account at least three roles: two clients and a social worker. The instructions given students for writing the simulation are generally similar to those included in Exhibit 2 (later in this article), with adaptations orienting it toward the social work aspects of the tasks and to the in-course use of the simulations. (Exhibit 2 is an example of a final course paper, not an in-course activity; however, the instructions regarding the step-by-step process of simulation design are the same.)

Beyond the challenging task of designing such a role play, the final simulations that students construct are utilized as the centerpieces of the following exercises. After the student-authors introduce the simulation to the class—briefing them on background and the chosen theories—a forty-five-minute simulation is conducted, in which the student tasked with the social worker role must apply one of the chosen theoretical models in his or her intervention techniques. After a break, the simulation is started from the beginning, but this time the student tasked with the social worker role needs to apply the *other* theoretical model in his or her intervention. This is followed by a class debriefing of the two simulations, focusing both on the relative strengths and weaknesses of the two theoretical models with regard to the case and on the social worker's skill in applying the models in a practice scenario. Given that designing and conducting the simulations are a major part of the course, students continue to analyze them as part of their term papers.

Integrating the Material of an Entire Course/Workshop

Another way of using simulation design for learning, which benefits greatly from the power of design to clarify relationships between discrete elements, is assigning

---

*The authors thank Dr. Atalia Mosek of Tel Hai College, Israel, for sharing this application of teaching by simulation-design with us.

simulation design as a mid-term assignment or as a course's final project. At this point in time, for courses in which simulations are used, participants are at the peak of their content knowledge; they will also be experienced with conducting simulations. This provides them with a sense for how simulations are constructed and how they play out. If you have assigned small design exercises along the way, they have this to build on as well. Given a generous time window, as final assignments are often granted, we have found that participants approach this assignment enthusiastically and creatively, as evidenced by the quantity of material produced, the creative production of support material, the intricacy of the story lines, and by their direct feedback. Exhibit 2 contains sample instructions used for a final project in a course on multi-party/multi-issue negotiation and mediation. These instructions could be used, with a few changes, for any kind of course or training workshop.

Exhibit 2. Instructions for Final Paper

Working *alone or in pairs*, you are expected to write a conflict and negotiation role-play simulation game of a general nature similar to those we have played in the group, according to the parameters set out below.

Writing a comprehensive role play requires theoretical knowledge about the process it focuses on, a practical understanding of how it works, and a feel for how the type of situation described might play out in real life. Simulation game designers and researchers have commented that the main beneficiaries from a simulation game are often the designers rather than the participants; this has been my experience as well. For more on this, read Druckman and Ebner (2008) at http://sag.sagepub.com/cgi/rapidpdf/1046878107311377v1.pdf or Druckman and Ebner (2010) at http://papers.ssrn.com/sol3/papers.cfm?abstract_id=1916791 (reading these article is certainly *not* necessary for performing the assignment; however, the authors explain and demonstrate the pedagogical value of the exercise).

You may choose any situation you like to build your scenario on. It can be real or wholly fictional. It might echo a real-life experience of your own or of someone you know or reflect a scenario from a book or a movie. It might come out of the pages of yesterday's newspaper or be a total figment of your imagination. It might be the type of situation you could encounter anywhere in the world or a uniquely local one. It might be an interpersonal situation or international in scope; it could involve a cross-cultural clash or something occurring between inhabitants of a fictional country (or planet). This might be an opportunity to design a conflict that suits your own preferred negotiation and conflict style process; storylines can be crafted to support cooperation or to induce competition, third-party roles might be weighted toward being transformative, adjudicative, problem solving, etc.

Mandatory Simulation Game Parameters

1. *At least* three distinct parties should be involved.
2. *At least* one of the parties should be a team, comprised of two or more roles.
3. There should be enough content to provide for *at least* an estimated one hour of role playing.
4. Define whether the situation will be negotiated directly between the parties or whether a third party intervener is included (in addition to the negotiating parties), and work this into the scenario.

Roles, Information, and Materials

I expect to see that all the different roles are detailed in such a manner that each potential role player will know what his or her background is and what is expected from him or her and such that an outside observer (me) will be able to review the entire package and obtain a situation overview. *How you choose to do this is entirely up to you.* You may choose to stick to a standard and familiar method, such as providing all players with some common information regarding the situation and in addition providing each player with private information regarding his or her own role (including separate information for individual members of the same team, as well as instructions for the third party, if one is involved). On the other hand, you may choose any alternative method and use any media you wish in order to accomplish this (tapes that self-destruct in five seconds, newspaper clippings etc.); creativity is certainly welcome. There is no minimum or maximum regarding the length of the roles or the amount of material accompanying them.

In addition, prepare a one- to two-page "Debriefing Guide" to accompany your simulation game. The guide should define the points you think a potential class debriefing of the simulation game might stress and describe what parts of the story line form the background to these points (e.g., "The importance of team preparation prior to negotiation: A and B (teammates) have different agendas, but if they don't bother to put this on the table between them, they might find themselves arguing in front of the other parties"). These points will actually be (I'm giving it away here . . .) elements you viewed as central while writing the scenario. The guide's inclusion is an important window for me into your analytical and creative process and will help me to understand what you set out to design.

Expectations

In general, the simulation game should build up a negotiation situation comprised of the elements we are familiar with. Build the parties' roles in a way that the obvious clashes or tensions between them are defined. Try to picture any stages of conflict escalation or of relationship deterioration the parties have gone through, and leave room for future development. Keep the ten elements of negotiation in mind. They can serve as your guiding points and are the main components of the situation. On the other hand, you do not have to describe the scenario down to the smallest detail. Keep in mind that role players need room to flesh out their roles with their own preferences and will fill in anything missing. There is no need to design a magic, hidden solution into the role play, as these are seldom to be found in reality.

Go beyond the current conflict. If the characters have a prior relationship, describe it so that the role players know what background they are coming from. Help them understand the "emotional package" they walk around with concerning the other parties.

Besides basic negotiation and conflict elements, the scenario should incorporate elements of complexity common to multi-party conflicts. Remember the simulations performed in class, the video clips we saw, and review your reading material, primarily Thompson and Lewicki. Design the conflict to incorporate coalition forming, intra-team dissonance, and other common traits of multi-party negotiation. If you wish, you may also choose to add in other elements of complexity: multiple issues, time pressure, communication limits, etc.

Assignment Goals and Grading

This is *not* a test of your writing capabilities or of your ability to produce outstanding literary accomplishments. Errors in spelling or grammar will *not* affect your grade, and your work will not be read through the eyes of a literary critic.

While an added value of this paper is to experience a situation through a trainer's eyes, it is *not* a test of how good a trainer or training-material designer you can be.

You will be graded on your ability to construct a conflict giving rise to a negotiation in a manner that brings to light the common elements of conflict and the common dynamics of negotiation that you have studied in the course; stresses the complexities we've discussed in the group; and portrays all of this in a "real-life-like" situation. The "real-life" aspect has two components: the realness of the conflict vis-à-vis the parties taking part in it (whether actual or imaginary characters) and the sense of reality you are able to convey to potential participants in the role play. The first measures your understanding of how complex conflict plays out in the real world, while the second focuses on understanding learning processes. While the grading will concentrate on the first, you would do well to keep the second in mind as you create the scenario.

Simplified Instructions

Simplified, the instructions are
1. Remember what we've learned.
2. Write a story, something realistic.
3. Keep to the parameters. Do it well.
4. Add a Debriefing Guide.

Good luck.

Simulation Design: In Practice

Having provided several frameworks for using simulation design as a learning exercise, we will now offer several suggestions for best practices in conducting these exercises.

Should this exercise be assigned individually or in pairs?

We have conducted these exercises both ways, and they work well either way. Working in pairs might increase task motivation and creativity; however, it takes longer and does not suit every participant's learning preference. This might best be left up to participants to decide.

Should this exercise be conducted in class, or outside of class hours?

The smaller-scoped versions, as we have mentioned, are quite suitable for in-class work. For longer versions, one needs to keep in mind that writing is a creative task, which often requires a suitable amount of time and calls for a certain frame of mind. As a result, the wider the scope of the assignment, the more it will be suitable to let participants design simulations on their own time as a take-home assignment. We have used this assignment in a distance-learning course in which students complete their work at their own pace.

To give a sense of time scale, designing simulations on the negotiating concepts discussed above, such as in the assignment in Exhibit 1, usually takes participants between forty-five minutes and an hour, not including the debriefing, and participants have often expressed a desire for more time. Course/workshop-ending projects are usually the result of several hours of design-work.

What should participants write about?

One question that often comes up when we employ this method for negotiation training is whether participants should base their scenarios on situations they have experienced or invent fictional scenarios based primarily on their knowledge of nego-tiation. In other areas of training, trainers are likely to face similar deliberations.

In our research, we hypothesized that the former approach (real-life scenar-ios) enhances concrete (situation-specific) learning, whereas the latter (fictional story lines) is beneficial for concept learning. It was also suggested that the lat-ter approach is more suitable for achieving overall learning goals. However, our research thus far has shown no differences in learning outcomes between the two types of scenarios (Druckman & Ebner, 2010); as a result it would probably be best to tell participants to choose whichever type of scenario they prefer and to expect that this freedom will affect motivation positively.

What should be done with the simulation designs?

Trainers can conduct a design exercise and provide feedback (see below). Based on class time available and participant motivation, trainers might also choose to have trainees exchange scenarios and observe the way that others role play their designs. Since time is often an issue, some participants are more eager than others to see their simulations played by classmates and class time can be conserved by role playing only those simulations.

How should participants receive feedback on a design?

Feedback can be provided individually in writing or by means of a group debrief-ing. We have also discovered that designers gain impressive amounts of insight by observing their simulation being played out by others, insight that can be captured in a class discussion or in a reflective paper.

Should participants submit any material beyond the simulation?

While our original experiments required students to prepare and submit the simu-lation scenarios only, we often ask participants in training workshops to imagine that they are writing a simulation to be used by trainers and to prepare a Trainer's Guide instructing the trainer how to set up, conduct, and debrief the simulation as designed. This adds a level of direct reflection to the exercise, which otherwise con-sists of participants operating at a more covert level, embedding and employing—but not naming—individual and related concepts in their writing.

What types of groups should this exercise be conducted with?

It is important to stress that, in our experience, not all participants enjoy the design exercise. Some feel that they were being pressured to produce original material in a short period of time. It will be helpful to explore a variety of procedures for conducting design writing, including allotting more time and perhaps other types of support. More compelling, perhaps, is that the exercise may be problematic in some cultures or contexts. Like any classroom innovation, the receptiveness of students or trainees is important to take into account. More generally, trainer mindfulness and specific preparation for each group are advised.

Should the exercise be conducted face-to-face or electronically?

We have conducted the exercises in both mediums. Advantages of the face-to-face format include immediate feedback, synchronous communication, and group process. The electronic format has the advantages of time for reflection before response, asynchronous communication (respond when convenient), and more precise, written communication. Both formats have been implemented without problems; students in both mediums have indicated that they enjoyed the challenges of design and role play. However, results obtained from recent preliminary experiments have shown smaller differences between designers and role players in learning and motivational benefits in the online form. Although an explanation for the different results is unclear and further experiments are needed, the early findings are suggestive: The designer advantages may be limited to a face-to-face synchronous interaction format. If substantiated in further studies, these findings have implications for the way that these exercises are conducted in training workshops.

Conclusion

Simulation design, which has received attention in the research and practice literatures, is relatively novel as a training tool. In the search for new methods to expand the trainer's toolbox, this approach, easily implemented due to the ubiquity of role play in training, and beneficial for learning and motivation, should be explored. While we have been able to demonstrate many of the benefits, and to isolate some best practices for maximizing learning and motivational gains, much remains unexplored. We invite trainers using this method to view their own work with groups as a laboratory, and conduct experiments to further refine the use of the method. We would welcome hearing about follow-up work, or even anecdotes of experiences with classroom use of simulation design.

References

Alexander, N., & LeBaron, M. (2009). Death of the role play. In C. Honeyman, J. Coben, & G. DePalo (Eds.), *Rethinking negotiation teaching: Innovations for context and culture.* St. Paul, MN: DRI Press.

Bhappu, A., Ebner, N., Kaufman, S., & Welsh, N. (2009). The strategic use of online communication technology to facilitate relational development in executive training courses on negotiation. In C. Honeyman, J. Coben, & G. DiPalo (Eds.), *Rethinking negotiation teaching: Innovations for context and culture.* St Paul, MN: DRI Press.

Cherryholmes, C. (1966). Some current research on effectiveness of educational simulations: Implications for alternative strategies. *American Behavioral Scientist, 10,* 4–7.

Druckman, D., & Ebner, N. (2008). Onstage, or behind the scenes? Relative learning benefits of simulation role-play and design. *Simulation & Gaming, 39*(4), 465–497.

Druckman, D., & Ebner, N. (2010). Enhancing concept learning: The simulation design experience. In C. Honeyman, J. Coben, & G. DiPalo (Eds.), *Venturing beyond the classroom: Vol. 2 in the rethinking negotiation teaching series.* St Paul, MN: DRI Press.

Druckman, D., & Ebner, N. (in press). Simulation: Learning through role playing and design. In D.J. Christie (Ed.), *Encyclopedia of peace psychology.* Hoboken, NJ: Wiley-Blackwell.

Ebner, N., & Efron, Y. (2010). Negotiation consulting: A 10-element toolbox for managers. In E. Biech (Ed.), *The 2013 Pfeiffer annual: Consulting.* San Francisco: Pfeiffer.

Ebner, N., & Kovach, K. (2010). Simulation 2.0: The resurrection. In C. Honeyman, J. Coben, & G. DiPalo (Eds.), *Venturing beyond the classroom: Vol. 2 in the rethinking negotiation teaching series.* St Paul, MN: DRI Press.

Greenblat, C.S. (1981). Teaching with simulation games: A review of claims and evidence. In C.S Greenblat & R.D. Duke (Eds.), *Principles and practices of gaming-simulation.* Thousand Oaks, CA: Sage.

Inbar, M., & Stoll, C.S. (1972). Designing a simulation. In M. Inbar & C.S. Stoll (Eds.), *Simulation and gaming in social science.* New York: The Free Press.

Patton, B. (2005). Negotiation. In M.L. Moffitt & R.C. Bordone (Eds.), *The handbook of dispute resolution.* San Francisco: Jossey-Bass.

Noam Ebner *is an assistant professor at the Werner Institute at Creighton University's School of Law, where he chairs the online master's program in negotiation and dispute resolution. He has consulted on many negotiation processes across a wide number of issues and industries and specializes in negotiation process conducted online. He has conducted negotiation training in more than one dozen countries, including the United States, Israel, Turkey, Costa Rica, Sweden, and Cyprus.*

Daniel Druckman *is a professor of public and international affairs at George Mason University and distinguished scholar at the University of Southern Queensland's Public Memory Research Centre. He has been scholar-in-residence at the Australian Centre for Peace and Conflict Studies at the University of Queensland in Brisbane, Australia. A prolific researcher, Daniel was the recipient of the 2003 Lifetime Achievement Award from the International Association for Conflict Management and has recently served as the association's president. His recent books include* Doing Research: Methods of Inquiry for Conflict Analysis *(Sage, 2005; best book award, IACM 2006),* Conflict *(2nd ed.), with Sandra Cheldelin and Larissa Fast (Continuum, 2008), and* Evaluating Peace Operations, *with Paul F. Diehl (Lynne Reinner, 2010).*

Leadership and Accountability Lecturette

Phil Van Horn

Summary

Leadership is power. Power is not leadership. The single variable that makes this paradox true is *accountability*. Leaders hold themselves accountable to others and to their institutions and therein derive the real power to influence events.

Accountability ultimately distinguishes leadership from other positions of power. Let's be clear at the outset: *leadership is power*. This blunt assertion may surprise and even alarm some readers, as recent trends in discussions, articles, and books on leadership dance all around the premise of leadership as power.

Rather, we read and hear, often, of *leadership characteristics*: imaginative, caring, inspiring, and more. These are certainly important characteristics of being a leader, and there are infinite character qualities that should be discovered and nurtured by aspiring and established leaders. But when you get right down to it, leadership's goal is *power*, the power to influence others and to bring one's will to bear on outcomes.

This assertion may be particularly unsettling to some, given the recent revelations of despotic horrors uncovered in the aftermath of revolts against tyrannies in Libya, Syria, Egypt, and others during the so-called "Arab Spring" of 2011. The photos and other evidence of cruel imprisonment, torture, and mass murder were accompanied with very little outrage and even less surprise from the Western hemisphere, for the environment that spawned these atrocities had, unfortunately, become all too familiar.

Ironically, the oppressive wielding of power demonstrates, precisely, the paradox of leadership: Leadership is power, and power is not leadership. The single factor that renders this paradox true is *accountability*.

Leaders intrinsically understand the incredible power derived from being held accountable: accountable to themselves, accountable to their families, accountable to their advisors and colleagues, and, most importantly, accountable to those they lead. They recognize that the will they bring to bear on events is, in actuality, not their will at all, but the will of their citizens, members, shareholders, or customers.

Tyrants, on the other hand, maintain their positions by intimidation, corruption, and sabotage, all clearly with one goal: self-preservation, which is the antithesis of accountability. As the timeless adage goes: "Power corrupts, and absolute power corrupts absolutely."

Just as tyranny exists on the world stage, so does it exist in management teams and boardrooms. It can manifest itself as easily as a group characteristic as it does individually. If there is one individual in the room who wields power for personal benefit, it can become endemic and disastrous. And it won't necessarily be the department manager or the chief executive.

To clarify this concept, consider the manager or supervisor who withholds necessary information from the rest of the management team. It happens because, unfortunately, in too many organizations, information is currency to be acquired and hoarded. Too many people believe that sharing information will weaken one's standing and that job security depends on releasing as little information as necessary. Those who withhold information don't believe in accountability to the other members of the team. On the contrary, they have predetermined the priorities of the entire team to be secondary, at best, and *knowingly* undermine the effectiveness of the leadership team. This is purely power-wielding for self-preservation.

On the other hand, *leaders* embrace their accountability to other members of the team and enthusiastically seek to achieve the goals that benefit the organization as a whole. Rather than excusing the withholding of information, they foster environments in which information is shared and solutions are sought through collaboration. They inspire in their actions as well as their words. They may not innovate so much as inspire innovation among others. Rather than seek credit, they enjoy and highlight the successes of others.

Leaders fully understand and accept the burden of having to make tough decisions that have no guaranteed outcomes. Most importantly, they accept being held accountable for those decisions. Leaders know that collaboration is not a substitute for leadership. On the contrary, collaboration empowers their decision making. When opposing positions are presented and the leader has to make the final call, the parties know the accountable leader will have weighed all information and will accept the consequences of the decision.

In the final analysis, power derived from accountable leadership is greater than autocratic power. Contrasted with the truthful adage that "absolute power corrupts, absolutely," accountable leaders own the power, not of one, but of *all* to whom they hold themselves accountable. That is *real* power.

Phil Van Horn *is president and CEO of Align® planning, consulting, training, and business services. He has educational and practical expertise in the areas of board development, team building, strategic planning, and leadership. His previous articles include Avoiding Board Traps (published in the 2007 Pfeiffer Annual: Training), Don't Let Your Clients Be Defined by Instrument Results, and Consulting Opportunities in the Nonprofit Sector (both published in the 2010 Pfeiffer Annual: Consulting). He received his B.A. in psychology from Westminster College and M.Ed. from the University of Missouri.*

Developing Values-Based Leaders

Homer H. Johnson

Summary

What is values-based leadership and how does it lead to organization success? This article provides insight into this increasingly popular approach to leadership by defining values-based leadership, explaining the major approaches to this form of leadership, and clarifying the process of developing values-based leaders.

In the past several years there has been considerable interest in an approach to leadership and leadership development that has values at its core. The approach is sometimes referred to as "Values-Based Leadership" (Johnson, 2012; Majer, 2004; O'Toole, 1995), or "Values-Driven Leadership" (Malphurs, 2004), or "Leading with Values" (Hess & Cameron, 2006; King & Murray, 2007;), or "Managing with Values" (Blanchard & O'Connor, 1997). Kraemer's (2011) book, *From Values to Action*, and Steven Covey's (1990) *Principle-Centered Leadership* could also be seen as variations of the values-based approach.

A basic assumption underlying these approaches to leadership is that one's leadership perspectives, decisions, and behavior are guided by a set of values. The term "values" in this context is usually defined as a general principle that is applicable across many situations. For example, integrity is a value that often appears on the list for values-based leaders. A person who exhibits high integrity probably would do so across many situations, ranging from his or her work organization to his or her family.

Certainly, one advantage in leading with values is that a leader does not have to remember a vast list of "do's" and "don'ts" to decide how he or she should behave in the numerous situations encountered every day. Rather, a limited set of general values will be sufficient, or at least provide a starting point, to inform the leader regarding the decision at hand. However, since values are usually so general, they may mean different things to different people. For example, the value of "justice" to Martin Luther King, Jr., most probably had a different meaning and implications than the same value ("justice") did to law enforcement officers in the South. Therefore, naming values is not sufficient in values-based approaches to leadership; rather, the values must also be explained.

Not much agreement has emerged regarding what values should be included in the values-based approach, nor has there been much attempt to provide a definition for the approach. For example, some authors use a fairly narrow definition and see the values approach as synonymous with ethical leadership. According to these authors, the values-based leader is one who behaves according to ethical principles, always choosing the ethical path when faced with a difficult decision. However, other authors have used a broader definition and included both ethical and moral values. Thus, the values-based leader is a person of moral character, one who exhibits traits of integrity, honesty, and fairness. Still other authors use an even broader description and define the values approach as including not only moral and ethical values but other values, such as "results-oriented," "empowerment," and "courage," which may be seen as the "values" of an effective leader.

Another distinction that separates approaches to values-based leadership is whether the values that the leader follows are prescriptive, in the sense that they are given to the leader, or does the leader discover the values? A well-known example of the prescriptive approach is the values that the U.S. Army expects its leaders to demonstrate, such as loyalty, duty, selfless service, and personal courage. Thus, all Army leaders are expected to demonstrate the same values, which are those "prescribed" by the Army. An alternative to the prescriptive approach is to have the leader "discover" his or her values, or the values he or she wants to follow, usually by a series of self-reflective exercises. A given leader may develop a set of values unique to him or her. In the discovery approach, the leader is not told what values he or she should follow; rather, the leader develops his or her own set of personal values.

The purpose of this article is to define values-based leadership; to explain why it is an important approach to leadership; and to explain the different approaches to developing values-based leaders.

Defining Values–Based Leadership

As noted above, there is no standard definition for the term "values-based leader," and, in fact, the term may refer to some very different approaches. In search of a standard definition, one probably can discount those approaches that emphasize ethical principles only. These approaches are probably too narrow to be described as values-based and should rather be labeled as ethical leadership. Moreover, the approaches to values-based leadership that encompass moral and character values would seem to also cover ethical behavior.

The argument for extending values-based leadership beyond just moral values is that leaders have to not only be honest with people and have integrity, but they have the responsibility for moving the organization forward and/or developing the people in the organization (or family). This is what we expect of leaders. Given this context, Johnson (2012) has proposed the following definition of values-based leadership.

Definition of Values-Based Leadership

Values-based leaders are those whose decisions and actions are guided by an integrated set of values that jointly enhance human dignity and organization success.

This definition suggests, first, that values-based leaders have an integrated set of values, that is, values that fit together and reinforce each other in a coherent system. Moreover, the values are geared to organization success, which is that which we expect of leaders. And finally, the values also enhance human dignity, which covers the moral aspects of values-based leadership.

It is also to be noted that the definition answers the question as to whether people who have had a destructive impact on the world, such as Hitler, could be considered values-based leaders. Hitler had very strong values, and additionally was a successful leader for the German nation, so wouldn't he qualify as a values-based leader? While it is true that he held strong values, many of his "values," such as Aryan supremacy and sending Jews to extermination camps, could hardly be considered "enhancing human dignity." As noted in the above definition, values-based leaders *jointly* enhance human dignity and organization success, and one would be hard pressed to include a person such as Hitler in that definition.

The Argument for Values-Based Leadership

One advantage of the values-based approach is that it provides the leader, or anyone for that matter, with a set of principles that is a base for his or her decision making and behavior. Whether the values are prescribed, as they are for the leaders in the U.S. Army, or are discovered through the leader's personal reflection, the values provide a filter for evaluating information or the actions of others; for deciding which course of action is most appropriate; and for acting or behaving.

Beyond that obvious advantage, Johnson (2012) makes six assumptions regarding this approach to leadership:

1. It is those people who have a strong personal values base who have made and will make important (positive) contributions to their families, organizations, and the world.

2. While the literature focuses on heroic leaders, the Martin Luther Kings and the Abraham Lincolns of the world, it is people showing leadership in the tasks of everyday life who will, in the long run, make for a better organization or a better world. While not diminishing the contributions of our heroes, most people are not focused on saving the world, but rather are focused on living their lives and doing their jobs. It is these "quiet leaders" who create better places for us to live and work.

3. Values and leadership come from inside the individual. Thus, if you want to make an impact, it is critical that you understand who you are and what you believe.

4. Values-based leadership includes both process and outcomes. An elementary school teacher should not only treat each student with dignity, but also make sure that students are learning in accordance with standards and potential.

5. Organizations can and do espouse values. Values become the basis for how organizations operate and are the foundation of their culture. The values are expressed in the policies and procedures, in leadership behavior, and a variety of little ways. Strong-values organizations are more successful in the long term than are weak-values organizations.

6. Values-based leaders create values-based organizations, groups, teams, families, and communities. By the standards they set, the decisions they make, the behaviors they exhibit, and the philosophy they espouse, values-based leaders have a significant influence on the behaviors of others and the workings of organizations.

Note that the approach advocated by Johnson involves discovering one's values, and thus the assumptions noted above are made with this approach in mind. However, the arguments are just as valid for one using the prescriptive approach—that values-based leaders will create better organizations and communities and families. Moreover, as noted above, anyone can be a values-based leader. In fact, it is the people working in the trenches, in families, communities, and schools, and in organizations who make this a better world. Joseph Badaracco (2002) called them "quiet leaders," people who quietly, without fanfare, enhance human dignity and organization effectiveness.

Prescriptive Approaches to Developing Values-Based Leaders

In a prescriptive approach to developing values-based leaders, the values that the leaders are expected to follow are given to them. There are a couple of variations of this approach. The first is a more general approach, often described in books on leadership, which outlines the several values that a person leading with values should possess. These values are assumed to apply to all leaders and all organizations. The second variation is more organization-specific and occurs when a business organization, or a military organization, or church has specified a set of values that it expects all leaders or managers of that organization to demonstrate. This approach is values-based in that all leaders in the organization are expected to demonstrate a set of values, in this case the same values. Moreover, these values are typically chosen by the leadership of the organization with the belief that if all leaders in the organization demonstrate these values, the organization will be successful.

With respect to the first variation described above, several approaches to leadership advocate general values that should be followed, and the implication is that a person practicing these values will become a better leader and will increase organization performance. For example, the theory of *servant leadership* suggests that a *servant leader* will demonstrate the values or practices of listening, empathy, healing, awareness, etc. (see Johnson, 2007, for specifics on the values). Here the focus is on a specific theory or form of leadership and there is little reference to organization success. However, there is an implicit assumption, as there is in most leadership theories, that being a servant leader will lead to organization success.

Likewise, Kraemer's (2011) book, *Leading with Values*, articulates four principles of values-based leadership: self-reflection, balance, true self-confidence, and genuine humility. These four principles are general enough that they could be applied to leaders and leadership in many different situations. Again, the assumption is made that the practice of these four principles is the key to successful leadership, which, in turn, will lead to organization success.

A more common variation of prescribed values cited above is when a set of leadership values is prescribed by the organization and all leaders and managers are expected to demonstrate those values. Moreover, there is a clearly acknowledged belief that if the leaders in the organization demonstrate the prescribed values, the organization will be successful. In fact, the values for the leaders to follow were specifically chosen because they were thought to be predictors of organization performance. A well-known example of this approach is the leadership values of the U.S. Army (2006). As listed in Table 1, there are seven values: loyalty, duty, respect, selfless service, honor, integrity, and personal courage. The Army clearly states that all leaders, at all levels, must follow these values.

The 2013 Pfeiffer Annual: Training
Copyright © 2013 by John Wiley & Sons, Inc. Reprinted by permission of Pfeiffer, an Imprint of Wiley. www.pfeiffer.com

Table 1. U.S. Army Leadership Values

Loyalty	Leaders who demonstrate loyalty bear allegiance to the constitution; observe higher head-quarters' priorities; and work within the system without manipulating it for personal gain.
Duty	Leaders who demonstrate devotion to duty fulfill all professional, legal, and moral obligations; comply with policies and directives; and continually pursue excellence.
Respect	Leaders who demonstrate respect create a climate of fairness and equal opportunity; show concern for and make an effort to check on the safety and well-being of others; and refrain from taking advantage of positions of authority.
Selfless Service	Leaders who demonstrate selfless service put the welfare of the nation, the Army, and subordinates before their own; sustain team morale; and give credit for success to others and accept responsibility for failure themselves.
Honor	Leaders who demonstrate honor live up to Army values; refrain from lying, cheating, or stealing; and never tolerate these actions by others.
Integrity	Leaders who demonstrate integrity do what is right legally and morally; possess high personal moral standards; and show consistently good moral judgment and behavior.
Personal Courage	Leaders who demonstrate personal courage show physical and moral bravery; take responsibility for decisions and actions; and accept responsibility for mistakes and shortcomings.

Another example of the prescriptive approach can be found in the leadership values of Allianz, an international financial services organization. The introduction to its leader values states:

> "The Leadership Values were introduced to raise the quality of leadership and accelerate the development of a high performance culture at Allianz, ensuring that leaders have a mutual understanding of our basic aims. They convey to every manager in the Group a clear framework linking business targets and desired leadership behavior." (Allianz, 2011)

The document continues by stating and explaining the five values, which are

- Align strategy and communication
- Promote a high performance culture
- Focus on our customers
- Develop our customers
- Build on mutual trust and feedback

Note that the introduction clearly states that the purpose of the values is to provide a framework to link leadership behaviors to business outcomes. Thus, the assumption here is that if all leaders at Allianz demonstrate these values, the company will be successful as a business.

The strategy for developing values-based leaders using the prescriptive approach is to first develop a set of values that will apply to all leaders and managers in the organization. These values should be connected to, or predictive of, organization success. The logic for having a limited set of values is that people will not be able to remember a large number of values. Moreover, if the set is too long, leaders might pick and choose which of the many values are the most important to observe and possibly ignore the others.

Once an organization has selected its values, communication and explanation are critical. If the values are new, meetings with managers in which the values are explained are essential. Often "values cards" are distributed. These are wallet-sized cards containing a list and a brief explanation the values expected of managers. New managers would be exposed to the values as part of a new manager workshop.

The values can now become a selection device for choosing new managers and leaders. That is, new managers are chosen, and managers are promoted, based on their demonstration of the leader values. Furthermore, the values may be part of the annual (or quarterly) performance review for managers and leaders of the organization.

Discovery Approaches to Values–Based Leadership

A second major approach to developing values-based leaders is to have the leader discover or formulate his or her values through a series of self-refection exercises. This approach is sometimes referred to as an "inside-out" approach in that the approach makes the assumption that leader development starts with having the leader understand his or her purpose in life, key values, and other beliefs. According to this approach, becoming a leader begins with a self-understanding and a self-reflection.

The argument for this approach is that before one can lead others, one must understand oneself. In particular, leaders must understand what they see as the purpose of their lives; what they would like to accomplish in their lifetimes; the values that they hold most dear; their beliefs about leaders and leadership; plus a variety of other issues such as what they do well and where they need to improve. It is only when leaders have a good understanding of who they are and what they believe that they become effective leaders.

Some of the principal authors advocating this approach are Cashman (1998), Lee and King (2001), Ruggero and Haley (2005), and Johnson (2012). The steps of this discovery process vary with the approach; however, all approaches involve a great deal of self-reflection and time. Most approaches suggest that the person write out the answers to a series of questions, and some ask that the person keep a daily or weekly journal. Table 2 outlines the steps of one discovery approach, that of Johnson (2012).

Table 2. Steps and Exercises for Becoming a Value-Based Leader

Step	Considerations
Step 1: Who were (are) the important people in your life?	Who were (are) the four or five people who most significantly impacted your life? Briefly describe each. Why were they important in your life? What did you learn from them that you would like to emulate?
Step 2: What is your purpose in life?	What is your life purpose? What would you like to accomplish in your life? Why would it be important (to you) to accomplish that?
Step 3: What are your life values?	What are your five or six most important life values? These are the values that you would use to guide your life.
	How would you "walk the talk" on each of these values? That is, if you were living these values to the fullest, what would we see you doing?
Step 4: What is leadership?	What is your definition of effective leadership? What are some of the most important responsibilities of a leader? What do effective leaders do that distinguishes them from leaders that are not effective?
Step 5: What are your leadership values?	What do you see as the most important values of leadership? These have to be your values, not something you read.
	If you were practicing these values to their fullest, what would we see you doing? That is, how would a person "walk the talk" on the values you have chosen? How will you "walk the talk" on your values? How will you live your values at home and at work?
Step 6: Communicating your values	How will you communicate your values to your employees, co-workers, and superiors? Or perhaps to friends or members of your family?
	How would you let them know that these are life and leadership values that you think are very important and to which they can hold you accountable?
Step 7: Assuming that you could (and want to) create a values-based work unit, or a values-based organization, how would you go about doing this?	What process would you use? Who will be involved? What outcome would you hope for? How will the values be communicated and explained? How will you make sure the values are actually practiced?

As noted in the table, this approach starts with having the person think about the important people in his or her life and what he or she learned from them. This exercise helps the person think about the past and important influences from his or he past. It also starts people thinking about values that they think are important, values that they probably learned from others.

Next, the person is asked to think about his or her purpose in life. What gives the person's life meaning? What energizes the person? What would the person like to accomplish in life?

The exercises continue with the person listing his or her important values and also describing what types of behaviors would be associated with these values. It is recommended that the person take some time between exercises and reflect on the questions. Further, writing out the answers to the exercises is usually very helpful. Some people keep a notebook so that they can jot down their thoughts on the questions.

Several approaches to this discovery approach have been proposed. Some of them focus more on leadership, and others focus more on understanding one's self. Perhaps most important in all discovery approaches is that the person begin a process of self-refection regarding purpose and values. Moreover, the process might be revisited periodically, perhaps every year, as a refresher course. This assures that one's purpose and one's values remain the focus of one's life.

Which Approach?

The question sometimes arises regarding which approach, prescriptive or discovery, is better for both developing values-based leaders or for actually leading with values. The answer is that both are equally valid and effective; however, they serve different purposes. The goal of the prescriptive approach, as noted in the Allianz example earlier, is to ensure that all managers "have a clear framework for linking business targets with desired leadership behavior." Thus, all managers are expected to demonstrate the chosen values, and the chosen values are expected to lead to business results.

On the other hand, the goal of the discovery approach is to have the person better understand who he or she is and the important values in his or her life. The argument for this approach is that leaders who understand their purpose and their values, and who have strong values systems, will be more effective leaders.

A disadvantage of the prescriptive approach is that a leader may not support the values dictated by the organization, or the organization may just pay lip service to these values. In either case, the values statement may not fulfill its promise of having all leaders in the organization espousing the same values—values related to organization success. A disadvantage of the discovery approach from an organization standpoint is that, while the organization might be filled with values-based leaders, they may not share the same values. In a worst-case scenario, the leaders may be pulling in different directions.

Continuing this discussion, could these two approaches conflict with one another? Certainly that is a possibility. Sometimes a person's personal values will be in conflict with the leader values of the organization to which he or she belongs. Trying to balance conflicting values is very stress-producing. The answer to this conflict is usually to change organizations and to find one in which one's personal and organization values are compatible. If one's values and the organization values are in sync, then one can lead a very meaningful and enjoyable life.

Conclusion

How do you develop values-based leaders? Having an understanding of what one believes, what is important in life, one's purpose in life, and what values one should follow is critical in the development of a leader. So starting with a discovery approach seems to be critical in leader development. Moreover, it also seems essential that the leader find an organization that also espouses these values and that asks all leaders to espouse these values. Only in such an environment can a leader live his or her purpose and values. The combination of the two—personal and organization values—would seem to be the key to living a fruitful life.

References

Army values. (2006, April 3). www.armystudyguide.com/content/army_board_study_
    guide_topics/leadership/army-values-3.shtml.

Allianz leadership values. (2011). www.allianz.com/en/about_allianz/strategy/leader-
    ship_values/page1.html.

Badaracco, J. (2002). *Leading quietly: An unorthodox guide to doing the right thing.*
    Boston: Harvard Business School Press.

Blanchard, K., & O'Connor, M. (1997). *Managing by values.* San Francisco:
    Berrett-Koehler.

Cashman, K. (1998). *Leadership from inside out.* Minneapolis: TCLG, LLC.

Covey, S.R. (1990). *Principle-centered leadership.* New York: Fireside.

Hess, E.D., & Cameron, K.S. (2006). *Leading with values.* New York: Cambridge
    University Press.

Johnson, H. (2007). Assessing your servant leadership skills. *The 2007 Pfeiffer annual:
    Training.* San Francisco: Pfeiffer.

Johnson, H. (2012). *Becoming a values-based leader.* Charlotte, NC: Information Age
    Publishing.

King, P., & Murray S. (2007). *Leading with your values.* Lakeville, MN: Galde Press.

Kraemer, H. (2011). *From values to action.* San Francisco: Jossey-Bass.

Lee, R., & King, S. (2001). *Discovering the leader in you.* San Francisco: Jossey-Bass.

Majer, K. (2004). *Values-based leadership.* San Diego, CA: Major Communications.

Malphurs, A. (2004). *Values-driven leadership.* Grand Rapids, MI: Baker Books.

O'Toole, J. (1995). *Leading change: An argument for values-based leadership.* San Francisco: Jossey-Bass.

Ruggero, E., & Haley, D. (2005). *The leader's compass: A personal leadership philosophy is your key to success.* King of Prussia, PA: Academy Leadership.

Homer H. Johnson, Ph.D., *is a professor of management in the School of Business Administration at Loyola University–Chicago, where he teaches courses in leadership and in strategy. He is the co-author (with Linda Stroh) of the best-selling book,* Basic Essentials of Effective Consulting, *and the author of the recent book* Developing Values-Based Leaders *from Information Age Publishers.*

I Have Seen the Future and It's Not What It Was Cracked Up to Be

Leonard D. Goodstein

Summary

A review of efforts to predict the future leads to the conclusion that the future is largely unknowable and efforts to predict the future are doomed to failure. The failures are due to the Law of Unintended Consequences, the Better Mousetrap Fallacy, and a generalized resistance to change. Preparing leaders for the future should concentrate on the process of getting ready for an uncertain future rather than the content of the future.

The process of preparing for an uncertain future involves three major elements: (1) learning to think and act strategically; (2) constantly working to increase one's self-knowledge; and (3) building and supporting a strong team. Applying these principles will help develop future-oriented leaders as well as assist mature leaders to avoid obsolescence.

Visions of the Future

Despite any difficulties and potential pitfalls, predictions of the future—by scientists, clerics, pundits, and others—have never been in short supply. A quick review of the extant literature on forecasting the future reveals both contradictions and utter failures. Among the early contradictions are the predictions of an apocalypse (Malthus, 1798) versus a utopia (Bentham, 1789) and, more recently, of endless technological progress (Martinez, 2010; Vinge, 1992) versus a dangerous robotic takeover (Joy, 2000). In such cases, both scenarios of the future cannot be correct, and preparing leaders for these diverse futures would be very different.

But futurology, despite such disparate views of the future, marches on. Following the publication of his initial book, *Future Shock*, in 1970, Alvin Toffler has created a cottage industry by publishing, speaking, and consulting with a new book every few years (e.g., Toffler & Toffler, 1975, 1980, 1983, 1985, 1990, 1995, 2006). And there are any number of competitors, each with a different vision of the future. Clearly, not all of these predictions can be correct. It gives one pause, to say the least.

Perhaps even more interesting are some of the specific predictions made by presumed experts. Here are some mind-blowing examples:

"Airplanes are interesting toys but of no military value."
—Marshall Foch, Commander-in-Chief, French Army, 1914.

"There is not the slightest indication that atomic energy will ever be obtainable. That would mean that the atom would have to be shattered at will."
—Albert Einstein, 1932.

"Who the hell wants to hear actors talk?"
—Harry Warner, CEO, Warner Bros., 1927.

"While theoretically and technically television may be feasible, commercially and financially, it is an impossibility."
—Lee DeForest, inventor of television, 1927.

"I think there is a world market for maybe five computers."
—Thomas E. Watson, Chairman, IBM Corporation, 1943.

"There is no reason for anyone to want a computer in their home."
—Ken Olson, CEO and founder, Digital Equipment Corporation, 1971.

These half dozen quotes (and I have lots more) illustrate the pitfalls inherent in predicting the future. And there has been a high cost to acting on at least some of these. The resistance of the French army to using airplanes undoubtedly prolonged World War I, and Olson's inability to see the potential use of home computers certainly was an important factor in the eventual failure of Digital Equipment Corporation.

A Personal, Retrospective View of the Future

Given both the contradictory views of the future and the inability of even well-informed experts to accurately forecast the future, I puzzled over how I had been prepared for my personal future—a present that is very, very different from my past. I thought of the many changes that I had experienced over my past eight and a half decades of life and found it useful to list at least those that I could identify as directly impacting my present life. Changes occurred from the trivial, e.g., ballpoint pens, to the profound, e.g., globalization, and on a multitude of fronts—political, social, technological—that I never imagined or even could have imagined.

Change and More Change

As I sit here in my air-conditioned home in Arizona working on this manuscript, I recall being a small child growing up in New York City, where the only places with air conditioning were movie theaters. Every Saturday, during the summers especially, I would go the movies to see a double feature (plus a serial) and, if the weather was extremely uncomfortable, I might see it all a second time. The ubiquity of air conditioning today makes it difficult to imagine a life without it, especially here in Arizona, but that's the nature of the adaptive process.

When a technological innovation leads to a large-scale discernable change in the way people live and work, such a change is usually regarded as a *disruptive technology*. The widespread adoption of home and office air conditioning discussed above would be regarded as such, as would railroads, commercial airlines, antibiotics, and the computer, to mention just a few.

On a broader front, there also have been changes that were not predicted. These include the demise of the Soviet Union, the changing role of women in Western societies, the end of segregation, and the coarsening of social interactions. A comment on each. While the USSR is gone, it is unclear what remains in its place. Certainly not a democracy based on the rule of law, but an authoritarian state with an unclear body politic. The barriers to women's entry into the workplace and politics are still evolving, but the changes are obvious and inescapable, as are the opportunities available to African Americans. Predicting a black president in 1948, when I first cast my vote, would lead to a question of the sanity of the person making the prediction.

And the pace of change is rapidly accelerating. For example, ENIAC, the first general-purpose computer, cost millions of dollars and occupied an enormous room in a secret U.S. Army facility. The smart phone that I regularly use has a more powerful computer and it was provided free by Verizon. Here's another example. Less than twenty years ago, as the Human Genome Project was being launched, it was estimated that sequencing the genome of a single person would take fifteen years and cost over $3 billion. Today, it can be done in less than twenty-four hours and costs less than $1,000. Who would ever have predicted anything like this?

But I do not see all the changes in society as positive, especially the coarsening of society, the erosion of the sensibilities and courtesies of the past. Journalist John Burns recently returned to live in the UK after serving for more than forty years as a foreign correspondent for *The New York Times*. In a recent essay (Burns, 2011), he noted that this coarsening was the most notable difference in the UK from his child-hood there. He further notes this may be the inevitable consequence of greater free-dom and a loosening of the class structure. My point here is that change is not always technological or without cost! And we may not always enjoy paying those costs.

The Information Age

Perhaps the most important of these disruptive technologies that has occurred in my lifetime has been the invention of the micro-processor and its many applica-tions, which have moved us from the Industrial Age to the Information Age—from the dial telephone to the smart phone, from film cameras to digital photography, from snail mail to instant messaging and email, from local to global. As I write this on my desktop computer, checking references on Google.com, moving sentences and paragraphs to and fro with a mouse click, it is hard to remember how I wrote my doctoral dissertation on a manual typewriter some sixty years ago in my non-air-conditioned apartment. Not only has my computer made it more convenient for me to write professionally (some of you may regard this as a mixed blessing, at best), but it enables me to pay almost all of my bills electronically, to keep in touch with old friends and to make new ones, to be involved currently in two start-up businesses that exist only in cyber-space. I have no question that the computer with its underlying soft- and hardware has revolutionized the way that I work and live. And very little of this was ever predicted when I was a young man.

Why Is It So Difficult to Predict the Future?

I believe that there are several reasons that make the future so unpredictable. One is that too many futurists focus solely on technology (e.g., Kaku, 2011; Martinez, 2011; Watson, 2010) and how technology will shape the future in one direction of another. How the technology is actually put to use all-too-often turns out to be another matter. As just one example, who would have predicted the role of cell phones in facilitating the Arab Spring of 2011? And few predictions of the future take into account the potential impact of the Law of Unintended Consequences.

The Law of Unintended Consequences

Many human actions, especially the introduction of disruptive technologies, bring about one or more unanticipated consequences. While the rise of easy electronic communications through email and electronic bill payment now seems obvious, who anticipated its impact on snail mail? (Indeed, who would have anticipated the emergence of the new label, "snail mail"?) From 2006 through 2010, the U.S.

Postal Service lost 20 percent of its volume, leading to a financial loss of $8 billion! This unintended loss will only increase over time and must be made up by tax revenues at a time when these are in short supply. The Postal Service is mandated to provide universal service, so its options to reduce costs are limited, and a solution to this dilemma is not obvious.

China's highly authoritarian government has tried to censor the Internet and email exchanges on topics that put it in a bad light. In July 2011, however, two high-speed passenger trains crashed near Wenzhou in Zhejiang Province, killing forty and injuring 192. A young girl happened to observe the crash and send a tweet (*weibo* in Chinese) to a number of her friends. Her initial tweet and the several that followed quickly went viral with over tens of millions of Chinese citizens eventually becoming involved. While the Chinese government has put a blackout on any news about the crash, it has been unable to stop the micro-bloggers. Had the Chinese government known in advance how such public discourse would impact its credibility, it would have been much less sanguine about the development of a country-wide telecommunications network.

As one additional example, the convenience and cost saving of electronic banking led most banks to quickly adopt e-banking and offer it to their customers. But the banks failed to take into account the potential security risks inherent in this system. According to a British government report (Shachtman, 2011), cybercrime in 2010 cost British businesses over US$ 43.5 billion! Clearly an unanticipated consequence, one that poses a serious risk to anyone who routinely uses e-banking, including this author.

The Better Mousetrap Fallacy

"Build a better mousetrap, and the world will beat a path to your door" is an aphorism usually attributed to Ralph Waldo Emerson in the late 19th Century. But history repeatedly has proven this adage to be false. The acceptance of a new technology is uncertain and uneven at best and depends on many factors, including how much the new technology differs from the existing one, who endorses and who opposes accepting the new technology, and the channels through which the technology is diffused. Interested readers should become acquainted with the work of Everett Rogers (Rogers & Rogers, 2003), arguably the leading authority on the diffusion of innovation, which provides many examples of successful and unsuccessful attempts at implementing innovations as well as a conceptual schema for understanding the process of diffusion.

As one example, consider the case of John Ericsson (1803–1889), a Swedish-American inventor, whose various inventions include the ship's propeller, the torpedo, and the rotating gun turret. When he proposed the now universally used ship propeller to the British Admiralty to replace the paddle wheel, it refused to adopt this new-fangled idea. He later was responsible for designing and building the U.S.S. Monitor, the first American iron-clad naval vessel. Its design was so unique that the U.S. Navy mocked it by calling it "a cheese box on a raft" and allowed it to be built only when Ericsson and his financial backers agreed to repay the Navy for all costs should it not be successful. Fortunately for all concerned, the innovation was successful despite the doubts expressed by many (Tierney, 2011).

As should be clear from this example, the adoption of a disruptive technology causes apprehension for those who support it. Who wants to be blamed for a failure? Especially one that costs a great deal of money, or even worse, human lives. Resistance to change makes psychological sense, but it is an important reason for the failures of many predictions to come true.

By now even the most casual reader should recognize that I do not believe that it is possible to predict the future with any degree of accuracy and that most efforts to prepare for a specific future are unlikely to succeed. The problem with most attempts to predict the future is that they focus on the *content* of the future and not on how to prepare for any future—on the *process* of preparing for the future. It is on that process of preparing for the future that I intend to devote the remainder of this article, especially how to position leaders for an unknown situation.

Preparing Leaders for an Uncertain Future

I began this essay by observing the many changes that I have experienced over a rather long and quite rich life, one in which I played a number of leadership roles, including directing a university counseling center, chairing a university psychology department, serving as president of a publishing company (University Associates, now Pfeiffer), serving as CEO of a large professional association, and working as a consultant to senior management in a wide variety of businesses and organizations during a period of enormous technological, social, and political change. Currently I am actively involved in three rather different ventures—an online, pre-employment assessment company where I share responsibility for product development, an organization that assesses and evaluates disruptive physicians (Goodstein & Shufeldt, 2011), and an organization that will provide virtual medical care over the Internet where I share responsibility for developing its mental health component.

On the basis of my long and varied experiences, what have I learned about preparing for an unknown future that would be useful to others?

I've thought long and hard about how to organize and compress my learning into a manageable message and have reduced my advice into three major categories, each with a variety of subthemes. They are (1) learn to think and act strategically;

(2) continually work to increase your self-understanding; and (3) build and support a strong team. All easier said than done!

Learn to Think and Act Strategically

A strategic leader needs to search for, locate, recognize, identify, store, and then use information to move his or her organization forward. The brain of a strategic leader is crammed with information about the organization, its markets, its competitors, its technologies, its strengths and weaknesses (including his or her own), and much more. The strategic leader brings this information to bear in making those decisions that will have significant impact on the long-range future of the organization. The failure of a leader to routinely conduct such surveillance puts the organization at extreme risk of becoming obsolescent, if not obsolete.

This should be a straightforward description of what senior managers of every organization do on a daily basis, but it is simply not the case. The daily work of most managers involves a constant series of confrontations with small, but vexing, problems requiring the managers' immediate attention. You leave a meeting and you are immediately confronted by several staff members, each waiting for you with his or her list of concerns that require your involvement. After a day of such firefighting, it is difficult to even imagine what your plans for the day originally were, but little, if any, of your actions meet the definition of strategic thinking and planning. And you still need to address the pile of technical reports, industry journals, newsletters, and the like that are a prime source of the information you need to acquire.

Create a Climate for Learning

This means that senior managers need to schedule both a time and a process for sorting out the wheat from the chaff, for thinking about the organization and its future holistically. A formal process of strategic planning is the typical way of accomplishing this at the organizational level. Senior managers also need to think about themselves, a process that requires something else—an off-site meeting with a mentor, executive coach, or a support group of peers that allows a respite from the endless firefighting. Such opportunities can and should lead to enhanced strategic thinking on the individual level. Without such time for reflection and deep thought, I believe both the manager and the organization are at risk.

Reflection allows us to reconsider our decisions and try to learn from our mistakes. Errors of judgment, failures to act decisively when the time is ripe, poorly thought-through action plans that lead to marginal successes, and so on will inevitably occur on your watch. Some even argue that if you have never had any failures as a leader, then you haven't been trying hard enough. But if you see each failure as a learning opportunity—to understand how and why you failed—you will sharply reduce the possibility of re-creating that same kind of failure. This learning, however, can only occur when you force yourself to take the opportunity for serious reflection, contemplation, and analysis.

Avoid Analysis/Paralysis

A related issue that deserves mention is that organizational leaders never have all the information they would like to have in order to make an informed decision. It's an uncertain world out there and there is always a question of how to decide in the face of such uncertainty. I have seen two major decision-making flaws over the years—snap judgments on the one hand and analysis/paralysis on the other.

Accepting the fact that we never will have all the information that we would like to have and still be willing to make a decision based on the facts at hand is one of the hallmarks of a strategic leader. This is when the storehouse of information referred to earlier comes into play. Such information prevents analysis/paralysis—the endless dithering about how to reduce the irreducible lack of knowledge. Most important decisions are made on the basis of *best guesses*, decisions based on the available facts plus what is often called *intuition*, but which really is that unspoken storehouse of knowledge based on experience and knowledge.

Avoiding snap judgments on the one hand, decisions that seem to lack a proper consideration of the facts at hand, and analysis/paralysis on the other is an important skill that can only be acquired as the leader comes to understand and trust his or her storehouse of information and realizes that the time for a decision has arrived.

Embrace Change

There is one certainty—the future will not be like the present and there's not much that you can do about it. But I have learned that I always can find something positive in every change that I experience. Giving up my faithful pre-war Royal typewriter was hard for me—it had been my reliable ally for very long time—but today I cannot imagine my present life without my desktop computer. I suspect that adaptability and looking for those positive elements in every change is necessary for leaders to cope with the future. An important learning for me, and I hope for you the reader, is to remember that the difficulties we encounter are often opportunities in disguise.

While I have never had an ambition, I have always been ambitious (Goodstein, 1999). All of the many jobs that I have had were offered to me as an opportunity that I knew little about. Usually happy in the job I had at the time, I was eager to accept the challenge of a new job, a new location, new people, and especially new problems to solve. Maintaining a problem-solving approach has been a constant in my career, and I know that many of the opportunities that have come my way have resulted from my prior successes in solving problems.

I look back at many of my jobs and I see many of my former colleagues still there doing much the same thing, apparently content. But my greatest fear has always been the fear of being bored, of not finding new opportunities to solve new problems. Of course, problems emerge on a regular basis, even when one holds the same job over time. But taking a new job, especially one that involves assuming a leadership role, guarantees you a multitude of opportunities to solve problems. At least that's my experience.

Increase Your Self-Knowledge

A second major process for preparing for the future is continually working to increase one's self-knowledge, developing a clear understanding of one's own strengths and weaknesses. Such self-knowledge gives one the opportunity to build on one's strengths and compensate for one's weaknesses. While it is far more satisfying to hear about one's strengths, learning about one's weaknesses is far more important for one's long-term success. But it is far more difficult to identify and manage one's weaknesses, especially as one rises in the management hierarchy. It is always difficult to confront supervisors or bosses about their weaknesses, and it is especially difficult to confront the CEO—too often seen as the embodiment of the organization.

Solicit Feedback

It is not easy for a leader to encourage fearful subordinates to tell him or her things that he or she does not want to hear! It is thus imperative that leaders make it as easy as possible for subordinates to raise concerns and problems. One useful tactic to encourage such feedback is the after-action review, a procedure initially used by the Israeli military to improve its combat performance. After each training exercise or actual skirmish, the military unit would review the operation, basically asking four questions: (1) What did we intend to do; (2) What did we actually do; (3) Why did that happen; and (4) How could we have done it better? In answering these questions, the unit leader always pushes to identify what he or she did that held the unit back, when mixed or unclear messages were sent, when the leader failed to show the necessary leadership, and so on. This process has largely been adopted by other militaries, including the U.S. Army, and become an essential process for developing successful top-level leaders. It is a process both for leaders to learn about their behavior and for organizations to learn how to operate more effectively.

It is easy to extrapolate this process to the non-military organizational world. After a marketing campaign, a new product rollout, a fund-raising effort, or whatever, the leader of such an effort can call for an after-action report in order to learn about how his or her behavior facilitated or limited the success of the effort. Adopting such a process as an organization routine can do much to identify the leader's weaknesses, create comfort among subordinates, and permit the necessary corrections. To complete a successful after-action review, the team needs to approach the review with a learning orientation, to be completely honest, and to avoid focusing on the trivial—all essentials for personal and organizational learning.

Another important way to identify and address one's weaknesses is through an independent, off-site evaluation by a team of qualified professionals. One such program is the week-long program offered by the Center for Creative Leadership, which involves the Center obtaining subordinate feedback on the leader, intensive psychological testing and observation, and a summary session for developing an ongoing plan of action. I know of no one who has gone through such a program who has not profited greatly from his or her participation.

Another way of gaining feedback is to have a seasoned consultant *shadow* you for several days—observing your behavior *in situ* and then reviewing and questioning you about what you did and why you did what you did. This is yet another process that pays rich dividends for the leader, as it brings home to the leader the usually unseen consequences of his or her behavior. This is an especially useful technique if it is followed up for a period of time. What is important to recognize in this context is the value of continually soliciting feedback in order to identify and better manage one's weaknesses.

Some Personal Examples

To illuminate this process of identifying strengths and weakness, let me offer my own as examples. One of my strengths is my skills in understanding people. I have always been intensely interested in people, in understanding them, in learning what makes them tick! I suspect that it is this interest that led me into a career as a professional psychologist. My graduate training helped me learn how to be a good, empathetic listener and how to put together the life story of the other person. Five decades of practice have greatly enhanced this strength. In my current work with disruptive physicians, I see senior professionals who have been sent for an evaluation, largely against their will. At the end of a long day of in-depth interviewing, reviewing of test results, and developing an action plan, the physician often will remark that he or she never expected to reveal as much about him- or herself as he or she did—a back-handed compliment. But I understand that this is one of my unique strengths and I use it professionally whenever I can.

One of my weaknesses—pointed out regularly by peers, subordinates, consultants, and especially my wife—is my impatience. While my impatience can often be a stimulus to action in an organizational setting, I have been forced by circumstances to recognize that my impatience sometimes has led to poor quality, premature decisions. All too often, my cry to "Let's get this show on the road" has led to a departure before we had all the necessary equipment on board! Like most weaknesses, my impatience is sometimes a goad to action, but more often a detriment, and I've had to learn how to better manage this weakness. One way has been to encourage others to let me know, in no uncertain terms, when it's still *not* time to "get the show on the road."

Avoid Turning Strengths into Weaknesses

Almost any strength can turn into a weakness when over-utilized. For example, consider conscientiousness. Decades of research has shown that *conscientiousness* is a primary factor leading to one's success at work. Showing up regularly, and on time, meeting deadlines, holding high standards for one's own work and that of others characterize the conscientious person and are critical factors in achieving success. But, as a leader, it is possible to turn conscientiousness from a strength into a weakness. One can be too demanding, impose standards impossible to meet, micromanage, and generally attempt to push subordinates faster and further than they can go. Finding the right balance in the application of each of our strengths is an important element of becoming a future successful leader.

With the rise of positive psychology, a view has emerged that leaders and those who are responsible for leadership development should focus their attention on maximizing leaders' strengths rather than trying to correct their weaknesses (e.g., Morris & Garrett, 2010; Rath & Conchie, 2009). The positive psychologists argue that identifying and understanding one's weakness can be painful and unpleasant and is a process that most people try to avoid. Therefore, why not simply focus on a person's strengths, while largely ignoring his or her weaknesses?

There is both strong anecdotal and research evidence that developing leaders by focusing only on their strengths is not a successful strategy. As I have just noted, strengths become weaknesses when overused. "Too much of a good thing" is an aphorism based on much experience. For example, McCall and Lombardo, in their comprehensive study of why managers become derailed, concluded "the same attributes that got these men to the top also did them in" (1983, p. 8). In a recent research report, Kaiser and Overfield (2011) found a strong tendency of managers to overutilize their strengths while underutilizing behaviors that would modulate their weaknesses, a strategy that led these managers to less positive outcomes.

Thus, despite the attractiveness of the positive psychology argument, I believe that preparing for effective, long-term leadership requires an understanding of both one's strengths and one's weaknesses. That understanding must then lead to a careful use of one's strengths and a continual effort to address one's weaknesses. Remember, any strength can become a weakness when inappropriately or excessively used.

Build a Strong Team

Building a strong team of individuals with complementary skills, different approaches to problem solving, and quite different personalities is essential to preparing both an organization and its leaders for an unknown future. Team members should be expert in their various areas of specialization. The marketing person should know the markets in which the organization can and should be operating. The financial person should be expert in understanding the fiscal position of the organization, in the management of cash flow, and so on. These various areas of expertise should be chosen to complement any weakness in the background and experience of the team leader.

Of even more importance, however, is the need for the team to work collaboratively to support the team leader in moving the organization toward its strategic goals. The members of a strong, healthy team are able to face and resolve their differences while avoiding the in-fighting, back-stabbing, and the petty politics that all too often characterize organizational life. Establishing an appropriate climate for teamwork and setting limits for bickering are essential component of building and leading such a team. Absolutely necessary is the ability to disagree without being disagreeable.

A strong senior management team is the ideal place to introduce and practice the after-action review described earlier. As the team utilizes the after-action review process, it creates a learning orientation for both the leader and the team, as well as serving as a model for teams elsewhere in the organization.

The ability of individual team members to confront the team leader when necessary is essential. Too many organizations are steered by top-level teams composed of "yes men," persons chosen by the team leader on the basis of friendship or their known passivity. The recent past is unfortunately replete with examples of corporate boards of directors who have passively agreed to go along with decisions that had disastrous consequences, both for the organization and for society at large, Rupert Murdoch's being a notable case in point.

Often an individual team member takes on, by force of personality or otherwise, the role of *devil's advocate*, questioning the logic of a decision, proposing alternatives, asking for additional information, and so on. Having someone to fill such a role is an important ingredient of a successful team, especially at the most senior levels of an organization. It is interesting to note that President Obama's Council of Economic Advisors had such a "naysayer" in Austan Goolsbee (McArdle, 2011), and many economists feel that he will be sorely missed.

Some leaders, understanding the need to have that role fulfilled and recognizing that there is no one on the team who naturally fills that role, will appoint a devil's advocate for each meeting. While such a solution is clearly an artificial one, it legitimizes open confrontation without negative consequences.

Trust

Arguably the most important issue in leading a team into the future successfully is trust. Trust is both a logical and a psychological process. Logically, I trust you because in my prior dealings with you I have experienced you to be a trustworthy person—predictable, true to your word, open, and safe. As a consequence this leads emotionally to feelings of closeness, agreeableness, friendship, and even love.

Trust means believing in what that person, says even when you do not have full knowledge of his or her intent, the basis for the statement, or what might occur to you as a consequence. Teams are successful only when a reasonably high level of trust has been established, and it is the leader's responsibility to model that trust— one of the reasons that micro-managing reduces trust in an organization.

Trust is a fragile commodity in most human encounters. It is very difficult to establish and very easy to break. When I trust you, I am exposing myself to some possible negative consequences, and therefore I am very guarded initially in my dealings with others. It is only over time that others can prove their trustworthiness by showing that they are reliable truth-tellers without hidden motives. Trust always means enabling others to take advantage of you, but expecting that they will not do so! Without trust, teams fail, organizations fail, and the future is in doubt.

How to Avoid Obsolescence

While the focus of my argument has been on leadership development, I wish to close with my advice to those who are in senior leadership positions and to those who counsel and consult with established leaders. The major question that needs to be addressed is how to avoid obsolescence, to remain current and relevant in a time of extraordinarily rapid change.

One of the most frequently told tales about avoiding obsolesce is that of the buggy whip manufacturers. As the late Ted Levitt (1960) explained in his now famous *Harvard Business Review* article, if they had only understood that they were in the vehicle acceleration business and not in the buggy whip manufacturing business, they would have better positioned themselves to move into the automotive age by producing accelerators, starters, or whatever for the newly invented automobile. Levitt, however, missed the real issue—what are the necessary skills and competencies necessary to move from making buggy whips to manufacturing electronic parts. Two related issues arise: (1) How many of these buggy whip manufacturers both understood the impact of the automotive revolution and (2) How many had the necessary competencies and resources to make such a move?

But what actually did happen to these buggy whip manufacturers? Interestingly enough, some have survived by continuing to manufacture and sell buggy whips, although the latest models have embedded LED lights! The bulk of them, however, simply failed and went out of business, and a few seemed to have figured it out, although in a very modified form—by identifying their basic competencies and grasping how to apply them to this new opportunity—the automobile. However, those who successfully made the transition to autos were not to be the buggy whip makers but the makers of parts for carriages.

Arguably, the single best example of this shift is the Timken Corporation, founded in the 1890s, that initially produced roller bearings for carriage wheels and is now a highly successful multinational supplier of roller bearings for all sorts of applications. They saw in the invention of the automobile an opportunity to adapt their competencies to this emerging technology and took advantage of it.

What is the moral of this story? Both individuals and businesses alike need to identify and hone their competencies and stand ready to adapt them to meet new market needs. Such transition is not easy to make. In the 1890s there were over thirteen thousand businesses involved in the wagon and carriage industry, and only a handful survived. Those who perished simply could not imagine the impact this new invention would have, were unable to identify their transferable competencies and how these competencies might be utilized, or were held back by legacy issues that prevented any transition from occurring. This failure to adapt lies at the root of many of the current problems, both of individuals and of businesses, that are either unable or unwilling to make the necessary modifications in their thinking and planning. The moral of this story would appear to be "Be neither a buggy whip nor a buggy whip maker!"

The Role of Technology in the Future

It would seem appropriate to close with a brief discussion about how leaders need to view the role of technology in the future. I can think of no business or industry that has not been greatly impacted over the past few decades by technology, but what about the future? Leaders of organizations need to be clear about their organizations' missions and, unless they are in the technology business itself, they need constantly question how an emerging technology can or might impact the way in which they do business.

It is important for leaders to be sensitive to the rise of new technologies; the constant question to raise is how that emerging technology can affect the ongoing success of the organization. Can adopting this new technology improve the quality of the product or service, increase market penetration, improve customer service, and so on? And is the cost of adoption—both financial and psychological—offset by the expected gains?

Rogers and Rogers (2003) have identified a five-stage process of the diffusion of innovation: (1) innovators, (2) early adopters, (3) early majority, (4) late majority, and (5) laggards. Leaders, in considering whether or not to adopt and implement a new technology into their organization, need to be clear on where in the five-step process the technology being considered stands. There are serious risks in being at either end of this continuum, and leaders must be aware of these risks. While it may seem attractive to be the "first kid on the block" to have the new gadget, these innovators often end up becoming beta sites for the technology without having any intention of having done so. A healthy skepticism about the newest and greatest usually goes a long way toward ensuring the future health of an organization and the future of the leader of that organization.

References

Bentham, J. (1789). *A fragment on government with an introduction to the principles of morals and legislation.* Oxford, England: Clarendon Press.

Burns, J.F. (2011, July 23). Rude Britannia. *New York Times*, pp. SR 1, 6.

Goodstein, L.D. (1999). Meandering to the top: A personal and professional odyssey. *Psychologist-Manager Journal, 3,* 71–83.

Goodstein, L.D., & Shufeldt, J. (2011). Dealing with disruptive physicians. *Journal of Urgent Care Management, 5,* 17–26.

Joy, B. (2000, April). Why the future doesn't need us. *Wired, 4,* 1–11.

Kaiser, R.E., & Overfield, D.V. (2011). Strengths, strengths overused, and lopsided leadership. *Consulting Psychology Journal, Practice and Research, 63,* 89–110.

Kaku, M. (2011). *Physics of the future: How science will shape human destiny and our daily lives by the year 2100.* New York: Doubleday.

Levitt, T. (1960, July/August). Marketing myopia. *Harvard Business Review*, pp. 45–56.

McCall, M.W., & Lombardo, M.M. (1983). *Off the track: Why and how successful executives get derailed.* Greensboro, NC: Center for Creative Leadership.

McCardle, M. (2011, September). Devil's advocate: Why the White House and Washington should miss departing economics adviser Austan Goolsbee. *The Atlantic*, pp. 40–44.

Malthus, T.R. (1798). *An essay on the principle of population.* London: J. Johnson.

Martinez, S.B. (2011). *Time of the quickening: Prophesies for the coming utopian age.* Rochester, VT: Bear and Co.

Morris, D., & Garrett, J. (2010). Strengths: Your leading edge. In A.P. Linley, S. Harrington, & N. Garcia (Eds.), *Oxford handbook of positive psychology and work* (pp. 95–105). New York: Oxford University Press.

Rath, T. & Conchie, B. (2009). *Strength-based leadership*. New York: Gallup Press.

Rogers, E.M., & Rogers. M. (2003). *Diffusion of innovations* (5th ed.). New York: The Free Press.

Shachtman, N. (2011, July 30). E-crimes sitting ducks. *Arizona Republic*, p. B5.

Tierney, J. (2011, August 6). A brief dry spell for the U.S.S. Monitor. *New York Times*, pp. D1, D4.

Toffler, A. (1970). *Future shock*. New York: Bantam Books.

Toffler, A., & Toffler, H. (1975). *The eco-spasm report*. New York: Bantam Books.

Toffler, A., & Toffler, H. (1980). *The third wave*. New York: Bantam Books.

Toffler, A., & Toffler, H. (1983). *Previews and promises*. New York: William Morrow.

Toffler, A., & Toffler, H. (1985). *The adaptive corporation*. New York: McGraw-Hill.

Toffler, A., & Toffler, H. (1990). *Powershift: Knowledge, wealth, and violence on the edge of the 21st century*. New York: Bantam Books.

Toffler, A., & Toffler, H. (1995). *War and anti-war*. New York: Warner Books.

Toffler, A., & Toffler, H. (2006). *Revolutionary wealth*. New York: Alfred Knopf.

Vinge, V. (1992). *Fire upon the deep*. New York: Tor/McMillan.

Watson, R. (2010). *Future files: A brief history of the next 60 years* (rev ed.). London: Nicholas Brealey.

Leonard D. Goodstein, Ph.D., *is a consulting psychologist located in Scottsdale, Arizona. He has been a faculty member at the University of Iowa and University of Cincinnati and Arizona State University. He later was president and CEO of University Associates (now Pfeiffer) and CEO and executive VP of the American Psychological Association. He is now president and CEO of Professional Assessment Services and Solutions (PASS), VP for product development of Psichometrics LLC, and western regional VP for mental health services, MeMD.*

Connecting the Dots
Developing Leaders Who See the Big Picture
Catherine J. Rezak

Summary

Do you remember those connect-the-dots puzzles you played with as a child? Each one appeared to be just a random scattering of black dots on a white page. No matter how hard you squinted or stared at those spots, you couldn't see the object or scene in front of you. But if you drew a line and connected the dots in the right order, a clear picture would suddenly emerge out of the chaos.

Trying to make sense of the uncertainty, complexity, ambiguity, volatility, and seeming chaos of the current business environment is a lot like tackling one of those puzzles. Understanding what is really going on and responding accordingly requires the ability to connect the dots astutely and accurately.

It's a tall order in today's business world.

An Unrecognizable New World

Within its most recent ten-year forecasts, the Institute for the Future (2010) predicted a decade of unprecedented change and reinvention on the horizon, pointing to widespread collapse of existing institutions and infrastructures, as well as radical transformation and the emergence of new systems. In addition to a protracted recovery from the recent economic crisis, the resulting fallout has put an end to business as usual. In its place is a "new normal" that not only looks markedly different from anything anyone has seen before, but also augurs the inevitability of a future world that will be very different from the world we know today.

To survive and thrive in this radically different, ever-changing landscape, businesses face more than just competition. They are buffeted by geopolitics and global instability, challenged by rapid technological advances, and set afloat in a rising tide of information that demands their constant attention. Myriad factors need to be examined—from the emergence of entirely new business models to morphing consumer attitudes and behaviors, social and political shifts, and new algorithms for mining and analyzing data. While some classic management strategies and skills will continue to be effective, leaders in this confusing and complex new world of business will most certainly need to lead differently.

Technology: Blurring the View?

Ironically, technology and the billions of bits and bytes of information it generates every day may be crippling leaders' ability to see business situations clearly and make critical decisions that can reap long-term benefits. The pace is so fast and furious and there's so much information coming at leaders all the time that they're becoming more scattered in their thinking.

In fact, information and data are so ubiquitous and digital distractions such a big part of our lives that our minds, according to Nicholas Carr (2011), author of the Pulitzer finalist *The Shallows: What the Internet Is Doing to Our Brains*, are no longer the same. We have become attuned to "the crazy quilt of web content" or what blogger and science fiction writer Cory Doctorow calls an "ecosystem of interruption technologies."

In the process, the very features that make the Internet so attractive and valuable as an information resource—interactivity, hyperlinking, searchability, multimedia—are literally changing our brains and diminishing our capacity to engage in the kind of deep reasoning and critical thought necessary to meet the challenges we face. Instead, they are distracting and dividing our attention and straining our cognitive abilities. Our capacity for learning suffers, and our understanding remains shallow. Carr concludes that the mental functions that are losing "the survival of the busiest" brain cells battle are those that support calm, linear thought—the ones we use for recognizing patterns, seeing the big picture, and engaging in critical and strategic thinking.

Based on scientific studies of the brain's lifelong plasticity, our brains are always in flux, adapting even to small shifts in our circumstances and behaviors and to changes in the tools we use. Unused circuits are pruned away and new habits are formed by repetition of a physical or mental activity. Calling it "the single most powerful mind-altering technology that has ever come into general use," Carr believes the Internet delivers precisely the kind of sensory and cognitive stimuli—repetitive, intensive, interactive, addictive—that result in strong and rapid alterations in the brain's circuits and functions.

"Dozens of studies by psychologists, neurobiologists, educators, and web designers point to the same conclusion: when we go online, we enter an environment that promotes cursory reading, hurried and distracted thinking, and superficial learning. It's possible to think deeply while surfing the 'Net, just as it's possible to think shallowly while reading a book, but that's not the type of thinking the technology encourages and rewards. . . . Our use of the Internet involves many paradoxes, but the one that promises to have the greatest long-term influence over how we think is this one: the 'Net seizes our attention only to scatter it" (Carr, 2011, p. 115).

And now is not the time for scattered thinking, especially from our leaders.

A New Kind of "Vision" for Leaders

Without a broad understanding of both the external and internal landscapes, leaders are more likely to develop the wrong capabilities, set the wrong goals, hire the wrong people, or enter the wrong markets. Worst of all, without a clear vision of financial and strategic objectives, they may fail to recognize the challenges the business is facing, the concerns of their people, and the impact of their decisions on the bottom line. That kind of leadership thinking won't help businesses survive in the challenging times ahead.

First and foremost, successful leaders will need the ability to connect a plethora of "dots" within a vast and dynamic global business ecosystem. Effective strategy will require a broader view, rather than tunnel vision and the ability to keep the details in perspective—not an easy task in an environment of ever-increasing information availability and diminishing time and opportunity to examine and think.

According to Loizos Heracleous, professor of strategy at England's Warwick Business School, "It all comes down to the ability to go up and down the ladder of abstraction . . . being able to see the big picture and the operational implications, which are signs of outstanding leaders and strategists" (1998, p. 481).

For business leaders, connecting the dots to see the big picture goes by many names—holistic thinking, gestalt, pattern recognition, strategic versus tactical thinking, to name a few.

Seeing the Big Picture

Peter Senge, director of the Center for Organizational Learning at the MIT Sloan School of Management, focuses on "systems thinking," a discipline for seeing wholes. "It is a framework for seeing interrelationships rather than things, for seeing patterns of change rather than static snapshots" (Senge, 1990, p. 68).

Others call it taking a "helicopter view," which is exactly what it sounds like. A helicopter view gives leaders the ability to intellectually rise above current business situations and see what's ahead, what's behind, and what surrounds them. They can discern a larger context, analyze dynamic interactions, and recognize overarching trends while still taking into account all important details and implications. In other words, they can see the forest—without losing sight of the individual trees—and navigate it successfully.

In his book *The Nature of Leadership*, former University of Illinois President B. Joseph White calls a helicopter view one of the five qualities great leaders share. He describes it as a sense of perspective. "Can the person put an immediate problem, question, or challenge into a larger context of the past, the future, things going on concurrently in other spheres, and, perhaps most important, the larger mission and purpose to which it relates? And can the person do it not just as an intellectual exercise but, rather, identify the practical consequences of context?" (White, 2007, pp. 137–138).

For Daniel Pink (2005), the best-selling author of *A Whole New Mind*, it is all about "symphony," one of the six key "high-concept, high-touch senses" needed for what he dubs the new "Conceptual Age." "What's in greatest demand today isn't analysis but synthesis—seeing the big picture and crossing boundaries, being able to combine disparate pieces into an arresting new whole," says Pink. "It's fast becoming a 'killer app' in business" (Pink, 2005, p. 66).

After nearly a century of Western society being dominated by a form of thinking that is narrowly reductive and deeply analytical, Pink sees big changes. He envisions us moving from the logical, computer-like capabilities of the Information Age to an "economy and a society built on the inventive, empathic, big-picture capabilities of what's rising in its place, the Conceptual Age." What's required in this emerging age is a "new set of aptitudes: forging relationships rather than executing transactions, tackling novel challenges instead of solving routine problems, and synthesizing the big picture rather than analyzing a single component." It also demands the meta-ability to "grasp the relationships between the relationships" (Pink, 2005, pp. 39–40).

Recognizing the Patterns

Both research and observation demonstrate that understanding the relationships between relationships—assimilating a disparate set of data, recognizing industry patterns, anticipating change, and being able to wrap one's mind around complicated phenomena and detect potential movements from seemingly random occurrences—has risen to the top as a core competency and competitive advantage for current and future leaders.

In *Working with Emotional Intelligence*, Daniel Goleman (1998) cites a study of executives at fifteen large companies. According to the research, "Just one cognitive ability distinguished star performers from average: pattern recognition, the 'big picture' thinking that allows leaders to pick out the meaningful trends from a welter of information around them and to think strategically far into the future." These star performers, says Goleman, "relied less on deductive, if-then reasoning" and more on intuitive, contextual reasoning (1998, p. 33).

Looking Inside as Well as Out

Whatever you call it, this ability to see the big picture isn't just an external exercise for business leaders. Just as it's important to have a clear view and understanding of the outside world—the business ecosystem in which an organization operates—it's also imperative to take a helicopter view and think critically about what's going on inside the business. Again, context is key.

In today's highly charged marketplace, leaders are challenged like never before to make the connection between what's happening in the world at large with the finer points of how the business functions internally. As their role in executing strategy continues to expand, they are accountable for making crucial, real-time decisions that directly affect financial outcomes at the unit and at the corporate level. To succeed, they need to have the insight and perception to balance the big picture with the day-to-day basics of doing business. The truth is, leaders can't impact bottom-line success if they are unable to accurately assess the competitive landscape or connect operational decisions and activities with key financial and business performance metrics and goals.

Where Business Acumen Fits in the Picture

The ability to engage in internal big-picture thinking and understand the organization's financial and strategic issues—the relationships between actions and consequences within a holistic context—is known as business acumen. Leaders who understand all the business drivers and key financial levers, as well as the relationships among them, are able to understand the total organization and how the individual parts work together.

What Is Business Acumen?

The dictionary defines acumen as "quickness, accuracy, and keenness of judgment or insight," especially in practical matters. The word comes from the Latin acuere—the root of acute—meaning "to sharpen."

Business acumen is an acute understanding of how a business works and what it takes for the enterprise to make money. It combines financial literacy (the ability to understand numbers on financial statements) with business literacy (recognizing how strategies, behaviors, actions, and decisions not only affect the numbers but also drive profitable and sustainable growth).

Consider this example: In team sports, players need to know how the game is scored. To affect the score, they need to know how to play the game. In business, financial literacy is understanding the score and business acumen is knowing how to impact it.

On any business team, managers with basic financial literacy can read a company's income statement by relying on a fundamental understanding of financial terms, ratios, and what the numbers represent. But that's about it.

Managers with business acumen, however, can interpret that income statement— what the numbers really mean—and act accordingly. With a solid understanding of industry, market, and financial information, they have a clear view of the company's current realities and potential opportunities. They are able to analyze and apply diverse financial data to the development of strategy. Most important, they can make decisions that lead to increases in profit or cash flow because they know how their actions affect the numbers and vice versa.

They have a clear understanding of not only how the business works but also how it sustains profitability. They make better decisions, influence top-line revenue generation, establish priorities, and take actions that align with organizational and marketplace strategy.

Leaders with business acumen are able to break down organizational silos, bridge communication gaps, and engage the employees they manage in understanding how the company operates and what each person can do to contribute to success.

On the other hand, without adequate business acumen, leaders can't align their priorities with those of the company or help employees connect with the company's vision and goals. Narrow focus on their own departments and job functions prevents them from understanding how what they do rolls up into a financial statement or affects their customers, so there is no sense of urgency. And when income statements, balance sheets, cash flow statements, asset management initiatives, and other financial concepts are misunderstood or misused—and when they don't grasp the connection between these financial concepts and corporate vision, goals, and strategies—they can't be effective leaders for the organization, themselves, or their teams.

Sharpening the View with Critical Thinking

Also under the umbrella of the big picture, critical thinking has been elevated to a core competency. Identified by the Department of Labor as a foundational skill and the "raw material" that underlies fundamental workplace competencies, critical thinking appears to be exactly what's needed from leaders navigating the volatility of the new economic order.

In her seminal book, *Thought and Knowledge*, Diane Halpern offers this definition of critical thinking:

> "Critical thinking is the use of those cognitive skills or strategies that increase the probability of a desirable outcome. It is used to describe thinking that is purposeful, reasoned, and goal-directed—the kind of thinking involved in solving problems, formulating inferences, calculating likelihoods, and making decisions. . . . It's the kind of thinking that makes desirable outcomes more likely." (2002, p. 6)

Critical thinking can enable leaders at every level to understand the impact of their decisions on the business as a whole and ensure both alignment with organizational goals and accountability for results. Leaders who are reasoned, purposeful, critical thinkers think differently about how their decisions and actions influence the business and impact the bottom line. Using an approach that is fair, objective, accurate, and based on information relevant to the situation, they know how to make sure the correct problems are addressed within acceptable risks.

Operating from a broad, systemic perspective, they understand what it takes to execute for results now, while fulfilling their obligations to positively affect the future. And they are able to balance department or team issues with broader company issues and embrace a larger responsibility for the success of the organization.

In a recent study from The Conference Board, 150 companies and more than eighty thought leaders weighed in on what they saw as the characteristics of leadership necessary to face the future. The results pointed to "an environment of extreme cognitive complexity in many industries, requiring extraordinary strategic thinking skills and the ability to make high-quality decisions quickly in the face of competitive pressures and uncertainty" (Barrett & Beeson, 2002, p. 33).

At the same time, in "Are They Really Ready to Work?"—a subsequent report from The Conference Board, in collaboration with Corporate Voices for Working Families, the Partnership for 21st Century Skills, and the Society for Human Resource Management—critical thinking was singled out by 77.8 percent of employers as the number one skill of increasing importance over the next five years (Casner-Lotto, Barrington, & Wright, 2006).

The Lack of Big-Picture Leadership

Despite the growing realization that seeing the big picture—and demonstrating the business acumen, critical thinking, and leadership accountability that accompany it—is vital for business survival in a turbulent environment, most business leaders haven't really mastered this strategic competency.

There's certainly evidence that the lack of big picture thinking is and has been a critical issue. The 9/11 Commission (National Commission, 2004) determined that the biggest failure in the days leading up to the terrorist attacks was a "failure of imagination." The data—the necessary pieces of the puzzle—were there, but no one connected the dots. Likewise, in the wake of the economic crisis, we all know too well what happens when decisions are based upon erroneous, partially false, or incomplete information and those in charge fail to think clearly and strategically about the full implications of what they're doing.

Filling the gap and developing the capability to interpret and find order in often chaotic masses of data, understand connections between seemingly separate elements, see new opportunities, or recognize when the world is changing, represents a critical need at an especially critical time.

Every two years Executive Development Associates (EDA) conducts a survey on the trends, growth, and evolution of executive development. The 2009/2010 EDA Trends in Executive Development, which asked senior executive development professionals to gauge the readiness of the next generation of leadership talent, revealed trouble on the horizon.

The survey identified "hot topics" in executive development. At the top of the list was leadership, followed by "business acumen, honing skills in strategy execution, leading/managing change, and talent management."

But when asked, "What competencies are your leaders lacking?" respondents indicated little confidence that leaders had what it takes to execute in these critical areas. Here's what they said was missing:

- Strategic thinking

- Leading change

- Ability to create a vision and engage others around it

- Ability to inspire

- Understanding the total enterprise and how the parts work together

EDA CEO Bonnie Hagemann succinctly describes this disconnect: "What a leader needs the most, the next leaders lack. . . . They can't think critically. They can't think at a high level and a low level at the same time" (Welch, 2010). Anecdotal evidence from the ranks of corporate executives supports the concern that current and emerging leaders lack the skills they need for the future. In "Leadership Matters," a 2009 paper published by Heidrick & Struggles International, one of the world's leading executive search and leadership advisory firms, CEO Kevin Kelly and Leo T. Csorba, an H&S partner, write:

> "Countless CEOs have confided in us that what keeps them up at night is whether their leaders are sufficiently developed to head off the next crisis. They worry about whether their leaders are able to make the tough decisions and take the necessary actions to not only drive earnings and revenue growth, but to mitigate risk and ward off ethical lapses.
>
> "Boards and executive teams must ensure that their future leaders are not only the smartest, most innovative guys and gals in the room, but also the wisest; not only the most confident, but also the most authentic; and not only the most driven, but also the most ambitious for the enterprise as a whole." (p. 6)

A New Leadership Development Focus

Given the gaps uncovered by EDA and other groups studying leadership competencies, as well as the strains on leadership capabilities exerted by the technology and the times we live in, the obvious assumption is that the traditional development process that businesses have relied on in the past to prepare leaders simply hasn't kept up or has merely scraped the surface.

That's why smart companies are revamping their leadership development initiatives to deal with these issues. To accelerate the development of high-potential individuals and raise leadership accountability to a whole new level of awareness and action, they are placing a new emphasis on big-picture and critical thinking in their leadership curricula.

The good news is that this kind of thinking is a skill that can be taught. According to Diane Halpern, an award-winning professor of psychology at Claremont McKenna College and a widely read author on the subject, "There is a large body of evidence showing that people can learn to think better. Of course, education makes us all more intelligent, but critical thinking is more focused. Everyone can learn to recognize and use the skills of critical thinking, and we can always get better" (2002, p. 55).

New competencies, however, may require a deeper, more analytical approach to training. The challenge today is not to discard what's been learned in the past, but to build upon traditional competencies with a whole new and more complex set of skills, tools, and sensitivities.

Learning to Think Like a Leader

The new generation of leaders needs to learn how to be discerning, how to think clearly and wisely, and how to be accountable for their impact on the business. The trick is reinvigorating the leadership curriculum with development experiences that transfer these thinking skills to current and emerging leaders who have not previously been helped to think this way.

Not surprisingly, when it comes to teaching things like high-level thinking skills, traditional management training often falls short. Emphasizing the "tactical" skills of managing—setting goals, communicating expectations, providing feedback—doesn't adequately prepare leaders to use the "strategic" skills of big-picture thinking, providing vision, and motivating others. While this type of skills training clearly has a role in executive development, it cannot accomplish the desired transformation to high-level thinking or provide opportunities to develop true leadership. These demanding requirements call for new learning methodologies.

Despite the urgency of the situation, however, it is hard for many firms to move away from their reliance on traditional leadership development models and consider new approaches. Their training isn't necessarily broken. But it may well be incomplete.

The vast majority of today's emerging leaders—middle or junior managers—have little exposure to the types of learning experiences that would nurture transformative leadership. They need learning initiatives that focus on deeper competency development by modeling complex, real-world contexts in which learners can experiment, reflect, and take new courses of action based on increasingly deeper awareness.

Relevance is essential. Research has demonstrated that people learn best when they are actively involved in the learning process and engaging in the behaviors to be learned. What's vital in developing deeper thinking skills in current and future leaders is framing those behaviors within a relevant, job-related context.

And the learning experience needs to be memorable. Conventional wisdom shows a huge gap between knowledge retained from traditional instructor-dependent classroom training and knowledge gained from more interactive learning experiences. According to some estimates, most people retain just about 5 percent of learning from a lecture, compared to about 75 percent when they are actively involved in their learning experience.

Clarity Comes with Active Learning

Given the considerable spike in learning retention from hands-on experience, it stands to reason that experiential or "discovery learning" is rapidly gaining a reputation for preparing future leaders more effectively. Incorporating game techniques, visuals, simulations, small-team exercises, and other participant-centered elements that enhance learning, accelerate skill acquisition, and ensure long-term retention, discovery learning has proven to be a powerful way to change perspectives and build higher-level thinking skills and insights. Learners are guided and motivated to explore information and concepts in order to construct new ideas, identify new relationships, and create new models of thinking and behavior.

Discovery Learning: A Powerful Learning Methodology

Despite the proliferation of e-learning and digital development opportunities, classroom-based learning still represents one of the most effective and important ways to deliver management-level education designed to develop critical leadership skills. When combined with dynamic discovery learning experiences, immersive and interactive (as opposed to instructor-dependent) classroom training provides a unique opportunity to actually engage in the behaviors being taught. When designed properly, these active learning experiences ensure that participants have to think clearly and deeply, not shallowly.

Discovery learning is highly experiential, incorporating game techniques, visuals, simulations, small-team exercises and other participant-centered elements that enhance learning, accelerate skill acquisition, and ensure long-term retention. Participants contend with real business obstacles, make decisions (and mistakes), and discover the impact of their actions. They practice in a compressed, safe environment without risk or real-world consequences. This kind of "learning by doing" enables them to not only absorb essential concepts but also transfer their knowledge directly to the workplace as changed behaviors.

Five Important Characteristics

- *Team Problem Solving:* Learners engage in problem solving with other learners, using their combined knowledge and experience to achieve a goal.
- *Hands-On Learning:* Active participation by learners in exploring information and ideas engages their brains in the learning process.
- *Guided Discovery:* Learners are guided along a path toward discovery of ideas, concepts, and information with:
  - ☐ A learning design that builds ever-increasing understanding and comprehension.
  - ☐ A learning facilitator who is a guide rather than a teacher.
- *Reflection and Connection:* Insights learned clearly connect to real workplace issues. Learners are given the time and tools to reflect and to plan on-the-job action.
- *Learner Accountability:* Learners are "in the driver's seat," responsible for their own learning and goal achievement.

For leaders undergoing this kind of development, the knowledge, insights, and skills that they acquire can pay big dividends for the company and for themselves. With a deeper understanding of the big picture, both externally and internally, corporate leaders are better equipped to think on a deeper and broader scale and successfully bridge to solving real workplace issues. They are able to make direct connections between what happened in the leadership development activity and what happens in the business. They also are better prepared to drive results, armed with a robust understanding of the company's financial and strategic performance drivers and a keen sense of accountability for achieving those goals.

Connecting the Dots Within Learning Organizations

By assessing current leadership development initiatives through the lens of what's required of the next generation of leaders—and addressing the gaps—learning organizations can exercise their own brand of big-picture thinking. Connecting the dots between robust, relevant, engaging learning and the creation of a holistic and insightful approach to strategy puts both organizations and their leaders in a much stronger position to succeed now and in the future.

Here are three steps that learning leaders can take to ensure that their leadership development initiatives fully align with the new knowledge and skills their leaders will need to succeed in the years ahead:

1. Develop your own helicopter view of the organization's leadership development approach and offerings. Reevaluate the curriculum to make sure it provides learning experiences that help leaders make the connection between how the organization fits within the business ecosystem at large, how it makes money and sustains profitability, and how their individual actions and decisions affect organizational success.

2. Explore new learning approaches that boost engagement and retention. Strengthen leadership development content with ample opportunities to engage in critical thinking behaviors, apply them to real-world situations, and analyze the consequences.

3. Connect the dots between experiential learning and organizational impact. Bolster leadership development delivery with active rather than passive learning experiences—small-team activities, challenge scenarios, simulations, game techniques, post-session action projects, and other discovery learning exercises that make it more intuitive to transfer learning to the job.

References

Barrett, A., & Beeson, J. (2002, April). *Developing business leaders for 2010* (Report #R-1315-02-ES). New York: The Conference Board.

Carr, N. (2011). *The shallows: What the internet is doing to our brains.* New York: W.W. Norton.

Casner-Lotto, J., Barrington, L., & Wright M., (2006). *Are they really ready to work?* New York: The Conference Board.

Executive Development Associates (2010). *The 2009/2010 EDA trends in executive development.* Oklahoma City, OK: Author.

Goleman, D. (1998). *Working with emotional intelligence.* New York: Bantam Books.

Halpern, D. (2002). *Thought and knowledge* (4th ed.). London: Psychology Press.

Heracleous, L. (1998). Strategic thinking or strategic planning? *Long Range Planning, 31*(3).

Institute for the Future. (2010). 2010 ten-year forecast: The future is a high-resolution game. www.iftf.org/tyf.

Kelly, K., & Csorba, L.T. (2009). *Leadership matters.* Chicago, IL: Heidrick & Struggles International.

National Commission on Terrorist Attacks upon the United States. (Philip Zelikow, Executive Director; Bonnie D. Jenkins, Counsel; Ernest R. May, Senior Advisor). (2004). *The 9/11 Commission Report.* New York: W.W. Norton.

Pink, D. (2005). *A whole new mind.* New York: Riverhead Books.

Senge, P. (1990). *The fifth discipline: The art and practice of the learning organization.* New York: Doubleday

Welch, M. (2010, March 3). Leadership trends survey reveals problems on the horizon. Womenetics.com.

White, B.J. (2007). *The nature of leadership.* New York: American Management Association.

Catherine J. Rezak *is chairman and co-founder of Paradigm Learning, a leader in learning innovation, offering unique education and communication programs to organizations around the world. Paradigm Learning's core methodology is discovery learning, a powerful approach that engages employees, accelerates learning, and increases retention. The company's flagship business acumen program, Zodiak®: The Game of Business Finance and Strategy, has been conducted with more than one million managers and employees worldwide. Other leadership development products and services are offered in the areas of critical thinking, talent leadership, change communication, accountability, employee engagement, and project management.*

Contributors

Karl Albrecht, Ph.D.
Karl Albrecht International
3728 Old Cobble Road
San Diego, CA 92111
  (858) 836-1500
  email: Karl@KarlAlbrecht.com

Dr. Charles Anderson
School of Social Science
Room 106
Kean University
1000 Morris Avenue
Union Township, NJ 07040
  (908) 737-4239
  email: canderso@kean.edu

Teri-E Belf
Founder and Executive Director
Success Unlimited Network®
2016 Lakebreeze Way
Reston, VA
  (703) 402-8762
  email: coach@belf.org
  URL: belfcoach.com, successunlimi
ednet.com, or wrinklewisdom.com

Tim Buividas, Ed.D.
Partner, Corporate Learning Institute
1615 North Stoddard Avenue
Wheaton, IL 60187
  (312) 615-2211
  email: tbuividas@corplearning.com

Susan Cain, Ed.D.
Partner, The Corporate Learning
  Institute
1615 North Stoddard Avenue
Wheaton, IL 60187
  (630) 347-6333
  email: scain@corplearning.com

Lily Cheng
PACE O.D. Consulting
1 Commonwealth Lane
#06-14, One Commonwealth
Singapore 149544
  +65 6278 8289
  email: lilycheng@pace-od.com

Peter Cheng
PACE O.D. Consulting
1 Commonwealth Lane
#06-14, One Commonwealth
Singapore 149544
  +65 6278 8289
  email: petercheng@pace-od.com

Allan H. Church, Ph.D.
PepsiCo Inc.
700 Anderson Hill Road
Purchase, NY 10577
  (914) 253-2236
  email: allan.church@pepsico.com

Shirley Copeland, Ed.D.
Learning Resource Group LLC
2361 Lonicera Way
Charlottesville, VA 22911-9044
  (434) 975-1834
  fax: (434) 975-1834
  email: shirleycopeland@embarqmail
  .com

Erica I. Desrosiers, Ph.D.
PepsiCo Inc.
700 Anderson Hill Road
Purchase, NY 10577
  (914) 253-2236
  email: Erica.Desrosiers@Pepsico.com

Daniel Druckman
10509 Gainsborough Road
Potomac, MD 20854
  (301) 983-8477
  email: dandruckman@yahoo.com

Noam Ebner
The Werner Institute
Creighton University School of Law
2500 California Plaza
Omaha, NE 68178
  email: NoamEbner@Creighton.edu

Daniel Eckstein, Ph.D.
P.O. Box 1000
Saba Dutch Caribbean
  (936) 577-9855
  email: d.eckstein@yahoo.com

Sarah Eckstein
1301 Iowa Street, Number 12
Ashland, OR 97520
  (541) 817-3824
  email: Seckstei1134@gmail.com

John Goldberg
711 Flint Way
Sacramento, CA 95818-2122
  (916) 595-1224
  email: johngoldberg@hotmail.com

Leonard D. Goodstein, Ph.D.
10220 East Buckskin Trail
Scottsdale, AZ 85255
  (202) 841-8290
  email: lengood@gmail.com

Kurt Iskrzychi
Career Builder
841 North York Road, Number 426
Elmhurst, IL 60126
  (309) 242-7027
  email: kiskrzycki@gmail.com

Homer H. Johnson, Ph.D.
School of Business Administration
Loyola University–Chicago
820 North Chicago Avenue
Chicago, IL 60611
  (312) 915-6682
  email: hjohnso@luc.edu

Deborah Spring Laurel
917 Vilas Avenue
Madison, WI 53715
  (608) 255-2010
  fax: (608) 260-2616
  email: dlaurel@laurelandassociates
  .com

Lauri Luoto
Psycon Corp.
Jaakonkatu 3 A
00100 Helsinki
Finland
  +358-40-7094938
  email: lauri.luoto@psycon.fi

J. Alexis Mamber
2561 Bullion Loop
Sanford, FL 32771
  (321)663-7079
  email: castmamber@hotmail.com

Marilyn Marles
1935 Mill Creek Road
Macungie, PA 18062
  (610) 398-0125
  email: marilyn@marlesgroup.com
  URL: www.marlesgroup.com

Mohandas Nair
A2 Kamdar Building
607 Gokhale Road(s)
Dadar, Mumbai, Maharashtra 400028
India
  91-22-24226307
  email: mohandasnair53@gmail.com

Phillip E. Nelson, Ph.D.
2016 Lakebreeze Way
Reston, VA 20191-4021
  (703) 716-5511
  email: pzxnelson@gmail.com

Deb Pastors
619 North Ridgeland Avenue
Oak Park, IL 60302
  (708) 406-9828
  email: debpastors@att.net

Kella B. Price, DBA, SPHR, CPLP
3532 Fairgreen Lane
Palmdale, CA 93551
  (252) 622-8119 or (661) 526-6578
  email: drkellabprice@gmail.com

Erwin Rausch
Kean University and Didactic Systems
P.O. Box 457
Cranford, NJ 07016
  (908) 276-5413
  email: didacticra@aol.com

Catherine J. Rezak
Paradigm Learning, Inc.
100 2nd Avenue South
St. Petersburg, FL 33701
  (727) 471-3170
  email: Cathy.Rezak@
  ParadigmLearning.com
  URL: www.ParadigmLearning.com

Lou Russell
Russell Martin & Associates
9084 Technology Drive
Fishers, IN 46038
  (317) 475-9311
  email: Lou@russellmarting.com
  URL: www.lourussell.com

Nicole Russo
2430 Vanderbilt Beach Road,
  #108-268
Naples, FL 34109
  (954) 445-6335
  email: nicolerusso@mac.com

Sandra A. Shelton
StrengthBank® Companies
6008 Welch Avenue, Suite 107
Fort Worth, TX 76133-3635
  (817) 230-4523
  fax: (877) 256-3811
  email: sandra.shelton@strengthbank
  .com

Ken Steiger
Steiger Training & Development
P.O. Box 452
Tully, NY 13159
   (315) 307-2506
   email: ken@SteigerTraining.com

Jennifer Straub
322 North Second Street
Sunbury, PA 17801
   (570) 205-1590
   email: jenns26@tds.net

Lisa Strick
Chief Idea Officer
The Idea Bungalow
2250 Bay Street
San Francisco, CA 94123
   (415) 655-9926
   email: Lisa@ideabungalow.com

Sacip Toker
Administrative and Organizational
   Studies Division
Instructional Technology Program
College of Education
Wayne State University
Detroit, MI 48202
   (313) 645 7112
   email: saciptoker@gmail.com

Michael D. Tuller, Ph.D.
PepsiCo Inc.
700 Anderson Hill Road
Purchase, NY 10577
   (914) 253-2236
   email: Michael.Tuller@pepsico.com

Phil Van Horn, CEO
The Align Team
1401 Airport Parkway, Suite 300
Cheyenne, WY 82001
307-772-9000
   (307) 772-9000
   (877) 322-5446 x 9000
   email: pvanhorn@TheAlignTeam.org
   URL: TheAlignTeam.org

Jan Yuill
Principal, Yuill & Associates
1081 Ambleside Drive, Suite 306
Ottawa, Ontario K2B 8C8
Canada
   (613) 721-8793
   fax: (613) 721-1410
   email: jan@yuill-associates.com

Sherene Zolno
25900 Pillsbury Rd SW
Vashon, WA 98070
   (206) 463-6374
   email: slzolno@comcast.net

Contents of the Companion Volume, *The 2013 Pfeiffer Annual: Consulting*

Editor's Choice

Inventories, Questionnaires, and Surveys

**Preparing Leaders for the Future Topics

Articles and Discussion Resources

---

†Cutting-Edge Topics

Pfeiffer Publications Guide

This guide is designed to familiarize you with the various types of Pfeiffer publications. The formats section describes the various types of products that we publish; the methodologies section describes the many different ways that content might be provided within a product. We also provide a list of the topic areas in which we publish.

FORMATS

In addition to its extensive book-publishing program, Pfeiffer offers content in an array of formats, from fieldbooks for the practitioner to complete, ready-to-use training packages that support group learning.

FIELDBOOK Designed to provide information and guidance to practitioners in the midst of action. Most fieldbooks are companions to another, sometimes earlier, work, from which its ideas are derived; the fieldbook makes practical what was theoretical in the original text. Fieldbooks can certainly be read from cover to cover. More likely, though, you'll find yourself bouncing around following a particular theme, or dipping in as the mood, and the situation, dictate.

HANDBOOK A contributed volume of work on a single topic, comprising an eclectic mix of ideas, case studies, and best practices sourced by practitioners and experts in the field.

An editor or team of editors usually is appointed to seek out contributors and to evaluate content for relevance to the topic. Think of a handbook not as a ready-to-eat meal, but as a cookbook of ingredients that enables you to create the most fitting experience for the occasion.

RESOURCE Materials designed to support group learning. They come in many forms: a complete, ready-to-use exercise (such as a game); a comprehensive resource on one topic (such as conflict management) containing a variety of methods and approaches; or a collection of like-minded activities (such as icebreakers) on multiple subjects and situations.

TRAINING PACKAGE An entire, ready-to-use learning program that focuses on a particular topic or skill. All packages comprise a guide for the facilitator/trainer and a workbook for the participants. Some packages are supported with additional media—such as video—or learning aids, instruments, or other devices to help participants understand concepts or practice and develop skills.

- *Facilitator/trainer's guide* Contains an introduction to the program, advice on how to organize and facilitate the learning event, and step-by-step instructor notes. The guide also contains copies of presentation materials—handouts, presentations, and overhead designs, for example—used in the program.

- *Participant's workbook* Contains exercises and reading materials that support the learning goal and serves as a valuable reference and support guide for participants in the weeks and months that follow the learning event. Typically, each participant will require his or her own workbook.

ELECTRONIC CD-ROMs and web-based products transform static Pfeiffer content into dynamic, interactive experiences. Designed to take advantage of the searchability, automation, and ease-of-use that technology provides, our e-products bring convenience and immediate accessibility to your workspace.

METHODOLOGIES

CASE STUDY A presentation, in narrative form, of an actual event that has occurred inside an organization. Case studies are not prescriptive, nor are they used to prove a point; they are designed to develop critical analysis and decision-making skills. A case study has a specific time frame, specifies a sequence of events, is narrative in structure, and contains a plot structure—an issue (what should be/have been done?). Use case studies when the goal is to enable participants to apply previously learned theories to the circumstances in the case, decide what is pertinent, identify the real issues, decide what should have been done, and develop a plan of action.

ENERGIZER A short activity that develops readiness for the next session or learning event. Energizers are most commonly used after a break or lunch to stimulate or refocus the group. Many involve some form of physical activity, so they are a useful way to counter post-lunch lethargy. Other uses include transitioning from one topic to another, where "mental" distancing is important.

EXPERIENTIAL LEARNING ACTIVITY (ELA) A facilitator-led intervention that moves participants through the learning cycle from experience to application (also known as a Structured Experience). ELAs are carefully thought-out designs in which there is a definite learning purpose and intended outcome. Each step—everything that participants do during the activity—facilitates the accomplishment of the stated goal. Each ELA includes complete instructions for facilitating the intervention and a clear statement of goals, suggested group size and timing, materials required, an explanation of the process, and, where appropriate, possible variations to the activity. (For more detail on Experiential Learning Activities, see the Introduction to the *Reference Guide to Handbooks and Annuals*, 1999 edition, Pfeiffer, San Francisco.)

GAME A group activity that has the purpose of fostering team spirit and togetherness in addition to the achievement of a pre-stated goal. Usually contrived—undertaking a desert expedition, for example—this type of learning method offers an engaging means for participants to demonstrate and practice business and inter-personal skills. Games are effective for team building and personal development mainly because the goal is subordinate to the process—the means through which participants reach decisions, collaborate, communicate, and generate trust and understanding. Games often engage teams in "friendly" competition.

ICEBREAKER A (usually) short activity designed to help participants overcome initial anxiety in a training session and/or to acquaint the participants with one another. An icebreaker can be a fun activity or can be tied to specific topics or training goals. While a useful tool in itself, the icebreaker comes into its own in situations where tension or resistance exists within a group.

INSTRUMENT A device used to assess, appraise, evaluate, describe, classify, and summarize various aspects of human behavior. The term used to describe an instrument depends primarily on its format and purpose. These terms include survey, questionnaire, inventory, diagnostic, survey, and poll. Some uses of instruments include providing instrumental feedback to group members, studying here-and-now processes or functioning within a group, manipulating group composition, and evaluating outcomes of training and other interventions.

Instruments are popular in the training and HR field because, in general, more growth can occur if an individual is provided with a method for focusing specifically on his or her own behavior. Instruments also are used to obtain information that will serve as a basis for change and to assist in workforce planning efforts.

Paper-and-pencil tests still dominate the instrument landscape with a typical package comprising a facilitator's guide, which offers advice on administering the instrument and interpreting the collected data, and an initial set of instruments. Additional instruments are available separately. Pfeiffer, though, is investing heavily in e-instruments. Electronic instrumentation provides effortless distribution and, for larger groups particularly, offers advantages over paper-and-pencil tests in the time it takes to analyze data and provide feedback.

LECTURETTE A short talk that provides an explanation of a principle, model, or process that is pertinent to the participants' current learning needs. A lecturette is intended to establish a common language bond between the trainer and the participants by providing a mutual frame of reference. Use a lecturette as an introduction to a group activity or event, as an interjection during an event, or as a handout.

MODEL A graphic depiction of a system or process and the relationship among its elements. Models provide a frame of reference and something more tangible, and more easily remembered, than a verbal explanation. They also give participants something to "go on," enabling them to track their own progress as they experience the dynamics, processes, and relationships being depicted in the model.

ROLE PLAY A technique in which people assume a role in a situation/scenario: a customer service rep in an angry-customer exchange, for example. The way in which the role is approached is then discussed and feedback is offered. The role play is often repeated using a different approach and/or incorporating changes made based on feedback received. In other words, role playing is a spontaneous interaction involving realistic behavior under artificial (and safe) conditions.

SIMULATION A methodology for understanding the interrelationships among components of a system or process. Simulations differ from games in that they test or use a model that depicts or mirrors some aspect of reality in form, if not necessarily in content. Learning occurs by studying the effects of change on one or more factors of the model. Simulations are commonly used to test hypotheses about what happens in a system—often referred to as "what if?" analysis—or to examine best-case/worst-case scenarios.

THEORY A presentation of an idea from a conjectural perspective. Theories are useful because they encourage us to examine behavior and phenomena through a different lens.

TOPICS

The twin goals of providing effective and practical solutions for workforce training and organization development and meeting the educational needs of training and human resource professionals shape Pfeiffer's publishing program. Core topics include the following:

Leadership & Management

Communication & Presentation

Coaching & Mentoring

Training & Development

E-Learning

Teams & Collaboration

OD & Strategic Planning

Human Resources

Consulting

Printed in the United States
By Bookmasters